Healthy, Wealthy, and Wise

1,001 Money-Saving Secrets to Curb Your Spending, Clear Up Financial Chaos, Improve Your Health, and Make Your Life Easier!

Publisher's Note

The editors of FC&A have taken careful measures to ensure the accuracy and usefulness of the information in this book. While every attempt was made to assure accuracy, some Web sites, addresses, telephone numbers, and other information may have changed since printing.

This book is intended for general information only. It does not constitute medical, legal, or financial advice or practice. We cannot guarantee the safety or effectiveness of any treatment or advice mentioned. Readers are urged to consult with their personal financial advisers, lawyers, and health care professionals.

The publisher and editors disclaim all liability (including any injuries, damages, or losses) resulting from the use of the information in this book.

"Now may the God of hope fill you with all joy and peace in believing, that you may abound in hope by the power of the Holy Spirit."

Romans 15:13

"Always remember that it is the Lord your God who gives you power to become rich, and he does it to fulfill the covenant he made with your ancestors."

Deuteronomy 8:18

Table of contents

Smart choices, super health

Sound savings, fit finances

Better buys, better living

Safe and sound prescriptions

Smart choices, super health

♦ ♦ ♦ ♦

In this section

• Safe and sound prescriptions

• Smart medical choices

• Nutritional know-how

• Healthy healing

♦ ♦ ♦ ♦

Beware of hidden drug hazards

A child is accidentally given his grandfather's antibiotic. A woman suffers a drug overdose because she filled two prescriptions for the same drug with different names.

More than 200,000 people die each year because of medication-related problems like these and another 2 million are seriously injured.

The Institute for Safe Medication Practices (ISMP) works to prevent medication disasters. Try their recommendations to protect yourself from drug-related dangers.

Speak up. Ask your doctor to tell you about the medicine he prescribes for you. Get answers to questions like these.

- What is the name of the medicine you have prescribed?

- What is the medication being prescribed for?

- How do I take the medicine?

- What are possible side effects, and what should I do if they occur?

- What foods, herbs, nutritional supplements, or other drugs should not be taken with this medicine?
- Should I avoid any specific activities, foods, or drugs while taking this medication?
- What should I do if I miss a dose?

If you are uncomfortable asking your doctor these questions, bring someone with you, recommends Hedy Cohen, registered nurse and Vice-President of the Institute for Safe Medication Practices. And bring a pencil and paper so you can take notes.

Share your concerns. Tell your doctor about any concerns you have. If a drug seems too expensive or a pill is too big to swallow, say so. A cheaper drug or an easy-to-swallow liquid may be available.

Mention allergies you have, as well as herbs, supplements, or over-the-counter (OTC) drugs you take. A safe herb or OTC medicine can turn dangerous when taken with some medications.

Don't crush or split a pill for any reason without first checking

---

⚠ Spot rising risk of dangers

The American Society of Consultant Pharmacists suggests medication-related problems may be more likely if you are over age 65 and several of these describe you.

- more than one doctor regularly prescribes your medicines
- you get prescriptions filled at more than one pharmacy
- you take five or more medications
- you take over 11 medicine doses daily
- you take medications for three or more medical problems
- your medicines or instructions on how to take them have changed four or more times this past year
- someone else brings your medicines to your home
- you don't know why you were prescribed one of your medications

with your doctor. Cohen warns about drug overdoses from pills that were meant to deliver a small dose of medication every few hours. Crushing the pill releases all the doses at once.

Write it down. To play it safe, make a list of all the prescription medicines, OTC drugs, and supplements you take. Update the list often just in case you have a health emergency. Show the list to any doctor or nurse who sees you. Also, show the list to any pharmacist who fills a prescription for you — or even better — use the same pharmacy all the time.

Keep your eyes open. Before you leave the drugstore, take your medicine out of the bag. "If it's a medication you've taken before, make sure it looks like the medication you took before," Cohen says. If it doesn't, check with your pharmacist. It could be the wrong medicine. If you start a new prescription, read the package and any information that comes with the drug. Ask the pharmacist to explain anything you don't understand.

Get a "brown bag" checkup. The ISMP also suggests showing your doctor or pharmacist all medicines and supplements you take to check for interactions or other possible problems. Schedule an appointment; put your medications, vitamins, and herbs in a bag; and take them with you.

Talk with an expert. Certified Geriatric Pharmacists, also called senior care pharmacists, can do all the things regular pharmacists do, but they specialize in medication problems unique to older adults.

According to Tom Clark, Director of Policy and Advocacy for the American Society of Consultant Pharmacists, a brown bag checkup with a Certified Geriatric Pharmacist could save you more money than the fee you pay for it. The pharmacist may find cheaper or safer alternatives to drugs you already take or spot cases where you're taking one drug to treat the side effects of another.

To find a Certified Geriatric Pharmacist near you, visit *www.seniorcarepharmacist.com.*

Keep on learning. For many more useful tips, information, and consumer alerts to help you avoid medication-related problems, check ISMP's consumer Web pages at *www.ismp.org/Pages/Consumer.html.*

Avoid accidental overdose

The life you save could be your own. To protect yourself from taking too much medicine — or not enough — follow this advice from the Food and Drug Administration.

- Never use a kitchen spoon for liquid medicine. You could get twice the dose you need because kitchen teaspoons aren't all the same size. Use measuring spoons instead.

- Check whether the instructions say teaspoon or tablespoon — one tablespoon equals three teaspoons.

- If a liquid medicine comes with a measuring cup, use it. Double-check the dose before you take it, because it's easy to confuse lines marking teaspoons and tablespoons. And don't risk using a dose cup from another medicine. Dose cups aren't all alike.

- Ask your pharmacist about purchasing a special spoon, dropper, or oral syringe to measure liquid drugs more accurately.

Watch out for impostors

Counterfeiting isn't just for money anymore. Now drugs can be counterfeit, too. According to estimates, more than 10 percent of drugs worldwide are counterfeit, and in some places, over 50 percent of the available drugs aren't the real thing.

Get the facts. A counterfeit version of a drug may not have enough of the active ingredient to do any good, or it may have no active ingredient at all. If you need the drug for an illness or medical condition, taking these counterfeits may be like taking no medicine at all.

A few counterfeits merely have fake packaging. Others have the wrong active ingredient, incorrect ingredients, or improper amounts of the right ingredients. They might also contain hazardous ingredients. These shortcomings can cause unexpected side effects, allergic reactions, or make your condition worse.

Weigh the risks. Although counterfeiting occurs less often in the United States than in other parts of the world, a few consumers and pharmacists reported bitter-tasting counterfeits of Lipitor in one incident. In another case, investigators snared a counterfeit version of Procrit. Instead of medication for anemia, cancer, or HIV, the counterfeit Procrit just contained water contaminated with bacteria.

The Food and Drug Administration (FDA) is already battling against the counterfeiters. An anti-counterfeiting task force now seeks ways to use modern technologies and other tools to keep counterfeit medicines out of your pharmacy and your medicine cabinet. What's more, the FDA has cracked down on counterfeiters so hard they have more than tripled their average number of counterfeit drug cases.

Protect yourself. You can protect yourself from counterfeit drug risks, too. Remember that counterfeiting can apply to brand name and generic medications and prescription and over-the-counter medicines.

Buy all prescription and over-the-counter medications from U.S. state licensed pharmacies. These include Web sites identified by the Verified Internet Pharmacy Practice Sites (VIPPS) hyperlink seal. To learn more about safely purchasing drugs online, see *Discover deep drug discounts at Internet pharmacies* on page 221.

⚠ **Beware of drugs that turn risky as you age**

Medications that were once safe could turn hazardous as you grow older. As the natural changes of aging kick in, some drugs may linger in your body longer. The latest "Beers Criteria" lists medications that can be unsafe for adults age 65 and up. These include dangerous medicines you can replace with safer substitutes, drugs that are ineffective for older adults, and medications to avoid if you have particular medical conditions. To find out whether you should make changes in your medicine routine, ask your doctor or pharmacist about the Beers Criteria.

The FDA warns that it can't guarantee the safety or effectiveness of medications bought online unless they have been purchased from a U.S. state licensed pharmacy.

Every time you get a new medicine, examine it closely. Keep your eyes peeled for unsealed containers or other changes in packaging. Check for differences in the shape, size, and color of the drug. If the medicine looks different, has a different taste, or if you experience side effects, contact your doctor or pharmacist.

Realize the full value of your statin

You've already declared war on high cholesterol by regularly taking the statin prescribed by your doctor. But researchers think you could shrink your LDL cholesterol even more if you also spread one of the new anti-cholesterol "sterol" margarines, like Benecol and Take Control, on your morning toast. As if that's not enough, here are extra ways to rack up more cholesterol-blasting power.

Think food. If you take lovastatin, another study suggests your body may use up to 50 percent more of the drug if you take it with food.

In addition, Finnish researchers found that eating a healthy diet and taking simvastatin works better than either approach by itself. The diet even counteracted some simvastatin side effects, like elevated insulin levels and depleted antioxidants. People in the study ate a modified Mediterranean diet rich in omega-3 fatty acids. It featured fish, lean meats, low-fat dairy products, fruits, vegetables, whole grains, and berries. The combination of simvastatin and the healthy diet slashed bad LDL cholesterol by 41 percent.

Get more might at night. British researchers found that taking simvastatin in the morning, instead of at night, could actually boost your cholesterol. If you take your statin in the morning, ask your doctor if switching to an evening dose could help.

Keep in touch. Remember — talk with your doctor before changing the way you take your statins. And report any numbness, tingling, or pain in your hands and feet to your doctor. These are symptoms of nerve damage, which can be a side effect of statins.

You'll also be glad to know lower LDL cho-lesterol and a reduced risk of heart disease and stroke may not be all you win if you take one of the "Fab 5" statins — atorvas-tatin (Lipitor), fluvastatin (Lescol), lovastatin (Mevacor),

---

Net drug info with these Web sites

For reliable drug information on the Internet, try the following sites. They have useful information like the best ways to take your drugs and how to avoid drug interactions. Just be sure to check with your doctor or pharmacist for additional information about your medications.

www.drugs.com

www.fda.gov/cder

www.drugdigest.org

To help you create handy schedules and checklists for taking medicines, surf to *www.mypillbox.org.* Be sure to write down your user number and password so you can keep using this valuable tool.

pravastatin (Pravachol), and simvastatin (Zocor). Here are more ways this drug might keep you healthy.

Cuts your Alzheimer's risk. If you already battle high cholesterol with statins, you may be cutting your odds of Alzheimer's disease, too. A Boston University study found that statins slashed risk of dementia by up to 70 percent. In spite of this, doctors don't recommend taking statins just to protect against dementia.

Shields your eyes. Your statins may battle macular degeneration, too. In a British study, people taking these prescription drugs were 11 times less likely to have age-related macular degeneration.

Strengthens your bones. Although more research is needed, some studies suggest that statins could help lower your risk of fractures.

Smooth ways to swallow pills

If you find pills are hard to swallow, try these helpful tips:

- Drink some water to wet your throat, place the pill on the back of your tongue, and take several more swallows of water.
- Don't tilt your head back when swallowing. Instead, bring your head forward so your chin nearly touches your chest.
- Chew some food, then place the pill in your mouth with the food, and swallow. Or take the pill in a spoonful of applesauce.
- Open gelatin capsules, and pour the powder into a cold drink, like tomato or orange juice, then drink it down.

Smart solutions for drug patch problems

Prescription patches can be tricky — even dangerous. That's why it's important to be savvy about using them.

"There have been cases of people dying from an overdose with some of the narcotic patches," says Teresa Rubio, pharmacist and member of the American Society of Health System Pharmacists.

But with these tips and tricks, you can use prescription patches more safely and effectively.

Avoid interactions. Ask your doctor the same questions you would for any other prescription. Be sure to mention all drugs, over-the-counter medicines, and herbal remedies you take, as well as any health conditions or illnesses you have.

Find out how, when, and where. Be clear on how to apply the patch and how often to change it. "Some patches have to be applied every week; some every three days or so," Rubio explains.

Ask where the patch should be applied. Rubio says where you put the patch on your body may determine how much medicine you get or how fast you get it. What's more, some patches must always be applied to a particular place while others must go in a different spot every time.

Only apply a patch to clean, dry skin that is free of creams and lotions.

Keep track. Make changing the patch a part of your regular routine, so you won't forget. Rubio even suggests keeping a log or marking the dates on your calendar. Write down when you changed the patch, where you applied the new one, and when you need to change the patch again.

Prevent an overdose. When it's time to change a patch, always remove the old one before putting on a new one. Otherwise, you could get doses from both patches — and that could be too much.

Steer clear of clear patches. Ask for colored patches instead of clear ones, if possible. Rubio says the FDA actually advises against the near-invisible patches because people don't see them and forget to take them off. Otherwise, Rubio says, "Ask your physician if you can write lightly on the patch so you know where it is and when you are supposed to take it off."

Decode your prescription

When your doctor writes you a prescription, does it look like a secret code? Here are a few common abbreviations you might see — along with their meanings.

a.c.	before meals
ad lib	as much as wanted
b.i.d.	twice a day
h.	hour
h.s.	at bedtime
p.	after
p.c.	after meals
p.o.	by mouth
p.r.n.	as necessary
q.	every
q.4 h.	every four hours
q.d.	every day
q.i.d.	four times a day
q.o.d.	every other day
Rx	prescription
stat.	immediately
t.i.d.	three times a day

Store wisely. Avoid keeping your extra patches above the kitchen sink or in the bathroom where moisture may affect the medicine. Find a cool, dry place, instead.

Pitch patches safely. To remove a patch, peel it off quickly. If it won't come off easily, use a little baby oil. "Try to touch as little of the adhesive as possible," says Rubio.

Don't throw them in the trash since patches can be toxic if swallowed by children or pets. "Fold the patch in half so the adhesive sticks to itself and then flush it down the toilet," Rubio advises.

Avoid two-part patch traps. Some patches come with two parts — the medicated patch and what's called an overlay. "For example, if a patch is round, the overlay would be round but larger," Rubio says. "You put the overlay on top of the patch to make sure it can't fall off or move around."

You must use both parts. If you apply the overlay without the patch, or attach the patch with tape instead of the overlay, you won't get the medicine as prescribed.

"The adhesive on the patch actually insures that the drug gets into your system like it's supposed to," Rubio explains. "Tape could interfere with some of the absorption of the drug."

"There are a lot of mistakes people tend to make with patches," Rubio says. "But patients are asking more and more questions about their health — and that is really positive."

Smart medical choices

Wise ways to handle a health crisis

It's hard to think clearly when you're facing a health emergency. So arm yourself with good advice now and you'll be more prepared if — and when — trouble strikes.

Know when to go. If you experience any of the following symptoms, call 911 immediately and do not try to drive yourself to the emergency room.

- sudden, severe shortness of breath
- sudden, severe chest pain
- a fall along with a severe blow to your head or with a loss of consciousness
- sudden weakness or numbness on one side of your body
- sudden dimness or loss of vision, particularly in one eye
- difficulty speaking
- sudden severe headache
- unexplained dizziness or unsteadiness

Use wait time wisely. "If possible, have someone stay with you while you are waiting for the ambulance to arrive," recommends Colleen Christmas, M.D., Assistant Professor of Medicine in the Division of Geriatric Medicine and Gerontology at Johns Hopkins University. "Try to remain calm."

"Either sit or recline so that if you pass out, you will not fall or injure yourself," she adds. "If you are very short of breath, it is often more comfortable to sit than to lie down. If you are feeling dizzy or light-headed, lie down with your feet elevated."

In addition, ask your family to collect any medical information that the emergency medical technicians (EMTs) or hospital staff might need.

- insurance information
- your doctor's name
- a list of your allergies
- your current medications — a list or the actual pill bottles
- emergency contact information
- written documents that explain how you want medical decisions made if you can't make them yourself

Then ask your family to gather essential personal items, such as hearing aids, eyeglasses, or dentures. "These items may make it easier for you to communicate with the staff in the hospital," Christmas says.

Work with the EMTs. "Your family should step back a little when the EMTs arrive — to allow them to do their evaluation and start treatments on you," explains Christmas. "They may need to start an IV or place an oxygen mask on you. Try to remain calm and cooperate as much as you can."

"The EMTs will have many questions about your current symptoms and your previous health history," she says. "Your family should listen carefully to your answers and provide any further information they may have."

For more on older adults and emergencies, Christmas says to visit the American Geriatric Society Foundation for Health in

Aging on the Internet at *www.healthinaging.org* or call them at 800-563-4916.

Pick the perfect physician

"I've had 16 surgeries so I have certainly gotten to know my share of doctors," says Kevin Soden, M.D., co-author of *Special Treatment: How to Get the Same High-Quality Health Care Your Doctor Gets.* "I think your relationship with your doctor is one of the most important you will have — outside of family, obviously — because it impacts the quality of your life and your health."

Imagine your dream doctor. Write down everything you want in a physician — for instance, she must work with a particular hospital or insurance plan, doesn't charge penalty fees for cancellations, or must be cheerful when answering your questions. Rank them in order of importance to you.

These are the top conditions that bring older adults to the emergency room, says Colleen Christmas, M.D., Assistant Professor of Medicine at Johns Hopkins University.

- chest pain

- worsening of chronic obstructive pulmonary diseases (COPD) such as emphysema, asthma, or chronic bronchitis

- congestive heart failure

- fainting or falls

- infections, especially upper respiratory infections and bladder infections

List some candidates. Use those physicians accepted by your insurance or managed care plan as a starting point. Then Soden suggests you ask friends, family, co-workers, and acquaintances about their doctors.

"Quite frankly," he says, "we all know doctors who we'd want to be treated by and some we don't want to be treated by."

If you are moving, ask your current physician if he can recommend any doctors in your new town.

Check them out. Examine the credentials of your possible doctors so you can come up with a few finalists. You can get the scoop on most doctors' board certifications, specialties, and other qualifications from the American Medical Association (AMA). Call 312-464-5000 or go to their *Physician Select* service on the Internet. That Web address is *www.ama-assn.org/aps/amahg.htm*.

Arrange an interview. "Call the office and schedule an appointment to talk to the doctor for 10 to 15 minutes," Soden says. "Tell them you'll pay for that time, but you need to do a little interview with the doctor." Realize that your insurance may not pay for this type of visit.

During this call, he says, you will find out what the office staff is like — how friendly and helpful they are over the phone. Confirm that they take your insurance and ask whether they are accepting new patients.

Soden suggests in the interview you also ask questions about office policies — like these.

- Does the doctor have hospital privileges?
- What hospital does he prefer to use?
- Who will handle your care if you have an emergency or need medical attention after office hours?

Go for a test drive. Whether you go to the office for an interview or an illness, examine the experience closely — just like you'd examine any major purchase before buying. Is it easy to get to the office? Is parking convenient? Notice how the staff treats you, what other patients say about the doctor, and anything else that could affect whether you will be satisfied.

Pay extra attention to the doctor's behavior. "Does he treat you courteously and with respect?" Soden asks. "Will he sit down and listen to you? Does he have the time to talk to you a little bit and is he good about answering your questions?" If so, you've probably found a pretty good doctor.

Get more from your doctor visits

"The weight is on both — the doctor to give clear communication, and the patient to ask for it and demand it," says Donna Phillips, a Partnership for Clear Health Communication member and Vice-President of the National Council on the Aging.

Find out how to improve those chats with your doctor so you can get more value from your doctor visits.

Translate doctor-ese. Does your doctor use so many medical terms you can't tell if she's speaking English or Latin? Ask for a clearer explanation. In fact, the Partnership for Clear Health Communication recommends that you ask these questions.

- What is my main problem?
- What do I need to do?
- Why is it important for me to do this?

"Ask these questions over and over again until you understand," suggests Phillips. The Partnership offers a brochure featuring these questions, space to write answers, and extra tips on getting the information you need. Learn more at the *www.askme3.org* Web site. To get the brochure, download it in PDF format at *www.askme3.org/pdfs.asp* or call 877-4-ASK-ME-3 to order a printed copy.

The Medical Library Association even has a brochure to help you translate doctor-ese into plain English. Read it on the Web at *www.mlanet.org.*

Ask questions. Don't wait until the end of a doctor visit to say you don't understand what's wrong or what to do to get better. Anytime you need more explanation, ask for it. Be ready to ask more questions to find out what you need to know. "If you can't understand and take action on medical information, then you won't benefit from the health care system," Phillips points out.

⚠️ **Act fast for greater stroke recovery**

Stroke sufferers treated with the drug tissue plasminogen activator (tPA) are more likely to recover completely experts say. Every second counts though, because the drug must be given within three hours of the first stroke symptoms and doctors must run tests beforehand.

"Both heart attack and stroke are very clearly best treated sooner rather than later," says Colleen Christmas, Assistant Professor of Medicine at Johns Hopkins University. "The later treatment starts, the more permanent damage is done."

Discuss all doubts. If you have doubts about a diagnosis or treatment, say so. Your doctor may know a perfectly good substitute.

Take doctor's orders home. Ask for written advice or instructions. Otherwise, take a pen and paper with you to the doctor's office so you can take notes.

Request easy reading. Ask your doctor how you can get brochures or other information about your health condition and treatments. Explain that you want information that's easy for anyone to understand. Your doctor might make some great suggestions — or she might have free publications she can give you on the spot.

Talk your way to a better diagnosis

Tell your doctor everything he needs to know, and you're more likely to get the answers you need and the best treatments for you.

Start early. Before you visit the doctor's office, write down your symptom along with answers to these questions.

- When did the symptom start?

- Has the symptom gotten better or worse?

- Is it constant or does it come and go? How long does it last?

- Does anything seem to trigger the symptom or make it worse?

- Did you start a new job, change your diet, or make other lifestyle changes around the time the symptom started?

These are the kinds of things your doctor will probably want to know. So either hand the list to him or refer to it while you talk with him.

Be direct. Keep these points in mind when you speak with the doctor.

- Bring up your most important concern at the start of your visit.

- Be honest with your doctor about your diet, smoking history, and other aspects of your lifestyle.

- If you're embarrassed about a topic, be upfront about that. Your doctor needs to know when a subject is hard for you to discuss.

Remember these tips the next time you go to the doctor. You may be surprised — and pleased — at the results.

Get a second opinion that's first-rate

Your doctor says you have a serious illness. Or maybe you need major surgery. If you choose to get a second opinion, use these tips to help you get a wise one.

Check your coverage. Find out if your insurer will cover the cost of the surgery or treatments your doctor recommended. Then check to see if they will pay for a second opinion.

Be straight-forward. Tell your doctor you want a second opinion. While that can seem intimidating, a good doctor won't be offended or insulted. "He should want you to feel better about your decision," says F. Dean Griffen, clinical surgeon and Chairman of the Patient Safety and Professional Liability Committee for the American College of Surgeons. "He should be good enough that he is confident he did his job right, and you'll come back to him."

"If the doctor you first saw would be offended or upset, that's a red flag," Griffen warns. "You need a second opinion more than ever."

Choose carefully. You can ask your doctor to recommend someone to give you a second opinion, or you can find someone on your own. Be sure you choose a doctor who is qualified to treat your condition. "You want him to be

⚠ Stop heart attack with aspirin — not coughing

Suddenly, you think you're having a heart attack. Don't waste precious seconds with repeated coughing or "cough CPR." Chew an aspirin instead. Research suggests up to 10,000 lives could be saved every year if more people chewed an aspirin at the first sign of a heart attack. Aspirin's salicylic acid helps prevent blood clots from forming. These clots can block the flow of blood to your heart. That could buy you life-saving minutes until you can get stronger medicine at the hospital. So remember, if you think you're having a heart attack, dial 911 and chew an aspirin.

Board Certified in the area that you have an interest," advises Griffen. Because most members of the American College of Surgeons (ACS) are Board Certified, he recommends you visit the Public Information section of *www.facs.org* to find ACS members near you. Also, if you know someone who had the surgery, treatment, or testing you might need, ask him about the doctor he used.

Tote your tests. Before you get a second opinion, ask if you can use the same X-rays or relevant tests from the first doctor. This request is not unusual, and it can save you a bundle. "Those tests are bought and paid for," Griffen points out. He even suggests you hand carry your X-ray films or copies of lab test results to your second opinion appointment.

Ask questions. To prepare for your appointment, write down questions you want to ask. For example, if you're debating about surgery, Griffen suggests seeking answers to questions like these:

- Why do I need surgery?
- Are there alternatives to this surgery?
- What risks come with this surgery?
- What risks do I face if I don't have the surgery?
- What can I expect after surgery? How could it affect my life? Will I need rehabilitation or other treatments?

Consider your options. If the second opinion disagrees with the first, you have three options. Some experts urge you to get a third opinion. Others say consult with the first doctor again. Or you can simply decide. "A second opinion is not necessarily your best opinion. Your first may be your best," Griffen says. "What you have to begin to do at that point is use your best judgment."

Take no chances. In an emergency, seconds count more than second opinions. Don't wait for a second opinion if you need emergency surgery.

Seek help for better sex life

Medications could be cheating you out of a good sex life. So could atherosclerosis. It's important to know what can cause sexual problems.

"I'd encourage an older woman or an older man to never assume that there is something wrong with them if there is a change in their sexual desire, their ability to engage in sexual activity, or their degree of satisfaction," says Bev Johnson, Ph.D., R.N., Associate Professor at the Seattle University School of Nursing.

Know the culprits. The top sexual issues older adults face today include side effects of medications, chronic health problems, the aging process, and sexually transmitted diseases.

"Health problems such as heart disease, diabetes, and arthritis all can potentially impact sexual function as well as sexual interest," Johnson says. For example, arthritis pain may limit what you can do during sex, or atherosclerosis could cause impotence.

Side effects from medications may also interfere with sex. "The sexual side effects could be decreased interest and decreased ability to actually engage in sexual activity," she explains. Yet, you may be able to change to a lower dose or switch to a new drug.

Sometimes sexual changes are a natural part of aging. Older women may have vaginal dryness, vaginal discharge, or low sexual interest, while men may get slower or less firm erections.

Talk with your doctor. How do you know when sexual changes are natural and when they're not? You don't. That's why it's important to discuss the matter with your doctor. Although that could be embarrassing, keep these hints in mind to make it easier.

- Remember that doctors hear about sexual issues all the time. Your doctor probably answered your question many times before.

- Ask for a pamphlet or other reading material that could help and ask where you can get more information. Try to be as clear and specific about your question or concern as you can.

- You may worry that your doctor is not qualified to help with your particular problem or he may be reluctant to handle sexual issues. If reasons like these stop you cold, ask for a referral to another doctor.

- If you are referred to a specialist — or choose to hunt for one yourself — contact the American Association of Sex Educators, Counselors, and Therapists. Find qualified health professionals listed at their Web site *www.aasect.org* or write them at P.O. Box 5488, Richmond, VA 23220-0488.

- Talk with a doctor who is the same gender as you are. If you're a woman and your regular doctor is a man, talk with a female gynecologist or to a woman nurse practitioner.

Learn all you can. After you make the appointment, do some research before you see the doctor. You'll feel better once you know a little more.

- Order the National Institute on Aging's free pamphlet, "Sexuality in Later Life" by calling 800-222-2225 or read it online at *www.niapublications.org*.

- Check out *www.sexualhealth.com*.

- Learn more about discussing sexual issues with your doctor by reading The National Council on the Aging's online article "Sex After 60: A Natural Part of Life." This is a *Seniors' Corner Health Tips* article you can find at *www.ncoa.org*.

Johnson recommends "Chapter 12. Where to Go for Help" in *The New Love and Sex After 60* by Robert N. Butler and Myrna I. Lewis. Check your local library or bookstore.

Hunt down a high-quality hospital

"There are some excellent hospitals and there are some not-so-good hospitals," says Kevin Soden, medical doctor and co-author of *Special Treatment: How to Get the Same High-Quality Health Care Your Doctor Gets.* "They can't all be number one in care. They all can't be number one in a particular surgical procedure, so do your homework."

Review hospital ratings. Soden recommends The Leapfrog Group *www.leapfroggroup.org* and Healthgrades *www.healthgrades.com.*

Visit The Leapfrog Group's Web site and you'll see how well hospitals meet standards for both quality and preventing medical errors. What's more, Leapfrog has recently added an exciting, new quality rating. Hospitals will be scored on how well they follow 27 of the National Quality Forum's Safe Practices. "These practices include 'creating a health care culture of safety,' having the right levels of nursing staff, and recommendations for hand washing to prevent infection," says Suzanne Delbanco, Executive Director of The Leapfrog Group.

Healthgrades rates hospitals on how rarely complications or deaths from selected types of surgery occur.

Check accreditation. Ask whether a hospital has accreditation from the Joint Commission on Accreditation of Healthcare Organizations (JCAHO). JCAHO evaluates the quality of each hospital's medical care, nursing care, patient safety program, special care units, pharmacy services, and more.

Find out about a hospital's accreditation and ratings by visiting the Quality Check Web site at *www.qualitycheck.org.* You'll find performance reports that include the hospital's contact information, accreditation details, overall performance rating, and how the hospital compares to other hospitals in many categories. To get a printed copy of the report, call the JCAHO Customer Service Center at 630-792-5800.

Count the nurses. Find out how many patients each nurse must care for. "Unfortunately, in some of the studies where the nurses were shorthanded, the risk of complications and the risk of death almost doubled," Soden comments.

Ask about experience. "Ask your doctor or surgeon about the specialties a particular hospital offers and how frequently the hospital provides the care or procedure that you require," advises Charles A. Mowll, JCAHO Executive Vice-President for Business Development, Government, and External Relations. "Ask about the hospital's success record in carrying out the specific medical procedure you need."

Hospital computers save lives

Hospitals that use computers to order medications, tests, and procedures may be safer. "The errors that can happen when prescribing medication can drop 88 percent when hospitals do this," says Suzanne Delbanco, Executive Director of The Leapfrog Group.

"It's like a ball team — if you only play ball once a year, you're not going to be as skilled as somebody who does it 50 times a year," Soden says. He suggests checking for the minimum number of surgeries recommended by The Leapfrog Group. "If your hospital isn't doing those numbers of procedures, then you're not going to be as well taken care of," he says.

Get more information. "Many hospitals have Web sites that outline their services and areas of expertise. You can always ring a hospital directly if you know the questions you need answers to. Hospitals that care about quality should be happy to help," says Delbanco. "Some states also collect and disseminate this information — check with the Department of Health in your state."

"Ask your doctor which hospital he or she would choose," Mowll says. "Then, ask why."

Top tips for a safer hospital stay

As many as 98,000 people die from medical errors each year, according to research. Mistakes range from surgery on the wrong patient to medication mix-ups.

"Assume that there is a potential for error at all times — and you're going to be the one to stop it before it happens," says Ilene Corina, President of Persons United Limiting Substandards and Errors in Healthcare and a Board member for the National Patient Safety Foundation.

Hospitals are working to prevent medical errors, but there are things you can do, too.

Bring help. Before you go to the hospital, ask a friend or family member to go with you as your advocate. "It has to be somebody who is going to speak up," Corina says. "Someone who is going to remember to ask questions." Your advocate tackles issues you don't feel well enough to handle. She guards against mistakes and jumps in if something seems wrong. She can also find answers, ask for clearer explanations, and take down instructions.

Remind caretakers. Dangerous bacteria can lurk on anyone's hands — from doctors to orderlies. Ask everyone who comes to tend you whether they've washed their hands. "In most cases, when I do it, they are grateful for the reminder," Corina says.

Ask and tell. "You definitely need to know who is in charge of your healthcare — who is the one person everybody is going to answer to," Corina says.

Yet, if you're not sure if that person — or any other caregiver — has important health information about you, speak up. You may be surprised at who needs to be reminded about your allergies or which over-the-counter medicines you take.

Monitor your medicines. "Check things like dosage of medication and ask the nurse who that medication is for — just like the nurse should be asking the patient's name and checking the wristband," Corina says. Follow the advice in *Beware of hidden drug hazards* on page 1, to prevent problems with medicines.

Be shrewd about surgery. Before the day of your surgery, understand exactly what will be done. Make sure that you, your doctor, and your surgeon agree on what should happen during surgery.

Dodge discharge danger. To be certain you know what to do after you go home, repeat the instructions, as you understand them, to your doctor or nurse. Remember to ask what to do if you have trouble after leaving the hospital.

Learn from JCAHO. Charles A. Mowll, Executive Vice-President for Business Development, Government, and External Relations for the Joint Commission on Accreditation of Healthcare Organizations (JCAHO) shares these recommendations from the JCAHO "Speak Up" program.

- Speak up if you have questions or concerns, and if you don't understand, ask again. It's your body and you have a right to know.

- Pay attention to the care you are receiving. Make sure you're getting the right treatments and medications by the right healthcare professionals. Don't assume anything.

- Educate yourself about your diagnosis, the medical tests you are undergoing, and your treatment plan.

- Use a hospital, clinic, surgery center, or other type of healthcare organization that has undergone a rigorous on-site evaluation against established state-of-the-art quality and safety standards, such as that provided by the Joint Commission.

- Participate in all decisions about your treatment. You are the center of the healthcare team.

For more information about ways to stay safe in the hospital, visit these Web sites:

Agency for Healthcare Research and Quality	www.ahrq.gov/consumer
National Patient Safety Foundation	www.npsf.org
Joint Commission on Accreditation of Healthcare Organizations	www.jcaho.org

Prevent infections after surgery

An infection at the site of your surgery can lengthen your hospital stay, boost your medical expenses — and kill you, according to a report from the Centers for Disease Control and Prevention (CDC). But hospitals are already working hard to help prevent these infections and you can, too.

Practice self-defense. A surgery-related infection is an inflammatory reaction that can occur within 30 days after surgery. These occur in 4 to 5 percent of all surgeries, say Marcia Postal-Ranney, R.N., Infection Control Practitioner and Gwen Hudson, R.N., Surgical Services Project Manager.

These registered nurses are members of the nationally recognized Surgical Infection Prevention team at Gwinnett Hospital System in Lawrenceville, Georgia. They offer these tips to help prevent post-surgery infections.

- Stop smoking.
- Maintain a healthy diet.
- Shower with an antiseptic soap the night before or morning of surgery.

- Follow the instructions of the doctors and nurses. Ask questions if there's something you don't understand.

- Wash your hands before touching the surgical site.

- Urge friends and family not to visit you if they are sick.

- Remind visitors to wash their hands when they enter your hospital room. And tell them not to use the bathroom in your room or sit on the hospital bed.

•Ask someone to write down the surgeon's instructions for what you should do after leaving the hospital. It is important to know when to change the bandage and visit the doctor, say Hudson and Postal-Ranney.

•Ask friends and family to help with housework or other chores until you feel strong enough to get back to your daily routine.

⚠ **Put herbs on hold before surgery**

Garlic, ginkgo, and ginseng are just three of the herbs that can make you bleed excessively during surgery. Other herbs such as valerian and kava kava might make your anesthesia pack a stronger punch — and long-term use of kava kava can cause liver damage. Echinacea might even slow your recovery.

Play it safe. Be sure to tell your doctor about any herbs you take or show him the packages so he can read the labels. Ask when you should stop taking the herbs and whether you need to taper off slowly.

Learn from the CDC. The CDC, located in Atlanta, is constantly discovering new ways to help keep people healthy. Follow these additional tips to prevent a surgical infection:

- Ask your doctor if you have time to lose weight before the surgery. You're more likely to get a surgical infection if you're overweight.

- Before the day of your surgery, be sure to tell your doctor if you're diabetic or if you suspect you might already have some kind of infection. Although these conditions may boost your odds of getting a surgical infection, your doctor can help lower the odds.

- Don't let anyone shave the part of your body that will be operated on. Trimming with clippers is allowed if hair has to be removed.

- Ask your hospital caretakers to wash their hands before tending to you, especially if they have to touch the surgical site.

- Find out how you can keep the pre-surgery part of your hospital stay as short as possible. The less time you spend in the hospital before the surgery, the less likely you are to get an infection.

Cut the fat out of your hospital bill

Receiving a hospital bill in the mail shouldn't send you back to the hospital. While billing mistakes can happen to anyone, you don't have to be a victim. Start protecting yourself from errors as soon as you're admitted to the hospital.

Record everything. "Keep a pad and pen next to your bed and make notes," recommends Cindy Holtzman, Director of Operations for Medical Refund Service, Inc., a medical bill overcharge and error review company in Marietta, Georgia.

She suggests you write down the names of medications you're given, the names of doctors who see you, when you get x-rays taken, and so on. Keep a record of anything you might be charged for. If you're concerned you might not be able to do this, ask friends or family members to help.

"Some services can be on the bill but never were rendered," Holtzman explains. Comparing your records to your hospital bill might help you catch those mistakes.

Grill your bill. When your hospital bill arrives, rip it open and start looking over the list of charges. If it's just a summary, ask the hospital for an itemized bill.

If that itemized bill is a confusing jumble of computer codes, Holtzman has a quick fix. "Call Patient Accounts and ask for explanations and details of the services performed."

Hunt for clues. Holtzman also has ideas to help you spot possible errors. "Check that the dates of service are correct, and look at all quantities listed."

For example, are you charged for 22 doses of a medication when you're sure you only had two? That's just one kind of typing error that might be in your bill. Keep an eye out for others, as well.

Watch for signs that you're billed twice for the same product or service. For example, Holtzman says you may find blankets, thermometers, and pillows billed separately when they were already included in the room charges.

Get professional help. "All hospitals have an audit department that will do an in-house audit on your bill," Holtzman points out. Keep in mind that they might find legitimate extra charges that were omitted from your original bill. But Holtzman adds, "Most of the time the error is in the favor of the patient."

Dispute the charge. If you think you've found a billing error, Holtzman says, "Call the Patient Accounts department and demand to speak to a supervisor." Ask them to investigate the possible error and to make a note of your call. Get the name of the person you talk with and write down the date and time you called.

"Also tell the supervisor to put a 30- or 60-day hold on the account until the dispute is resolved and a corrected balance obtained," Holtzman adds. That means while the dispute is under investigation, your bill won't be submitted to a collection agency or considered past due.

Keep medical information private

Imagine how your life would change if your medical records were widely published and anyone could read them. You'd probably get more calls from telemarketers trying to sell you health products. Your records could even attract scam artists or scare off a potential employer. Fortunately, regulation to prevent such problems is now part of HIPAA (Health Insurance Portability and Accountability Act). It's called the Privacy Rule.

According to the Privacy Rights Clearinghouse in San Diego, the Privacy Rule applies to any information that health plans and health care providers keep regarding your current, past, and future mental and physical health.

Health care providers and health plans include doctor's offices, hospitals, health insurers, and pharmacies. But the Privacy Rule does not affect life insurance companies, health Web sites, the Medical Information Bureau, or agencies that supply social security benefits.

So what does this privacy protection mean for you? The Privacy Rights Clearinghouse offers some guidance.

Dig for details. Find out everything you can about the privacy practices of your health care provider and health plan. Ask how your health information is distributed — both inside the office and elsewhere.

Your health plan and health care providers should give you a privacy policy notice that explains how your medical information is used and shared. It should also explain how to file a complaint with your health care provider and the Department of Health and Human Services (DHHS) if your privacy rights are violated.

Read this notice carefully and ask questions about anything you don't understand.

Examine authorizations. Health plans and health care providers don't need an authorization to use or disclose information just to give you treatment. So if you're asked to sign an authorization to distribute your information, read it with a critical eye. Authorizations to share your health information should not determine whether you get treatment. Only sign the authorization if it benefits you.

Check your records. Take advantage of your right to see and review your medical records. Check them for accuracy and ask for any errors to be corrected. You may have to pay to get a copy of your records, but the Privacy Rule puts a limit on fees.

Know your health care rights

You're entitled to quality care, a clean, safe environment, and other important things when you visit a hospital. Find out about these rights and how you can help the hospital staff care for you better. It's all in the American Hospital Association (AHA) brochure *The Patient Care Partnership: Understanding Expectations, Rights and Responsibilities.*

Visit the AHA's Web site at *www.aha.org* and click on *Communicating with Patients.* From there you can download the brochure.

Right a wrong. If you feel your privacy rights have been violated, file a complaint. You cannot be denied treatment for filing a complaint, but you must file within 180 days of the violation.

Try filing with your health providers first to see if they'll answer your concern quickly. If that fails, submit a complaint to the DHHS Office of Civil Rights. Write them at U.S. Department of Health and Human Services, Office of Civil Rights, 200 Independence Avenue, S.W., Washington, D.C. 20201.

For more on the HIPAA Privacy Rule, surf to *www.privacyrights.org* and read the Privacy Rights Clearinghouse fact sheet, *HIPAA Basics: Medical Privacy in the Electronic Age.* To find out if your state laws give you even more privacy protection than the HIPAA Privacy Rule, contact your state government or visit *www.privacyrights.org.*

Verify insurance watchdog's records

You may not know much about the Medical Information Bureau (MIB), but they might have information about you. What's more, MIB is a watchdog for insurance application fraud, so you need to be certain your record is accurate. Get the scoop on how MIB gets information, the details they keep, and what to do to make sure your record is right.

Follow a paper trail. "MIB is a not-for-profit association of approximately 500 life insurance companies located throughout North America," explains David Aronson, Director of Corporate Communications at MIB. When you apply for life or health insurance from one of those companies, your insurance forms may include an authorization to send data to MIB. Once you sign, the insurance company can send MIB medical facts and other details related to your insurance application.

Don't worry. But you won't find medical records at MIB. Instead, MIB records contain codes. Most codes represent medical information that could affect your health or length of life — such as blood pressure or weight. A few codes are reserved for nonmedical information, like a poor driving record or involvement in hazardous sports. Yet, if you were once a daredevil skydiver, don't worry. MIB deletes information after seven years.

Check your record. You can find out whether MIB has a record about you, but you'll need to do a little paperwork.

Although the HIPAA Privacy Rule doesn't apply to MIB, they still check that the person requesting your record is really you — and not just someone pretending to be you. That's why you have to fill out MIB's Application for Disclosure form before you can see your record. Getting the form is easy. Just contact their disclosure office or visit their Web site.

"You can send an e-mail request to disclosure@mib.com or you can call MIB directly," says Aronson. "The number for U.S. disclosure is 617-426-3660. In Canada, the phone number is 416-597-0590." You can also visit *www.mib.com* to find out how to download the form in PDF format. (You may need free software from *www.adobe.com* to view and print documents in this format.)

You are automatically entitled to a free copy of your record if your insurance company says you've been denied coverage or charged a much higher premium based on information obtained from MIB. Otherwise, MIB usually charges around $9 for the record report. But this may change under new regulations. So if you call or e-mail, ask whether you must pay a fee. If you download the form, be sure to check fee information on the Web site.

Fill out the application form and sign it carefully before mailing it to MIB. MIB uses your written signature to verify your identity.

Fix a flaw. If you find an error in your record, contact MIB and ask for a Request for Reinvestigation form. Use that form to tell MIB which part of your record is wrong. MIB will trace the information back to its source. If they can confirm an error in your record, they'll correct it.

MRIs: no need for worries

An MRI (Magnetic Resonance Imaging) scan can help discover the reason for your back pain, recent stroke, or even why you have headaches. "It's a tool that lets radiologists look into a person's body without surgery," says Dr. Ramon E. Figueroa,

Professor of Radiology and Chief of Neuroradiology at the Medical College of Georgia.

Instead of radiation or X-rays, the MRI scan uses a magnetic field, radio waves, and a computer to make detailed pictures. Doctors can detect brain and spine disorders, track down joint problems in knees, hips, or shoulders, diagnose acute strokes, and more.

Find out how to prepare for an MRI, what to expect, and what you can do to get first-class results.

Pick the right type. You may be able to choose from three kinds of MRIs.

- Closed MRI. You lie on a padded couch that slides into a tunnel for your scan. A powerful magnet generates a high-quality, clear image. If you suffer from claustrophobia, this type of MRI can be a problem.

- Open MRI. These machines are open on the sides and well tolerated by most people. However, they generate a much weaker magnetic field and Figueroa cautions, "As a general rule, the images on an open MRI will be less sharp."

- Portable MRI. These smaller devices can scan just one part of your body — such as a hand or foot — and are most useful in pinpointing infections and tumors of soft tissue.

Shed light on abnormal test results

You just found out your blood test or medical test results are "abnormal." Before you worry, discuss these questions with your doctor.

- Did I have a list of things to do before the test? A list of things to avoid? Did I follow those instructions carefully?

- Are the test results abnormal enough to be a real concern?

- Do I have a habit, health condition, or another circumstance that could skew the test results?

Although not yet widely available, new MRI devices allow you to stand or sit comfortably in large open rooms or chair-like structures.

Mention your metals. Before the MRI, tell your doctor or the staff if you have a pacemaker, aneurysm clip, metal implant, or any metallic foreign object in your body, such as metal shrapnel, iron filings, or bullet fragments. These make an MRI too dangerous for you. If you are wearing anything metallic — including jewelry — remove it before the scan.

Come prepared. "MRI is well tolerated by most people, since nothing is touching you or pressing upon you inside of the scanner," Figueroa says. However, tell your doctor or the MRI staff if you're worried about claustrophobia. Your doctor can prescribe a mild sedative like Valium to help.

As the MRI takes pictures, you may hear tapping, knocking, or other sounds. If you think this racket might bother you, ask for headphones or earplugs. They can tone down both noise and nerves.

Figueroa says the average scan takes about 40 minutes. During that time, you must keep very still, so tell the technician if this is difficult for you.

Get good results. Make sure a qualified person performs and interprets your scan. "Look for a radiologist certified by the American Board of Radiology," advises Figueroa. "This means a person fully trained and tested to perform high quality imaging studies. You and your insurance will be paying for the test, so you may as well get the most qualified person to supervise and read it."

Skip a Pap test or two

"We recommend women get Pap tests every year, starting about 3 years after they start having sexual intercourse," says Debbie

Saslow, Ph.D., Director of Breast and Cervical Cancer Control for the American Cancer Society (ACS).

But she says you might be able to skip your Pap test this year if:

- you're over 30 and your last three Pap results were normal. Then, the ACS says get a Pap every 2 to 3 years.
- you've had a hysterectomy with your cervix removed. If the surgery was ordered because you had cervical cancer, however, this may not apply.
- you're over 70 and have been getting normal Pap test results for the last 10 years.

On the other hand, Saslow stresses that you should still get a Pap test every year if:

- you had a recent Pap test result that found a serious abnormality or any high-grade abnormal result.
- you take drugs that suppress your immune system — chemotherapy drugs, for example.
- your mother took the drug DES (diethylstilbestrol) during pregnancy.
- you are HIV positive.

Remember, if detected at an early stage, cervical cancer is one of the most successfully treated cancers. Talk to your doctor about your risks and options.

ACS says mammograms save lives

Breast cancer will strike more than 200,000 women this year. And yet, a simple test can have a huge impact on saving lives from this disease. "Mammograms are the best tool we have to find breast cancer early," says Debbie Saslow, Ph.D., Director of

Breast and Cervical Cancer Control for the American Cancer Society (ACS). If you've questioned whether or not you should schedule your mammogram this year, let the ACS be your guide.

Topple the age myths. "Any woman over 40 who is in fairly good health should get a mammogram every year," says Saslow. "While fewer women in their 40s will get breast cancer," she explains, "it's better to start at that age because there are more years of life saved by detecting and treating it early."

Breast cancer is usually more aggressive in younger women than in older women, but Saslow points out, "Risk of cancer — and risk of death from cancer — increase with age. So mammograms are very important for women in their 60s and 70s — and even 80s."

In addition, she says, "The chance of a false positive result decreases with age because of something called density. The breast tissue tends to become less dense on a mammogram with age, making it easier for a radiologist to read and see if anything abnormal is present."

Consider your risk. Some women should start having mammograms before 40 and be especially diligent about scheduling them and discussing additional screening techniques.

"Women with a strong family history of breast and/or ovarian cancer, women who know they have a breast cancer gene in their family, and survivors of Hodgkin's disease who received radiation treatment as young women should start early with mammograms," says Saslow. "Our new guidelines have a lot of specific guidance for these women and their doctors."

Evaluate your health. If a woman is in poor physical or mental health, Saslow says weigh the benefits of a mammogram against the drawbacks. The procedure may be too taxing or traumatic.

Know the limitations. "Mammograms, like most medical tests, are not perfect," Saslow says. "They find about 75 to 85 percent of breast cancers, not 100 percent. If a woman feels a lump in her breast that is not seen on a mammogram — whether the mammogram can find it or not — that lump needs to be checked out."

False positives can be very upsetting, too, but Saslow explains why that possibility shouldn't keep women from getting mammograms. "For every cancer that a mammogram finds, maybe 10 potential abnormalities will be found that turn out not to be cancer."

"If we followed up fewer abnormalities," she says, "there would be fewer false positives but we would also miss more cancers."

Stay informed. "The American Cancer Society recently developed guidance for physicians and interested patients about life expectancy, competing health concerns, and breast cancer screening," says Saslow. For more information on the limitations and benefits of breast cancer screening, Saslow says to visit the ACS Web site, *www.cancer.org*, or call them toll-free at 800-ACS-2345.

"Mammograms do not prevent cancer," she says, "but they are very good at finding breast cancer at an early enough point to successfully treat with the most options."

Nutritional know-how

Sweet treat your heart will love

If it tastes good, it must be bad for you — or so you thought. New research shows that eating a small amount of dark chocolate is good for your heart.

Chocolate is made from cocoa, which is high in antioxidant flavonoids. Recent studies show that flavonoids can decrease bad LDL cholesterol and increase good HDL cholesterol. They also improve blood flow and reduce your risk of forming blood clots that lead to heart attack and stroke.

Unfortunately, not all chocolate is created equal. Cocoa powder and dark chocolate seem to offer the most heart-healthy benefits. You'll want to stay away from milk chocolate. Researchers found that eating milk chocolate or drinking milk with dark chocolate interferes with the absorption of antioxidants, canceling out some of the health benefits.

Researchers also discovered that during the making of chocolate, certain processing and handling methods destroy flavonoids. However, the cocoa in Dove dark chocolate, called Cocoapro, is specially processed to retain more flavonoids. When buying chocolate, look for the Cocoapro logo.

If you're concerned about calories, look for small pieces of dark chocolate with less fat, such as Dove's dark chocolate Promises. One piece has 42 calories and a little more than 2 grams of fat.

Just remember to go easy on the chocolate. A heart-healthy diet is based on fresh fruits and vegetables, whole grains, and low-fat dairy products.

You'll also be glad to know flavonoids aren't just good for your heart. Flavonoid-rich foods can lower your risk of lung cancer, prostate cancer, asthma, and type 2 diabetes.

Cut health risks with green tea

It's hard to believe something as soothing as a warm cup of tea could protect you from disease, but it's true. And for thousands of years the Asian world has known the health secrets of this simple beverage.

According to legend, the Chinese Emperor Shen-Nung discovered this tasty drink by accident in 2737 BC. As the story goes, the emperor was boiling a kettle of water on a terrace when some leaves from a nearby bush happened to drift by and fall into the water.

The emperor tasted the brew and found it delicious. It wasn't long before people were adding the leaves to kettles all over China and the Far East and enjoying the protective benefits of this plant.

Both black and green teas are made from the same bush, native to China and India, *Camellia sinensis*. Green tea is different only in how it's prepared. Unlike black tea, which is fermented, green tea leaves are steamed soon after being picked. This steaming process helps preserve the plant's antioxidants, called tannins or polyphenols.

Many scientists believe green tea antioxidants are more powerful than those found in most vegetables. Green tea also contains B vitamins and vitamin C and is lower in caffeine than black tea. Because of the powerful ability of one of its antioxidants to fight cell-damaging free radicals, this natural drink is gaining a reputation as a warrior against aging and disease.

Halt heart disease and stroke. While you are lingering over another cup, green tea is working to lower your blood pressure and cholesterol. That means less risk of suffering a heart attack or stroke. A long-term study of older men in the Netherlands showed a relationship between heart disease and stroke risk and how much fruit, vegetables, and tea the men consumed. Those with the highest intake of these antioxidant-rich foods were the least likely to die from heart disease or stroke.

Researchers think an amino acid in green tea, called theanine, is responsible for keeping blood less sticky so it can move smoothly through your arteries. Preventing plaque build-up this way can reduce your risk of heart disease, stroke, and other health problems.

Contain cancer. If cancer is a frequent visitor to your family tree, green tea might be your new best friend. Studies show it fights cancers of the breast, stomach, colon, prostate, and skin. But it doesn't stop there. Green tea can even help chemotherapy patients get the most out of their treatment. Often during chemotherapy, cancer cells stop responding to the drugs. But a study in Germany showed green tea could make the resistant cancer cells start responding again.

Benefit your bones. Did you know your teacup can be a powerful weapon against osteoporosis? More than 1,000 tea-drinking women in England had their bone density measured. Surprisingly, they had stronger bones than the women who avoided tea. And even though these women were drinking black tea, the benefit came from antioxidants found in both green and black teas. In addition, it didn't seem to matter if the women smoked, used hormone replacement therapy, drank coffee, or added milk to their tea — the results were the same.

Fight the doldrums with flax

What in the world is flax? Remember all those mummy movies you saw as a kid? Well, those mummies were wrapped in flax — or specifically, linen — which comes from the flax plant along with flaxseed and flaxseed oil.

Of course, the plant's seeds are where you get your health benefits. They're a great source of the omega-3 fatty acids your body craves, and they provide a big boost of fiber as well.

"I started to use flax because my mother used it, and she's 78, healthy, and beautiful," says Chicago actress/model Susan Franz, a flax enthusiast. "I've been eating flax for 10 years, I would say pretty much every day. Besides, it helps to keep me regular." As Franz notes, flaxseed's rich supply of fiber helps to keep you on time, every time.

Many people like to grind the seed into flour and use it for baking breads, muffins, cakes, or even pancakes. But if that's too much trouble, just add it to your food or recipes. "I sprinkle it on my cereal and in my cookies, but I especially like it sprinkled on ice cream," says Franz.

It's best to crush or grind the flaxseed before eating, though. Otherwise your body won't absorb all the nutrients as the flax passes through your system.

Flaxseed oil is another way to get a good dose of essential omega-3. You can use flaxseed oil on salads or on vegetables in place of butter. Don't cook with flaxseed oil, though, because it breaks down in high heat and could be harmful.

Attack arthritis with omega-3. When your body's fatty acids are balanced, it helps prevent the breakdown of your immune system, which can cause rheumatoid arthritis. Research has shown that a diet high in flaxseed oil also may reduce inflammation. "I feel it helps my arthritis," Franz says. "It's one of those foods that works for you in subtle ways."

Fortify your mind with flax. Around 100 years ago, doctors discovered that the lack of vitamin B in diets contributed to mental problems and exhaustion. Additional research found that your body needs omega-3 acids to use vitamin B.

When patients with manic depression and fear of open spaces were given one to six tablespoons of flaxseed oil daily, most got noticeably better. Some reported feeling calm for the first time in years. "It's a natural mood enhancer," Franz agrees. "When I don't take it I can tell. Although it may not cure anybody's depression, it does elevate your mood."

So take Franz's advice, and sprinkle some flaxseed on your next scoop of fat-free ice cream. You'll give your body and mind a much-needed boost.

Grab garlic for your health

Some people say a clove of garlic a day keeps health problems away. According to garlic grower Loyd Hubbard of the Gnos Garlic Company, it's true. "Garlic is a natural antibiotic and detoxifier," says Hubbard. "In addition, it can purify the blood naturally and lower blood cholesterol."

Garlic is the number three spice used in America, but its strengths go far beyond its use as a savory food seasoning. In fact, garlic may protect you from just about everything, from the common cold to heart disease.

Why is garlic so special? Crushing garlic produces a powerful, penicillin-like compound called allicin. The allicin breaks down to create several sulfur compounds plus a substance called ajoene, giving garlic its distinctive smell. In addition, garlic is a good source of selenium, and it's chock-full of antioxidants that protect your body. Here are six ways garlic helps wallop health problems.

Strike at atherosclerosis. The build-up of cholesterol in the heart's arteries is the leading cause of death in the Western world. Garlic helps to lower cholesterol and blood pressure, protecting the heart's arteries from potential disaster.

Control cholesterol. Slash your cholesterol — even without drugs — just by eating two vegetables you can grow right in your garden. Garlic goes after your bad LDL cholesterol without harming your good HDL cholesterol. Garlic's cousin, the onion, may also lower cholesterol. Onions have plenty of flavonoids, including quercetin, which stop LDL cholesterol from oxidizing and blocking your arteries.

> ### Nature's herbal healers
>
> Sometimes herbs work as well as or better than their drug counterparts. Here are five healing herbs to try.
>
> - Garlic — Lowers cholesterol, stops blood from clumping, and slows the stiffening of your arteries.
>
> - Peppermint — Makes a great-tasting tea that relieves indigestion, upset stomach, and even gas.
>
> - Valerian — Soothes your mind and helps relieve tension while giving you a good night's sleep.
>
> - Ginger — Relieves motion sickness, including dizziness, nausea, and vomiting.
>
> - Saw Palmetto — Increases urine flow while decreasing urination frequency. Plus it may reduce prostate size.

Lower blood pressure. Garlic lowers cholesterol, which allows your blood to flow more freely through your arteries. That means lower blood pressure and less stress on your heart.

Pulverize clots. Ajoene, along with other compounds, stops blood from clumping and clotting. This also allows your blood to keep flowing, reducing the risk of heart attack or stroke.

Battle bacteria. Allicin is a potent antibiotic that kills a variety of bacteria, viruses, fungi, mold, yeasts, and parasites. Some of garlic's victims include *H. pylori, Salmonella, Staphylococcus, E. coli,* and *Candida.*

Strengthen immunity. Garlic can boost your immune system so you're less likely to get sick with colds or flu. So don't reach for that box of tissues — grab some garlic instead.

All these benefits are a boost to your health, but if you don't like the taste, you probably still won't eat it. So, what's the best-tasting garlic to cook with? Hubbard recommends elephant garlic, which is considered the Vidalia onion of garlic because you can eat the bulb raw.

"Elephant garlic is the best garlic to cook with," Hubbard says. "It has a smoother, milder, sweeter flavor that doesn't overpower the main dish. It's the specialty garlic for the connoisseur. Some of our best customers are executive chefs in four-star restaurants."

When cooking with any fresh garlic, mince or crush it, and wait 10 to 15 minutes before cooking it to get the full health benefits. If you can't eat fresh garlic, try supplements that contain aged garlic extract.

Behold the wonders of ginger

Ginger ale became a popular beverage when James Vernor of Detroit concocted America's oldest soft drink just after the Civil War. In fact, ginger ale was the nation's most popular soft drink until prohibition. Then it became linked with alcohol and was ignored by the nondrinking public.

Unlike most ginger ales of the time, Vernor's managed to survive and gain popularity. Although ginger ale never became number one again, it still remains a popular drink.

Today, Vernor's is one of the few ginger ales that actually contains real ginger. Most use ginger flavoring, which doesn't provide ginger's stomach-soothing benefits.

Calm a queasy stomach. Ginger fights motion sickness without annoying side effects. It relieves dizziness, nausea, and vomiting when you're in just about anything that moves — a boat, plane, or car. By relaxing the nerves and muscles in your digestive tract, ginger promises one quiet ride. Ginger may also prevent nausea from surgery, chemotherapy, and morning sickness.

Unfortunately, ginger doesn't work for everyone. To see if it helps you, try ginger supplements or candied ginger. You can buy supplements at any natural food store. Herbal experts recommend taking two 500-milligram (mg) pills about an hour before travel. If you still feel sick, take one or two more every four hours. You can find candied ginger at most grocery stores and Asian markets. A piece of candied ginger an inch square by one-quarter inch thick is equal to a 500-mg pill.

Just be sure to talk with your doctor before taking ginger supplements — and never take large doses.

Natural ginger ale

Most ginger ale soft drinks contain ginger flavoring — not the actual ginger root. Here's a tasty ginger ale recipe that will give you the benefits of real ginger.

1 teaspoon finely ground fresh ginger root

1/4 cup sugar

3 cups plain water

1/4 teaspoon lemon juice

1 cup carbonated water (optional)

Bring ginger and water to a boil. Simmer for 20 minutes on low heat. Strain ginger water through a sieve into a bowl. Stir in sugar and lemon juice, and add carbonated water if desired.

Soothe aches and pains. Researchers in Denmark suggest ginger could relieve everyday muscle pain and migraines, as well as take the ache and inflammation out of arthritis — without any side effects. It's no wonder the Arthritis Foundation lists ginger as an effective herbal remedy for pain. Just to be on the safe side, talk with your doctor before trading in your medication for ginger.

Shut out cancer. Ginger is chock-full of nutrients called phytochemicals. Many of these phytochemicals are well-known antioxidants that could ward off diseases, like cancer. Scientists discovered that ginger contains at least 12 different phytochemicals, making it one of the most potent food sources of antioxidants. Out of the dozen, curcumin is known as a potential tumor fighter. Like all antioxidants, it helps your body capture and flush out cancer-causing free radicals.

'Exotic' seasoning keeps you healthy

Whether you're the adventurous type or not, you might want to spice up your life with curry powder. This blend of spices, herbs, and seeds, including chili peppers, cumin, nutmeg, cloves, fennel seed, mace, cayenne, sesame seed, black pepper, saffron, and turmeric, offers important health benefits as well as great taste.

You can find curry powder at your local grocers or natural food store. Here are a few things you'll want to know before you start cooking.

- There are two styles of curry powder — standard, which is spicy, and Madras, which is spicy hot.
- You can get rid of curry powder's raw taste by sautéing it in a dab of butter before adding it to your recipe.
- Sprinkle a pinch of curry powder on any food to give it an exotic flavor.

- Curry gets hotter the longer it stands, so don't wait too long to enjoy its savory taste.

The main ingredient in curry powder — turmeric — gives curried dishes their yellow color. More importantly, turmeric contains curcumin, a powerful antioxidant. Curcumin and other phytochemicals in turmeric may reduce inflammation, safeguard your liver, and improve digestion.

Reduce swelling. Many herbalists say if you want relief from pain and swelling try turmeric. It could work as well as ibuprofen and other nonsteroidal anti-inflammatory drugs (NSAIDs), but without side effects.

Turmeric might even be powerful enough to fight the stiffness and swelling of rheumatoid arthritis and osteoarthritis, according to the Arthritis Foundation.

Rejuvenate your liver. This incredible organ spends a lifetime keeping your blood clean. During all that time, what keeps your liver clean? One answer could be turmeric and its team of antioxidants. They put the kibosh on free radicals and other toxic chemicals before they can harm your liver.

Aid digestion. If you get stomach pain after eating fatty foods, turmeric might offer some relief. This type of indigestion results from a poor flow of bile from your liver to your gallbladder. Turmeric gets your bile flowing, which could relieve your pain. In fact, it works so well some

---

⚠️ Avoid arthritis triggers

When it comes to arthritis, you're better off avoiding foods that may aggravate your condition. Possible trigger foods include milk, shrimp, wheat products, and certain meats, as well as nightshade vegetables like tomatoes, potatoes, eggplant, and bell peppers. Try cutting out these eight pain-inducing foods one at a time to see if your condition improves.

herbal experts recommend dissolving up to a half tablespoon (about 3 grams) of turmeric in warm milk and drinking it every day to relieve indigestion.

However, if your symptoms are severe, they could indicate a more serious condition, like gallstones. Before you treat yourself with turmeric, check with your doctor.

Apples: the ultimate health food

Go ahead, bite into one. Don't you just love its texture, its crispness, and its sweet succulent flavor? Whether it's a Granny Smith, a McIntosh, or a Red Delicious, an apple can add a tasty dose of fun to your day.

Filled with fiber, vitamins, minerals, and antioxidants, an apple is also fat-free, cholesterol-free, and low in sodium. In other words, it's one of the healthiest snacks you can eat.

"Apples are the ultimate in healthy convenience food," says Anna Maenner, Executive Director of the Wisconsin Apple Grower's Association. "They're easy to carry and they stay crisp in the refrigerator or wherever you want to take them."

They can also be part of a great family experience if you're lucky enough to have an orchard nearby. Just pack a picnic lunch, load the grandkids into the car, and drive over for an afternoon of apple-picking fun. When you're done, you may even find a gift shop, bakery, petting zoo, or wagon ride to finish off your day.

"Orchards have learned to diversify," Maenner says about the variety of activities now available. "They are finding creative ways to get consumers to come to their orchards more often and to spend more time there when they do come."

To keep your apples fresh, Maenner recommends storing them in your refrigerator's crisper drawer in a vented plastic bag. "Don't just dump them into the crisper," she says. "They'll pick up the odors of the other vegetables."

By getting into an apple-a-day habit, here are some of the ways your body will benefit.

Become more regular. Experts say you can prevent many illnesses just by avoiding chronic constipation. In fact, just one apple with its skin contains 4 to 5 grams of fiber — the important nutrient that keeps you as regular as your morning cup of coffee.

So if you want to be on time all the time, try replacing your afternoon snack with a crisp delicious apple.

Fend off arthritis. Modern countries have replaced fruits and vegetables with fast, processed foods, and large parts of their populations suffer from arthritis. Nutrition experts think this is no coincidence. The problem may be a trace mineral called boron, which is absorbed from the soil by many plants, including apples.

> ### Best way to clean fruits and vegetables
>
> To make your produce safer to eat, thoroughly rinse it under running water to remove contaminants. This may not eliminate bacteria completely, but it will reduce their number. Clean sturdy fruits and vegetables, like apples and potatoes, with a vegetable brush.
>
> Also, don't clean your produce with soap or liquid dishwashing detergent. And think twice before using expensive fruit and vegetable rinses, which claim to remove dirt, pesticides, and bacteria. Instead, soak your produce in an inexpensive vinegar bath for about 15 minutes. Just don't use vinegar on fruit with little pores or hairs. It might affect the taste.

Most people get 1 to 2 milligrams (mg) of boron a day. But experts believe you need 3 to 10 mg to affect your risk of arthritis. To make your joint-saving quota of boron, pair an apple with other boron-rich foods like peanut butter and raisins.

Lower heart disease risk. The magnesium and potassium in apples help regulate your blood pressure and your heartbeat. But it's the flavonoid quercetin that seems to do the most good. It protects your artery walls from damage and keeps your blood flowing smoothly. Research has shown that eating flavonoid-rich foods like apples helps lower your risk of heart disease.

Discover the sweetness of figs

Try to picture an inside-out strawberry. Hard to do, isn't it? But that's exactly what you'll see when you cut into a fig. If you've never tried one, you're missing out on an incredibly sweet and chewy taste sensation.

"I eat them because of the fiber and minerals they have, and I love their sweet taste," says Ghaida Barazi, an accountant and fig aficionado. "I eat them dried all year-round, but I really love to eat them fresh during fig season."

Figs have been used throughout the ages as a wholesome snack and for baking tasty desserts. Barazi likes to eat them as jam, but not the type you're used to. To create this jam, you make syrup out of water, sugar, and lemon juice, then add the whole figs and boil them.

"The fig softens and becomes a sweet dessert that you can spoon up," says Barazi. "They taste great and satisfy my sweet tooth in a healthy way."

Figs offer a powerhouse of nutrients and are a sweet way to get exactly what your body desires. And because they're fat-free, sodium-free, and cholesterol-free, they benefit not only your health but your waistline, too.

Guard against heart disease. Figs contain more fiber and minerals than most other common fruits. Recent studies have shown that fiber may help lower your cholesterol, which can slash your risk of heart disease.

Figs also contain phytosterols that help decrease natural cholesterol production in your body. Plus, the polyphenols in figs, which act like antioxidants, are known to stop low-density lipoprotein (LDL) cholesterol from oxidizing and building up in your arteries.

In addition, eating figs regularly may help keep your blood pressure under control. The combination of potassium and calcium in figs, along with eating less sodium, can give your body the one-two punch it needs.

Battle high blood sugar. As a diabetic, you need to think twice about everything you eat. But you can feel confident eating figs because they're naturally low in carbohydrates and high in fiber. Fiber lowers your glucose by slowing the amount your body absorbs through your small intestines.

A recent study found that diabetics who ate a high-fiber diet — 50 grams per day — helped keep their blood sugar, insulin, and cholesterol under control.

Tackle kidney stones. If you suffer from kidney stones, you should avoid high-oxalate foods like spinach, tomatoes, peanuts, coffee, tea, and chocolate. But if you do choose to eat them, have a few figs as well. Their high calcium content will help keep your body from absorbing the oxalate.

You also have a higher risk of developing kidney stones when your body is low in potassium. Eating potassium-rich figs is a good way to prevent stones from forming.

Power up with a handful of grapes

Remember the episode of *I Love Lucy* where she squashes grapes with her feet in a large vat? Grapes have been used in many ways in movie and TV land, but some of the best ways never received star billing.

For example, grapes can be the center of some great-tasting recipes. How about hot, steaming pancakes covered in grape syrup? Or maybe a slice of tasty grape cheesecake? During Hanukkah you can make Perfect Passover Grape Pie.

For something really different, try combining fresh grapes, cilantro, and chili peppers for a grape salsa that will rival any tomato-based version.

You can find great grape recipes like these simply by searching online or browsing through your local bookstore. But the easiest way to enjoy grapes is to simply pluck them off the stems and pop them into your mouth. Eat some every day, and your body will burst with good health.

Squash heart disease. Can you say resveratrol? When it comes to grapes, this plant estrogen is a disease-battling hero. Found in the skins, it helps prevent heart disease by fighting inflammation and preventing blood clots.

Grape skins also contain the powerful flavonoid quercetin. It's an antioxidant that helps stop cholesterol from building up in your arteries and blocking blood flow to your heart and brain. It also keeps your blood from becoming sticky and clumping together, which lowers your risk of stroke.

Because red wine uses the grape skin during processing, researchers believe it may help ward off heart disease. Several European studies suggest a glass or two a day will lower your risk of dying from heart disease by about 40 percent.

Non-alcoholic wine and grape juice have about half the flavonoids of red wine but are still chock-full of antioxidants. Try substituting grape juice for your morning orange juice for a heart-healthy start to your day.

Squeeze out cancer. Resveratrol is also a superhero when it comes to battling cancer. This phytoestrogen thwarts cancer by acting as an antioxidant and fighting inflammation, cell mutation, and tumors.

Add in the powerful antioxidant actions of quercetin and other flavonoids, and the dangerous free radicals that damage your cells and cause cancer won't stand a chance.

Pulverize kidney stones. Kidney stones are said to be one of the most painful conditions you can have. By drinking more, you help flush the toxins that cause stones out of your system.

Surprisingly, red wine may help more than most other fluids, Harvard researchers say. Their studies show that a daily glass of red wine may cut the risk of stone formation by 39 percent for men and 59 percent for women.

If you don't drink alcohol, be sure to take advantage of the antioxidant power of grape juice.

Boost your body with oranges

We should all plunge into health-oriented grocery shopping with the enthusiasm of a 14-year-old girl at the local mall, right? Well, maybe not, but the importance of adding healthy foods to your diet goes far beyond the pains of shopping.

If you regularly add oranges to your shopping cart, you've already made a good start. They are loaded with vitamin C, carotenoids, folate, fiber, and potassium — all essential nutrients for a healthy body.

Vitamin C in particular is a body booster. But, surprisingly, fresh oranges may not be the best way to get this vitamin. The amount of vitamin C in oranges differs from one variety to the next. Plus, it breaks down over time and with changing temperatures.

A recent study has shown that frozen concentrate orange juice may be your best source. Researchers examined different brands of frozen concentrate and ready-to-drink cartons of orange juice. They found that the frozen juice mixed with water contained more vitamin C than ready-to-drink juices. Plus, it retained the vitamin C longer.

So the next time you visit the grocery store, head to the frozen-food aisle to pick up your OJ. You'll not only save money over ready-to-drink brands, you'll get more vitamin C for your buck. And here are some of the healthy ways you'll benefit.

Fight colds. The high level of vitamin C in oranges spurs your body's immune system into action, lessening the severity and length of a cold.

Studies also show that vitamin C foods like oranges, strawberries, peppers, and spinach can lower the amount of histamine in your blood. That will help clear up your allergy symptoms, including your stuffy nose, without your having to rely on drugs.

Cancel cataracts. Vitamin C may help in slowing or stalling the onset of cataracts, which is a fogginess in the lens of your eye. Taking a combination of vitamin C and vitamin A is even better — it seems to stop cataracts in their tracks.

Axe arthritis. If you suffer from arthritis, vitamin C can come to the rescue. It builds and repairs the cartilage, ligaments, and tendons around your bones. And its powerful antioxidant abilities keep your tissues from aging as quickly, which slows down the development of osteoarthritis.

Boost your energy. Your brain also uses vitamin C to produce serotonin, a chemical that helps you sleep and makes you feel good. Without enough, you may feel tired and lack energy.

Halt heart disease. The antioxidant powers of vitamin C may lower your low-density lipoprotein (LDL) or bad cholesterol. It may also lower your blood pressure and improve blood flow, shrinking your risk of stroke.

Slash cancer risk. Studies show the antioxidant powers of vitamin C may protect you from cancers of the stomach, throat, lung, bladder, and pancreas.

Douse heartburn pain with orange peels

Did you know heartburn medications inhibit your body's absorption of several minerals? "We have one of the largest rates of osteoporosis in the world, and we're giving people medications every single day that block the absorption of calcium," says Dr. Decker Weiss, a naturopathic physician in Phoenix.

Recent studies of a product made from orange peels, called Heartburn Free, show that orange peel's active compound, d-limonene, relieves occasional heartburn, acid indigestion, and upset stomach without sacrificing the minerals your body needs.

You can find Heartburn Free at health food stores. If you have constant heartburn, or an ulcer, talk with your doctor before using it.

Nutrition-packed avocados beat disease

Football fans eat more than 40 million pounds of avocados during a Super Bowl game. The guacamole alone would be enough to bury a football field from end zone to end zone to a depth of more than 7 feet.

The Super Bowl generates the biggest demand for avocados all year. In fact, an "AvoBowl" taste-off is held a few days before the game featuring guacamole recipes created for each Super Bowl team. The team with the best-tasting guacamole has won the NFL championship five out of eight times.

Those aren't bad odds — but eating avocados could give you even better odds for a long, healthy life.

Tackle bad cholesterol. The avocado is high in fat — 30 grams per fruit, but it's mostly monounsaturated fat. This fat helps protect good HDL cholesterol, while wiping out the bad LDL cholesterol that clogs your arteries. That means you not only lower your bad cholesterol, you also improve your ratio of good HDL to total cholesterol.

But there's more than just monounsaturated fat at work. An avocado contains 10 grams of fiber, as well as a plant chemical called beta-sitosterol. These both help lower cholesterol. Throw in vitamins C and E — powerful antioxidants that prevent dangerous free radicals from reacting with the cholesterol in your blood — and it all adds up to a healthier heart.

> ### Super avocado tips
>
> To ripen avocados, place them in a paper bag with an apple for a few days. You'll know they're ripe when the skin is dark and it yields to gentle pressure. Don't buy avocados with dark blemishes on the skin.
>
> You can freeze avocado puree. Just add a tablespoon of lemon juice, to prevent discoloration, for every two pureed avocados. Place the prepared puree in a freezer container with no more than a half-inch of airspace. Use the puree within four to five months.

If you're on a cholesterol-lowering diet, in addition to avocados, add heart-healthy artichokes and sweet potatoes to help reduce your cholesterol levels.

Sideline diabetes. Eating high-fiber foods, like avocados, can benefit people with type 2 diabetes in several ways. One study published in *The New England Journal of Medicine* found that a high-fiber diet (50 grams a day) lowered cholesterol, triglyceride, glucose, and insulin levels. Avocados have earned the backing of the American Diabetes Association.

Blitz strokes. When it comes to taking on a deadly killer like stroke, who wants to play fair? Gang up on stroke with avocado's three heavyweights — potassium, magnesium, and fiber.

In the Health Professionals Follow-Up Study, which included more than 43,000 men, researchers found that the men who got the most potassium in their diet were 38 percent less likely to have a stroke as those who got the least. Results were a little lower for fiber (30 percent) and magnesium (30 percent).

3 great reasons to eat artichokes

The first time you eat an artichoke, you may be a little intimidated. It looks rather strange. Fortunately, beauty is only skin-deep. Hiding inside is a nutritious, nutty-flavored treat.

One medium artichoke has about 60 calories. It's a good source of potassium, magnesium, and vitamin C, which are important for heart health. And, like most fruits and vegetables, it's packed with powerful antioxidants that fight disease.

Outwit bad cholesterol. One of your liver's main functions is to produce bile, which breaks down fats and cholesterol in the food you eat. But a liver that doesn't produce enough bile lets too much cholesterol get by.

Artichokes can help your liver produce more bile, which might lower your cholesterol. What's more, a German study showed that taking artichoke extract for six weeks caused bad LDL cholesterol to fall by more than 22 percent.

Stabilize blood sugar. In addition to breaking down fatty foods, your liver also stores extra glucose in the form of glycogen, then turns it back to glucose whenever blood supplies are low. This is a great system in a perfectly working body. But some people have livers cranking out glucose their blood doesn't need. This overproduction can lead to diabetes and other health problems.

Animal studies show that artichokes keep the liver from producing too much glucose. Although more studies need to be done, scientists think artichokes might someday help people with non-insulin-dependent diabetes.

Calm indigestion. Bile is also necessary for good digestion. If your liver doesn't produce enough bile, your food won't break down properly, and you end up with stomach pains and indigestion. Several studies have shown dramatic improvements in people with poor digestion after being treated with artichoke extract. You might also get relief by eating an artichoke with your dinner.

Buying fresh artichokes

Select artichokes with a soft, green color and tightly packed leaves. Avoid those that look wilted or moldy.

Use your fresh artichokes within a few days. You can keep them looking and tasting fresher for up to two weeks by sprinkling a few drops of water on them. Store in an airtight plastic bag in your refrigerator.

Not sure how to cook artichokes? It's easy. Steam or boil them until tender, about 30 minutes. If you're in a hurry, cook them in your microwave. First, rinse them with water to add moisture. Then wrap each one in microwaveable-plastic wrap. For four artichokes, microwave on high for 10 to 15 minutes or until the meaty part at the base of the artichoke is tender.

Here are some tips on the proper way to eat an artichoke.

- Pluck off a petal.
- Hold the pointed end between your fingers and place it in your mouth.
- Gently scrape the petal between your teeth to remove the flavorful tasty pulp.
- When you reach the heart, scrape off the soft fuzz with a spoon. Then dig in and enjoy every bite.

Improve your life with beans

"Beans, beans, good for your heart. If you eat them, it shows you're smart." OK, so that's not the way the rhyme goes, but it's true. You'd be hard pressed to find a more cost-effective, nutrient-packed vegetable than beans.

"Beans are an excellent source of protein, vitamins, and minerals," says Dr. James Anderson, a medical professor at the University of Kentucky and author of *High-Fiber Fitness Plan.* "Beans are naturally low in fat and provide more protein per penny than any other food. They are also great sources of both soluble and insoluble fiber."

If you're fairly new to bean eating, start with canned beans. They come in many varieties and flavors and require little effort to prepare. "Canned beans cook more quickly and are also a nutritious alternative to dried beans," says Anderson. "They can be easily added to many soups, stews, and casseroles."

Once you get hooked on their flavor and texture, plan ahead. Instead of bringing fatty meats home from the supermarket, buy a variety of beans to use as side dishes or to plan meals around. Look for cookbooks that feature bean recipes you can use for fast and delicious meals.

Discover what fiber can do for you. The good news is you can eat as much fiber as your body can handle. Fiber has absolutely no calories, and your body needs it to function at its peak. So the fact that beans are full of both insoluble and soluble fiber is a big plus.

Insoluble fiber is the part of fruits, vegetables, and grains that your body can't digest. It helps to move food through the intestines and out of your body. Soluble fiber is found in fruits, beans, peas, and some vegetables. Both types of fiber help to regulate blood sugar in your body.

Dump your extra cholesterol. Like a superhero, beans come to the heart's rescue faster than a speeding clump of cholesterol. Anderson says the soluble fiber in beans removes extra cholesterol from your body, plus it keeps your body from producing too much cholesterol.

Halt hemorrhoids for good. "Constipation can be a major problem for some people and contributes to hemorrhoids, varicose veins, and diverticular disease of the colon," says Anderson. Eating plenty of fiber helps to increase stool bulk, and it also speeds up its passage through the intestines.

Protect yourself against cancer. Diet is one area of your life you can control, and eating right may help you avoid certain diseases, including cancer. If you're a red meat eater, for example, research has shown you can lower your risk of colon cancer by eating beans three times a week.

So make beans a regular part of your meals. You'll feel better about yourself and your lifestyle, while at the same time enjoying the great health benefits beans provide.

Carrots: the right way to snack

Whether you're munching on potato chips while catching the big game, or gulping down soda and popcorn with your sweetheart at the movies, you're taking part in America's favorite pastime — snacking.

"For many people, three meals a day just isn't enough, so it is absolutely fine to snack," says Lola O'Rourke, a registered dietitian and spokesperson for the American Dietetic Association. But, she adds, it's important to choose the right kind of snacks.

Snacking on carrots and other fruits and vegetables can be a healthy way to give you energy and additional nutrients between meals. "Carrots are high in fiber, high in antioxidants, beta carotene — they are certainly a good snack food," says O'Rourke.

She says a snack should consist of more than just carbohydrates, though. "They will be satisfying for only a short period of time," she explains. "If you really want something that is going to hold you for a few hours, try to include some protein and a small amount of healthy fat as well."

She suggests a homemade cereal, fruit, and nut mix as a good option for a snack. "That would provide plenty of fiber, protein, carbohydrates, fat, vitamins, and minerals. And it's something that can be carried around with you as well."

When you decide to go from snacking on potato chips or buttered popcorn to healthier snacks, O'Rourke recommends making gradual changes. Try baked potato chips and a low-fat dip or plain popcorn.

If you like the popular new energy bars, make sure you read the labels, and choose those that are lower in saturated fat, O'Rourke suggests. And if you're concerned about your cholesterol, look for snack bars with oats, which contain soluble fiber that helps get rid of the artery-clogging plaque.

Chase cholesterol away. Snacking on healthy fiber-filled foods like carrots is a way to lower your cholesterol levels and keep them down for good. And that means less chance of heart problems. A recent Scottish heart study showed that people who had a high daily intake of fiber — 25 to 40 grams in a 2,000 to 3,000 calorie diet — could slash their risk of heart disease by 30 percent.

Fight breast and lung cancer. A study by the National Institute of Environmental Health Sciences found that people who snacked on cooked carrots twice a week lowered their risk of developing breast cancer by 40 percent. And researchers say the more carrots you eat, the more beta carotene you'll take in, which means the more protection you'll have against disease.

If you're a non-smoker, you should definitely consider a daily dose of carrots. They can help lower your risk of lung cancer from second-hand smoke and air pollution. This time it's alpha carotene, beta carotene's cousin, that provides the antioxidant powers.

Fend off cataracts. You can protect yourself from cataracts and other vision problems by eating carrots. They contain carotenoids, such as beta carotene, which your body converts into vitamin A. Vitamin A guards against free radical damage that can lead to vision problems.

Harvest the power of pumpkin

Pumpkin pie has taken center stage at Thanksgiving dinner ever since the Pilgrims baked a pumpkin filled with milk, honey, and spices. But if you only eat pumpkin at Thanksgiving, you're missing out on many health benefits.

The pumpkin is rich in beta carotene and alpha carotene, which are converted to vitamin A in your body. It's high in fiber, low in calories, and a good source of several important minerals — iron, potassium, and magnesium. Here are three ways pumpkin helps keep you healthy.

Defend your prostate. Munch a handful of pumpkin seeds every day, as men in the Ukraine do, and you may be able to side-step prostate problems.

Scientists say the seeds contain zinc and chemicals called cucurbitacins, which could interfere with the production of dihydrotestosterone (DHT), a hormone responsible for prostate growth. Benign prostatic hyperplasia (BPH), a noncancerous enlargement of the prostate gland, is so common that 90 percent of men who reach age 85 will have at least a mild case of BPH.

You can prepare your own pumpkin seeds fresh from the pumpkin by rinsing them in a colander and adding a small amount of salt, garlic salt, or cayenne pepper. Spread them out on a cookie sheet. Set your oven to 250 degrees and dry them for about 20 to 30 minutes. Don't roast them at high temperatures. The heat can destroy the potency of the seeds' nutrients.

Protect your heart. Pumpkin may help protect your heart because of its high beta carotene content. One study of almost 5,000 elderly people in the Netherlands found that those who ate the most foods rich in beta carotene were 45 percent less likely to have a heart attack than those who ate the least amount.

If you are thinking of taking beta carotene supplements, better think again. Researchers say supplements may not have the same effects.

Ease achy joints. If your joints ache, try adding a little pumpkin seed oil to your diet. The essential fatty acids in pumpkin seed oil, linoleic acid (omega-6) and linolenic acid (omega-3), may help fight arthritis.

One study on arthritic rats found that supplements of pumpkin seed oil reduced signs of arthritis. The rats given pumpkin seed oil also had 44 percent less swelling in their paws.

While no recent studies have been done on the effect of pumpkin seed oil on arthritis in humans, it may be a natural, easy way to get a little relief. You can buy pumpkin seed oil for cooking or in supplement form.

Learn a lesson from Popeye

Spinach growers credit Popeye with saving the spinach industry after he "muskled" his way into cartoons in 1929. Ever since his humble celluloid beginning, Popeye has been showing kids of all ages that eating spinach is a smart idea. It's loaded with nutrients, including iron, magnesium, folate, beta carotene, vitamin C, and vitamin K.

You'll probably find both organic and nonorganic spinach at your grocery store. Organic fruits and vegetables are usually more expensive. Yet, many people buy them to avoid contaminants, like synthetic pesticide and fertilizer residue.

You can use the following USDA guidelines to help you understand organic labeling.

- 100 percent organic — no synthetic pesticides, herbicides, chemical fertilizers, antibiotics, hormones, additives, or preservatives
- Organic — contains 95 percent or more organically produced ingredients
- Made with organic ingredients — at least 70 percent of the product is organic

- If less than 70 percent of the product is organic, the word "organic" can't appear on the front of the package, but it can appear in the list of ingredients.

Although spinach won't give you the strength of 10 men, this nutritional knockout could help keep your heart, bones, and eyes healthy.

Keep heart disease away. High levels of a substance called homocysteine in your blood means you're more likely to develop heart disease. Fortunately, folate, a B vitamin, can help lower levels of heart-damaging homocysteine. Studies have found that spinach and other leafy greens are good sources of folate. Fresh is best since cooking and processing tend to drain this important nutrient from foods. If you don't like vegetables, eat fortified breakfast cereals or take a supplement to increase your daily folate intake.

Strengthen your bones. If you want to keep your bones strong and cut your risk of suffering a hip fracture, get more vitamin K in your diet. Not surprisingly, eating spinach is a great way to do it.

Just be careful if you're taking the blood-thinning drug warfarin. Too much vitamin K could seriously affect the way warfarin works. It's best to eat spinach and other leafy greens in moderation and talk with your doctor about any major changes in your diet.

Prevent vision loss. Your eye's retina is extremely rich in the carotenoids lutein and zeaxanthin. Experts believe these antioxidants protect your eye from light damage and also support the blood vessels to your retina. Boosting the amount of lutein and zeaxanthin in your body can keep your retina strong and efficient — able to fight off the damage that may cause macular degeneration.

Spinach and collard greens, both containing high amounts of lutein and zeaxanthin, were the foods most closely linked to this protection.

Damage from free radicals may also cause cataracts, a clouding of your lens. But once again, lutein and zeaxanthin come to the rescue. A 10-year study of 36,000 men found that those who ate the most spinach were protected from this damage.

Get sweet on sweet potatoes

A rose is a rose by any other name, but you can't say that about a sweet potato. It isn't a potato, or even a cousin of a potato. It's related to the morning glory.

Sweet potatoes are naturally delicious and loaded with vitamins, minerals, and fiber. The next time you decide to bake a potato, try baking a sweet potato instead. It's more than a tasty side dish.

Wash and dry your potato, then rub with oil. Prick the skin in a few places with a fork and place on a cookie sheet. Bake at 400 degrees for 30 to 50 minutes.

Battle heart disease. Sweet potatoes are loaded with potassium, beta carotene, folate, and vitamins C and B6 — five keys to lowering your blood pressure and keeping your arteries flowing smoothly. On top of this, a sweet potato has more than 3 grams of fiber. You can help protect yourself from heart disease by eating a variety of fiber-rich fruits and vegetables every day.

Fend off cataracts. A sweet potato's bright orange color means it has lots of beta carotene. Your body turns beta carotene into vitamin A, which is critical for healthy eyes.

"Vitamin A is an antioxidant," explains Dr. Richard G. Cumming, head researcher of the Blue Mountains Eye Study in Sydney, Australia. "Our study supports the view that antioxidant vitamins might help prevent cataracts. However, it suggests that other nutrients are also important." A good way to keep your eyes healthy, says Cumming, is to eat a well-balanced diet. The sweet potato is an excellent food to include because it is rich in beta carotene and other important nutrients.

Fortify brittle bones. It's never too late to fight osteoporosis. To prevent or slow down this brittle-bone disease, eat a diet packed with five disease fighters — potassium, magnesium, fiber, vitamin C, and beta carotene. Unlike many other foods, sweet potatoes contain all five.

To add even more bone-building power, top a baked sweet potato with a slice of your favorite low-fat cheese and a handful of chopped parsley. The cheese will add calcium, the original osteoporosis fighter. The parsley will replace some of the vitamin C lost in baking.

Find the perfect sweet potato

Sweet potatoes are available all year. Select sweet potatoes that are firm and evenly shaped, with even skin coloration. Choose those with a deep orange color. Avoid any with signs of decay.

Don't store your sweet potatoes in the refrigerator. Instead, store them in a cool, dry, well-ventilated container, preferably at around 55 degrees Fahrenheit. A cool basement or garage works great. Use your sweet potatoes within a week or two of purchasing to get the best flavor.

Fish: still a healthy choice

Fish has long been touted as a healthy food. But stories of harmful pollutants in salmon, tuna, and other fish may make you think twice about indulging in your favorite seafood.

One high-profile study reported that farmed salmon has significantly more pollutants than salmon caught in the wild. Since much of the salmon sold in stores and restaurants is farm-raised, this report has caused considerable concern.

Some experts, though, say the study's impact is not only unclear, but controversial. They point out that the amount of contaminants depended on where the fish were found. Plus, the levels in both the farmed and wild salmon were within the safety standards provided by the U.S. Food and Drug Administration. The study used Environmental Protection Agency limits, which are 40 times lower, to support its recommendation against eating farmed salmon.

"I don't think the general population needs to be terribly concerned about buying salmon and eating it," says Randall Manning, Environmental Toxicology Coordinator for the state of Georgia. "I still think it's a good food source that should be part of a healthy, well-balanced diet."

That's not to say you should ignore possible hazards in the fish you eat. "Our best advice is to become educated about fish and contaminants in your area," Manning says. "We don't want to discourage fish consumption. There are too many good things about fish — high protein, low fat, good fatty acids, etc. What we want to do is educate people to make the best choices."

Manning has these tips for allaying your fish fears:

- Choose fish from areas that are "relatively" clean. Your local Health Department should have information on which fish are best to eat for specific areas.

- Choose fish that are likely to have low levels of contaminants. These include younger fish and pan fish, rather than old bottom feeders (trash fish) and large top predators.

"If absolutely no information is available for a given area, I always fall back on the old saying 'everything in moderation' — meaning we want variety in our diets. I wouldn't eat a lot of any one thing. I would be trying to mix things up."

So go ahead and enjoy your grilled salmon steak as well as other types of fish. By including these in your diet, you'll bolster your body against heart attack, stroke, diabetes, and depression. Here are two specific ways fish benefits your health.

Flush out your arteries. Fish oil keeps your blood from sticking together, which helps your veins stay open and your heart beat regularly. Smooth-flowing blood will help prevent heart attacks and strokes.

One long-term study found that people who ate at least one serving of fish a week were half as likely to die of a sudden heart attack as those who ate less than one serving of fish per month.

Relieve arthritis pain. Omega-3, found in fish oil, has been touted as one of the most powerful anti-aging agents. It improves your brain function and joint mobility while protecting you from arthritis.

Several studies have found that omega-3 can help relieve joint pain and stiffness caused by arthritis. One study even showed that it might help prevent it. Women who ate at least one to two servings of fish each week were 22 percent less likely to get arthritis, compared with those who ate less fish.

Land the freshest fish

Look for the following signs of freshness when buying fish.

- moist, slippery, and shiny skin, with bright coloring and firmly attached scales

- bright red gills, a fresh smell, and clear eyes that have not sunk into the surrounding skin

- firm flesh on whole fish, fillets, and steaks, which bounces back when pressed

- moist flesh on fillets and steaks, with an even white or red coloring

Fish tastes best when cooked fresh, but you can wrap it in wax paper and refrigerate it for up to two days. You can also freeze it for up to six months.

If you're not a fish enthusiast, taking 3 to 5 grams of fish oil capsules a day will help you hook some powerful omega-3 fatty acids. Be patient though — it may take several weeks before you notice an improvement.

Choose olive oil for smart cooking

Today's home cooks are getting smart. Statistics show a record number of them are using olive oil instead of high-saturated-fat vegetable oils. In fact, the North American Olive Oil Association says 34 percent of all homes use olive oil, and recent sales are at all-time highs.

If you want to join the rank of smart cooks, add olive oil to your list of must-have ingredients. Don't worry if you feel lost when you see all the varieties on the supermarket shelf. By focusing on three main types, you'll have an easier choice.

- Extra virgin olive oil is made from ripe olives that are pressed immediately after harvesting. It has a strong, robust, fruity flavor, and the most full-bodied taste and aroma of any olive oil. Buy the darkest color to get the most phytonutrients, and drizzle it over salad or vegetables.

- Virgin olive oil is more golden in color and is an all-purpose cooking oil. It has a milder flavor and a hint of fruitiness.

- Extra light olive oil is a light golden color and has a mild olive flavor. It's an excellent cooking oil and can be used in place of vegetable oil in most recipes.

Keep several varieties on hand to meet all your cooking needs. Olive oil tastes best when used soon after opening, but most can last up to two years. Be sure to check the expiration date before buying. Store your "liquid gold" in an airtight container in a cool, dark place. It does not need to be refrigerated.

Because it has healthy monounsaturated fats, olive oil is a good substitute for butter and margarine. Using it may help reduce your risk of heart disease and breast cancer.

Strike at heart disease. Olive oil contains 77 percent monounsaturated fat. Research has shown this type of fat may lower bad LDL cholesterol in your blood. HDL cholesterol, the kind that helps keep your arteries clear, is left untouched. Olive oil also may help keep your blood from clotting, which may lower your blood pressure and risk of stroke.

Target rheumatoid arthritis. It is unclear if the monounsaturated fat in olive oil stops inflammation in your joints or if olive oil's antioxidant powers lock up dangerous free radicals. But in one clinical study, those who ate the least olive oil were more than twice as likely to develop arthritis. A combination of fresh vegetables stir-fried in olive oil seems to especially benefit arthritis sufferers.

Curb diabetes. Olive oil may reduce your risk of developing type 2 (noninsulin-dependent) diabetes by cutting the amount of LDL, total cholesterol, and triglycerides (fats) in your blood. In addition, it may also lower your high blood sugar level, which is a key symptom of diabetes.

Simple way to supercharge your health

Do you feel run down? Does your body ache? You can increase your "vim and vigor" by taking the most popular dietary supplement sold in America — a multivitamin.

This potent pill can provide the extra nutritional punch you need each day by supplying necessary vitamins you may lack in your diet. It also provides minerals your body needs like calcium, phosphorus, and magnesium for strong bones and potassium to regulate blood pressure.

"Protection from cataracts, cancer, heart attacks, better immunity, improved memory — these summarize some of the important health benefits that can be achieved by taking a good multivitamin," says Bill Sardi, author of *What's Best,* an in-depth look at the multivitamin industry. A consumer advocate, Sardi is also on the board of experts for Purity Products.

Taking a multivitamin does not mean you should ignore a healthy diet, however. "The best diet will not do what a multivitamin can do, nor will a vitamin pill completely make up for a poor diet. They are mutually exclusive," Sardi explains.

Vitamins battle arthritis pain

Are you sick and tired of spending too much time and money on doctors and drugs that fail to cure your arthritis? Researchers have pinpointed a vitamin remedy that offers the pain relief of traditional arthritis medicines at a fraction of the cost. People taking a daily supplement of 6,400 micrograms (mcg) of folic acid (B9) and 20 mcg of cobalamin (B12) had as much gripping power in their hands as people who took NSAIDs like aspirin or ibuprofen. Plus they had fewer tender joints. The best part? No side effects.

If you've shopped for multivitamins in the past, you've probably stood in the aisle and scratched your head. Multivitamins come in so many brands and forms — which one is right for you?

Pick the right multi. "Most multivitamins are poorly formulated, offer impotent dosages, and are unbalanced or incomplete," Sardi warns. "Learn more about what comprises a good multivitamin so you can make an informed choice."

ConsumerLab is one agency that helps by providing industry testing of supplements. Look for the flask-shaped CL Seal of Approved Quality on a product's label.

But don't let that be your only guide. If you're interested in a particular multivitamin, go to that company's Web site, and see if they've had an independent lab test their products for quantity and quality. Above all, select a product with the right ingredients for your needs.

Check absorption. Pills and tablets don't always break down in your body, especially in seniors with low stomach acid levels, Sardi says. Liquids are absorbed faster, but not always better. Plus, they're prone to a limited shelf life and contamination. Gel caps appear to work best, he notes.

"Studies show gelatin capsules which contain powdered ingredients exhibit about 30 percent better absorption. They are preferred."

Pay attention to your age. Seniors have special nutritional needs because they don't have the immune system they had when younger.

"Seniors are at the top of the list every time you examine the data on who gets sick from flu outbreaks or who gets ill when drinking water is contaminated," Sardi says. "It's very important for seniors to take supplemental selenium, zinc, vitamin C, and vitamin E to boost their immunity."

Just because you're over 50 doesn't mean you have to feel like it. Taking multivitamins especially formulated for older adults may

---

Smart supplement storage

You've spent decent money for good high-quality supplements. So protect your investment by storing them properly. Follow these tips from consumer advocate Bill Sardi.

- Store supplements in a cool, dark, dry environment. B vitamins, especially, are easily destroyed by light and heat.

- Never store your supplements in the refrigerator. The moisture may cause fungal spoilage.

- On the road, place them in a hard pill carrier so they don't get squashed in a purse or pocket.

- Always use your supplements before their expiration date. If you see brown specks on your pills, it's time to throw them out.

not only make you feel healthier, they may help you feel younger, too.

Minerals: a bottled-water bonus

Bottled water has become so popular that you can find a convenient size no matter what your needs. But you'll also find a vast difference in the contents. How do you choose?

Look at the mineral content, advises Bill Sardi, author of *In Search of the World's Best Water*. Most bottled waters are about the same, so finding one with added minerals will give you the most benefit for your buck.

"The mineral content is what's important, and this is often listed in very small type on the back of the label," says Sardi.

He says most American bottled waters are purified tap water, although some do come from springs or deep-water sources. If the label says "purified," you'll know it's just glorified tap water, he says.

If that's the case, then why drink bottled water instead of tap? "Bottled waters have an advantage in that they can be engineered to provide health benefits," he explains. "For example, the addition of magnesium to bottled water may drastically reduce the occurrence of sudden-death heart attack."

Sardi says water delivers minerals to the body quickly and in a form more available to the cells. "This may be important when it comes to rehydrating an individual who is low in sodium or magnesium following sweating or physical exertion."

He recommends looking for bottled water that has more than 40 milligrams (mg) of magnesium per liter, and no more than 25 mg of sodium.

Unfortunately, most American bottled waters are low in minerals, he says. "For comparison, European bottled waters are much richer in mineral content. Throughout Europe people drink bottled water and experience extra health benefits."

Whichever type you choose, take the bottle with you, and sip it throughout the day.

⚠️ **Avoid water bottle hazards**

Carrying a personal water bottle is a good way to stay hydrated. But reusing it without washing it may hurt your health more than help. A recent study has shown that unwashed bottles may allow bacteria to form inside, possibly from the germs on your hands and mouth.

Remember to wash your water bottle daily in soap and hot water. Or keep several on hand so you can use one while the others take a spin through the dishwasher.

Studies have shown that drinking six to eight glasses of water a day helps regulate your body temperature, lubricate your digestive tract, and maintain pressure in your eyes. Keeping your water intake up also may help prevent headaches, fatigue, lack of concentration, and an elevated heart rate.

And the next time your arthritis bothers you, think about taking a long, healthy drink. Water molecules like to spread out and form a cushion that helps lubricate your joints, which may soothe arthritis pain.

If you enjoy the taste and convenience of bottled water, pick a size and shape that's easy to carry with you throughout the day. Just be sure to choose a brand with extra minerals for a healthful bonus.

Healthy healing

Trust top health Web sites

"An informed consumer is a better patient," says M.J. Tooey, Executive Director of the Health Sciences and Human Services Library at the University of Maryland, and a member of the Medical Library Association (MLA). "As it turns out, medical information is one of the most highly sought types of Web-based information. But just as with cars or other products, consumers need to be educated how to find good health information."

The Internet puts all the newest medical breakthroughs right at your fingertips, yet Tooey says the biggest challenge is the quantity of information and your ability to sift through it all for what's accurate.

Focus your search. Type your health question into an Internet search engine and it may come up with thousands of "hits." Tooey offers some advice. "Use the advanced search feature so you can combine multiple words or even phrases."

Then be patient and look through the hits. A recent study found only 35 percent of the top search results offered scientific, unbiased information. Tooey says, "Learn to evaluate the hits by looking at the Web addresses." She advises you go to sites with these suffixes first.

.gov — a government-sponsored site

.edu — a site sponsored by an educational institution

.org — a professional organization or non-profit company

Look for a stamp of approval. The Health on the Net (HON) Foundation is a not-for-profit organization that, among other things, reviews Web-based medical information. If a site displays the HON seal, it means the site meets their strict rules of conduct. For more information about the HON code, go to *www.hon.ch.*

Check out sponsorship. All commercial sites — identified by ".com" in their Web address — should clearly state who sponsors them. While these sites are in the business of making money, Tooey says, "Many commercial Web sites have valuable and credible information." In fact, hospitals often have ".com" in their address.

Large pharmaceutical companies will finance and post research information on their sites, as well. Just remember they may have a financial interest in any products they recommend.

Discover free medical dollars

Find out if you qualify for deeply discounted drugs and medical services by going to *www.benefitscheckup.org.* This online service run by the National Council on Aging lists over 1,000 federal, state, and local private and public programs offering health and financial assistance, tax-saving programs, transportation assistance, and others for seniors. You can also find savings on over 1,450 prescription medications.

The questionnaire asks for an estimate of your assets and expenses to see if you qualify for certain programs — but you never enter your name or other private information.

Pay attention to dates. "Health information changes constantly," says Tooey. "And Web sites should reflect the most up-to-date information." When the page was last revised is usually clearly posted, often at the bottom of the site.

Get the facts. Reliable articles sound like newspaper reports, not opinion pieces. They are usually clear and exact, and can be easily verified with a professional source. Tooey warns, "Information represented as an opinion should be clearly stated and the source should be identified as a qualified professional or organization."

Start with the best. The MLA recommends these as seven of the best sites for seniors to find medical information on the Internet. For the complete list go to *www.mlanet.org*.

Centers for Disease Control and Prevention	www.cdc.gov
Health Web	http://healthweb.org
HealthFinder	www.healthfinder.gov
Mayo Clinic	www.mayoclinic.com
Medem	http://medem.com
MEDLINEplus	http://medlineplus.gov
New York Online Access to Health	www.noah-health.org

According to Tooey, it is always appropriate for a patient to take information they find on the Web to their doctor. "Consumer health information," she says, "is a starting point for discussing any treatments or information with your physician."

Clinical trials offer free health care

Imagine a world where you don't have to pay big bucks for medication, and your checkups and other health services are free. That's exactly the world of clinical trials — research studies where people test how safe and effective new medical treatments are.

"There are great benefits to participating in clinical trials," says Ken Getz, co-author of *Informed Consent: A Guide to the Risks and Benefits of Volunteering for Clinical Trials*. "But there are also risks that every volunteer needs to know and understand."

Learn the pros and cons. As a trial participant, you try new medicines and treatments that might not be available otherwise, and you are under the care of leading doctors in their field. As an added bonus, you have the satisfaction of contributing to the advancement of science.

But before you jump in with both feet, there are some factors Getz says you should be aware of.

- The doctor's priority is to study the drug, not treat your condition. So you are less a patient, and more a participant.

- You may receive a placebo — an inactive substance — instead of the active medication.

- You may have to stop your current medication to take the study drug.

- You may experience side effects.

- You may be required to keep a detailed diary of your experiences.

- You may have to travel to more than one study location.

Keep in mind, too, that you may need a companion to drive you to and from the studies. Consider the commitment of time they will have to make.

Ask the researcher these questions before you commit to a clinical trial:

- Will this treatment interact or interfere with my current medications?

- How many visits will I have to make?

- How far do I have to drive?

- Who pays for transportation?

- Will I get paid for participating?

- Will this treatment affect my health insurance?

- What is known about this drug?

- Who is in charge of this investigation and will they benefit financially from it?

- Has the research center ever had an FDA audit and what were the results?

- Can I continue using this drug after the trial is over?

Understand your rights. As Getz says in his book, any volunteer who participates in a clinical trial has rights. These include your right:

- to be told the general purpose, risks, and benefits of the trial as well as more specific details, before you join.

- to ask for and receive clarification from the researcher at any time.

- to withdraw at any time.

In fact, the FDA requires you sign a consent form detailing the purpose, procedures, risks, and benefits. Getz suggests you look it over carefully with your doctor and family members.

Find a trial. They are often advertised in the paper, or your doctor may recommend one to you. If you want to search for a specific trial, there are plenty of Internet sites designed to help you.

Getz, who is founder of CenterWatch, an information gateway for clinical trials, recommends starting with these three.

www.clinicaltrials.gov	lists government-funded and privately supported studies
www.cc.nih.gov	lists studies conducted at the National Institutes of Health
www.CenterWatch.com	lists industry-funded studies

Pick the perfect alternative healer

Complementary and Alternative Medicine (CAM) may solve a problem conventional medicine can't. From herbal remedies to acupuncture, CAM is becoming more and more available.

A therapy is considered alternative if it replaces a standard medical intervention. A complementary one is simply added on to your current treatment plan.

The National Center for Complementary and Alternative Medicine suggests you follow these steps to ensure you get reliable and safe care.

Clear it with your doc. If you feel a CAM approach might suit you better than the one you are on, talk to your doctor about it. Often he can recommend a practitioner or even prescribe a therapy directly. Inform him of any supplements or treatments — no matter how minor — you are on so he can discuss possible interactions.

Make sure you're covered. Health insurance doesn't necessarily pay for all alternative treatments. Call your provider to ask what they cover. Often they will recommend a practitioner paid for under their plan.

Call before you commit. When you make an appointment, ask for details of the practitioner's training and certification. A medical doctor who specializes in alternative methods is ideal. Ask how many patients she sees in a day and how long you can expect to speak with her. Also inquire if the practitioner is familiar or has previous experience with your condition.

Meet face to face. A visit to an alternative clinic is much like a doctor's visit — come prepared, and you will leave better informed.

- Carry your medical information with you, so you can fill out the medical history chart.

- Write down your questions ahead of time. Bring a friend or carry a tape recorder to make sure you don't miss important information. Take plenty of notes while the doctor explains her proposed treatment, and speak up if something is unclear.

- Make sure your doctor covers all the details — including how long it will take before you see results. Ask about side effects, interactions with medications, and equipment you may need to purchase.

- If at all possible, request medical studies that support the treatment your practitioner recommends.

Decide if it's a fit. Just because you saw the doctor, doesn't mean you have to follow her advice. Think back over your appointment and ask yourself these questions.

- Was the doctor easy to talk to? Were you comfortable asking questions?

- Did she take enough time to get all the details of your condition?

- Was the doctor candid about how alternative and conventional treatments might help you get well?

- Does the treatment seem reasonable to you, and were all the costs and time investment explained to your satisfaction?

Beware the quack. View your practitioner with suspicion if she does not mention any risks but makes grand promises of a swift and easy recovery. If she says her treatment will cure all your medical problems or tries to discredit regular medical practice, be prepared to move on.

Stay strong into your senior years

"Exercise is better than any pill you can take for disease," says Kara Witzke, a representative of the American Council on Exercise (ACE) and Assistant Professor of Physical Fitness at Norfolk State University. "It lowers blood pressure, blood sugar, and cholesterol; increases metabolism and muscle mass; decreases body fat; improves circulation; and makes daily activities so much easier to perform. And," she exclaims, "it increases your independence."

It's never too late to begin. See how easily you can gain the benefits of exercise.

Start out safely. "Any male over 40 and female over 50 should have a physical before beginning anything vigorous," recommends Witzke. "However, most people can begin a walking program without physician approval — as long as they are relatively healthy."

Throw away misconceptions. Exercise isn't about leotards and sweat. Rediscover the oh-so-important benefits of non-strenuous daily exercise. The little things you do to stay active can ensure lifelong health and happiness. Witzke's advice is to do something simple and familiar.

- If you like to walk, join a mall walking club, or park at the end of the parking lot and walk to the store when you shop.

- If you garden, stretch before you start, bend at the knees to lift your tools, and breathe deeply.

- If you like to sway to the music, just add a couple steps and dance in the privacy of your home.

Add some muscle. You don't have to grow old suffering from arthritis of the hips or knees. "A loss of muscular strength is the number one reason why older adults lose their independence," says Witzke.

However, with simple strength training exercises — and a bit of time — older muscle can grow strong just like young muscle. "Exercises can be as simple as standing up and sitting down in a chair, doing lunges next to a chair, or calf raises while holding on to a chair," suggests Witzke.

Build up your core. If you want to flatten a bulging belly and strengthen stomach muscles — while strengthening your back — try this simple exercise.

Stand up straight and pull your stomach muscles up and in. Hold this pose for 10 seconds, then relax. Repeat four or five times a day. It's much easier than sit-ups.

"Stay away from gimmicky ab devices," warns Witzke. "Consult a personal trainer or attend a fitness class where you will learn effective ab exercises without using any equipment."

Join a class. Many community centers have age-appropriate classes with people and music you can enjoy. "Don't underestimate the power of social exercise," says Witzke. "Staying involved in one's community and with peers is very important as we age."

Break it up. The Centers for Disease Control and Prevention, the American College of Sports Medicine, and the U.S. Surgeon General recommend you get at least 30 minutes of moderate exercise a day to maintain good health. You can divide that into three short sessions of 10 minutes each. You don't need to get breathless, either. Just exert enough energy to elevate your heartbeat moderately.

Get health club savvy with critical questions

"I know a lot of gyms that don't cater to seniors," says Tim Culwell, a spokesperson for the American Council on Exercise (ACE). What a mistake it would be to find that out after you've signed a yearlong membership contract.

That's why it's so important you get answers to questions like these before you join a health club.

Is there a trial period? "A lot of gyms offer a two-week free membership — some even up to a month," says Culwell. Use this time to make sure the club lives up to all its promises and suits your style.

Are there different membership options? See if you can get an "equipment only" or "equipment and pool only" subscription if you don't plan on using all the amenities the club has to offer.

How busy is the facility when I want to come? Visit the gym at approximately the same time you would once you became a member. "You probably want to avoid the early morning and the prime times," warns Culwell. "In some gyms that's anywhere between 4:30 and 7:00 p.m. Most clubs," he adds, "are going to be busy in that 8:30 to 10:00 a.m. range and right at the lunch hour." See how long you have to wait to use machines.

Do the classes suit my fitness goals? "The majority of clubs don't have senior programs because it's not a mainstream attraction," says Culwell. If that's the case, he recommends you try the local YMCA or community center instead.

Are the personal trainers qualified? Look for college degrees in a health-related field and certification by ACE or the American College of Sports Medicine.

Will personal trainers help me? "Be sure there is staff available to tend to you and show you the equipment," Culwell advises. "Ask if you will have to pay extra to have the kind of attention you deserve and need outside of the membership."

Is the staff trained in first aid? They should all know CPR and how to use a defibrillator if the club owns one.

Are the facilities clean and comfortable? Check the locker rooms, showers, pool, and spa areas. See if the machines are well cared for — in good condition and cleaned regularly. Make sure it is cool in the workout areas with plenty of ventilation.

What are the details of the membership contract? Check how long you are committed, the opt-outs — like suspension for medical reasons or if you move away — and any sign-up fee.

"If you don't find out what you need to within the first couple of weeks of free membership," says Culwell, "then maybe you need to go month to month — even if you pay a slight premium. Better safe than sorry." Once you are satisfied the club suits your personality and fitness goals, sign up. It could be the most important health decision you make all year.

Retire right: 5 tips to staying happy

Trading your time card for a remote control may sound like bliss, but retirement often leaves people restless, not content. To transition smoothly from a busy career to a life of leisure you need a plan of action and a destination.

Columnist Stan Hinden emphasizes making wise financial decisions in his book *How to Retire Happy*, but also offers these mental preparation tips.

Don't quit all at once. Ease gradually into your new schedule, Hinden says. Ask your employer to shift you into part time or flextime work. If that is not an option, take a part-time job once you quit. This will give you a chance to explore new possibilities before you cut loose from the moorings of job and responsibility.

Give time to charity. Many retirees find the greatest advantage to retirement is time for community service. You may want to donate your hard-earned expertise to a local charity. Think of it as your chance to choose work that matches your values.

Rest after you leap. Retirement is a major life change, so don't complicate it with too many large decisions at the same time. If you're considering relocating to a warmer climate, Hinden suggests you explore all your options for several years before you commit.

Plan for togetherness. Before the big day comes, consider what it will be like to be home with your spouse 24 hours a day.

Although it can be a wonderful thing, constant companionship can strain a marriage, especially if one spouse is unoccupied while the other is busy. Make sure you have a plan for your time, your chores, and your activities.

Cultivate other interests. Develop new hobbies in the years leading up to your retirement — both as a couple and individually. The North Carolina Center for Creative Retirement suggests you take continuing education courses in areas you think will interest you. It's important to find out before you retire that you don't care for philosophy or painting. Classes also give you a chance to enlarge your circle of friends. This will compensate for the co-workers you no longer see.

You will soon grow comfortable with your more casual lifestyle, and find that your calendar is as full as it used to be, but with more pursuits of your choosing — like social engagements, time with the kids and grandkids, travel, sports, or volunteering.

5 herbs keep memory from failing

Commercial memory enhancers are a million-dollar industry, complete with chemicals, side effects, and gimmicks. But these five herbs can boost your brain's performance naturally — and they've held up to scientific scrutiny.

Save your memory with a simple pill

The real cause of Alzheimer's disease may be brain inflammation. And that could explain why simple over-the-counter products like aspirin, ibuprofen, and other nonsteroidal anti-inflammatory drugs (NSAIDs) can help focus your memory.

Just as NSAIDs reduce the swelling of arthritis, some experts believe they fight inflammation in your brain that can damage memory.

Talk to your doctor about making this simple anti-headache pill part of your daily routine. Long-term use can lead to serious side effects, including internal bleeding.

Upgrade your recall with ginkgo. An extract from the leaf of this exotic Chinese tree can increase the circulation to your brain and improve your memory skills. Look carefully at the label before you buy a supplement — make sure it's pure ginkgo biloba extract (GBE or GBX). A good one will have between 24 and 26 percent flavonoid glycosides and 5 to 7 percent terpene lactones. Take three doses of 40 milligrams (mg) a day for best results. Just be sure you don't use ginkgo if you already take blood-thinning medications, like aspirin or warfarin.

Rev up with ginseng. Studies show this root can boost your energy and improve your concentration. Look for Asian (*panax ginseng*) or American (*panax quinquefolius*) ginseng, since they are the most thoroughly researched types. Ginseng products come in many forms — capsules, teas, chewing gum, extract, and more. Again, check labels to make sure you're getting between 4 and 7 percent of the active ingredient ginsenoside in every dose. Don't take ginseng and ginkgo at the same time. Together they can thin your blood too much.

Soothe arthritis with arnica

Besides having beautiful yellow flowers, arnica is a natural and effective pain remedy that can ease your arthritis and speed healing.

To make an arnica compress for achy joints, dilute a tablespoon of arnica tincture in two cups of water. Soak gauze pads and apply to the affected area. You can buy arnica tincture at health food stores or pharmacies that sell natural medicines.

Be careful though. Some people are sensitive to arnica and may develop a rash from using a compress. Make sure you don't apply it to broken skin. And only use it externally. Swallowing arnica could make your blood pressure skyrocket, possibly causing a heart attack.

Think clearly with lemon balm. New research out of England says powdered, dried lemon balm leaf (*melissa officinalis*) can not only improve your memory skills, but make you feel calmer as well. The study found that about 1600 milligrams gave the most benefit.

Stay smart with sage. You might call it an old wives' tale — enhance your memory with sage. But now scientific evidence bears it out. Sage oil capsules immediately improved word recall in a group of British volunteers. Best of all, they suffered none of the side effects that most memory-boosting medications can cause.

Re-energize with rosemary. Here's an easy to grow remedy you probably already have in your garden. It seems that just the smell of rosemary can make you more alert and jumpstart your memory. Simmer some leaves or essential oil in water to release the woody fragrance. It will keep your mind sharp as a tack and leave you feeling content.

Take care while you give care

Over 60 percent of caregivers suffer from signs of depression. In addition, they take more medication for anxiety than others their age. This is nothing to feel guilty about — the pressure to look after a family member who is ill or disabled is enormously draining. But experts say it is vital you take care of yourself as you care for another.

The Family Caregiver Alliance, National Center on Caregiving is a support network that can help. Their Manager of Communications, Bonnie Lawrence, has some useful suggestions.

Accept your feelings. As a caregiver, you may be angry and frustrated because you don't have enough time to do everything that is expected of you. You may feel tied down or depressed. Lawrence says these feelings are normal. You can and should discuss them openly with a fellow caregiver or with a counselor.

Kiss guilt goodbye. Don't feel to blame because you can't provide a certain level of care. There is no such thing as a perfect caregiver — trying to be one will just exhaust you. Take time instead to nurture yourself. Spend an hour or an afternoon alone, go for walks, read a book, eat some ice cream, have tea with a friend. Don't lose sight of who you are, since that is the greatest gift you give your family.

Develop a routine. A daily schedule can help you juggle all the demands on your time and keep your family informed of the tasks you do on a regular basis. Once they recognize your time constraints, they will be more understanding when you cannot be everywhere at once.

Know your limits. Say "no" to demands that will drain — rather than nurture — you. Let others throw the holiday feast and save your energy for things important to you and your loved one.

Get some rest. Lack of sleep will make you sick and cause even more stress. You may grow grumpy or even careless. If you or your loved one can't sleep through the night, ask your doctor for medication.

Stay physically active. If your body gets rundown, you risk an injury that will make it impossible for you to care for your family. Regular exercise will keep you strong and healthy, release feel-good chemicals in your body, and give you a much-needed break.

Say yes to outside help. Caregiving can make you feel isolated and withdraw from friends and loved ones. Lawrence says you must learn to accept help. Keep a list of simple duties handy in case someone offers. For instance, your daughter may be able to pick up prescriptions, or a visiting nurse give an insulin shot. It frees up your time, and gives them a chance to invest in your loved one. Tap into family service organizations and eldercare programs. They often have access to government aid that will help foot the bill for respite care.

Remember you are not alone. There are numerous support groups for people just like you who spend much of their time providing care for others. To find one, contact your local Agency on Aging, or get valuable information on these Web sites.

Eldercare Locator	www.eldercare.gov
Family Caregiver Alliance	www.caregiver.org
National Alliance for Caregiving	www.caregiving.org

Help for grandparents who become parents — again

More than 2.5 million grandparents are raising grandchildren — often without financial or emotional support from others. But you don't have to do it alone. Here are a few resources to consider.

Foster them at home. "If you qualify as a foster parent — which sometimes can be an ordeal — then you receive the same benefits and supports as other foster parents," says Kaja Snell, Manager of Generations United National Center on Grandparents and Other Relatives Raising Children, a nonprofit organization promoting intergenerational public policies and programs. Fostering means a regular monthly check and access to state services. But once a child is in the foster care system, the state controls a good deal of their future.

While you do have other legal options — adoption, guardianship, and legal custody — they all involve suing for status, and can draw state attention to your grandchild's parent. Make sure you understand all the repercussions before you approach social services. Once the ball is rolling, there may be no way to stop it.

Find government assistance. Even if you keep your guardianship informal, you can still apply for government funds. For instance, ask about a program called TANF, or Temporary Aid for Needy Families. You can get money and benefits through this program, but in most cases you must be working to receive them. There is also a time limit. Call your state social service office to find out if you qualify.

Tap into senior support. "If you've exhausted all of your resources and child welfare, look into what the aging networks are doing in your community," Snell recommends. Often senior support centers have money or aid they set aside specifically for a situation such as yours. For instance, through a program called the National Family Caregivers Support Program or NFCSP, your local Area Agency on Aging (AAA) can give out money the government has earmarked for adults over 60 who are raising a child.

Get insurance coverage. If your grandchild is not covered under your health insurance, ask about CHIP (Children's Health Insurance Program). This state administered program provides health insurance for children who don't qualify for it under Medicare.

Receive medical attention. If you don't have legal status, you may have problems taking your grandchild to the doctor. Many states have a medical consent law that gives you permission to approve care for your grandchild. See the Generations United (GU) Web site at *www.gu.org* for a list of states.

Sign them up for school. A similar directive, called the education consent law, will give you the authority to enroll a child in school. Only a few states have this law. See the GU Web site for a list.

Ask for respite. Don't use your retirement savings to care for your grandchild. There are plenty of programs in place to help with the costs of parenting so you don't endanger your security in later years.

Sometimes the aid is there and you just have to know how to ask for it. Snell suggests you use the word "respite."

"Respite is the buzzword that any sort of community, faith-based group, state, or federal program responds to," she says. "For instance, they may have a respite program, but not a babysitting program."

Don't neglect yourself. Children that aren't raised by their parents often have emotional as well as physical issues. According to Snell, you're doing much more than just parenting again — you are caregiving, which is more demanding. Don't try to do it all alone. Get help from your community or church, and create a web of support around you and your grandchild. After all, you face one of the hardest — and most important — jobs anyone can have.

To get more details on programs that can help you, go to the GU website at *www.gu.org* and click on *Kinship Care*.

Update your medicine cabinet for safety's sake

More important than a stocked pantry is a revamped medicine cabinet. It can mean the difference between sickness and health. If you haven't taken a close look inside yours lately, it's past time.

Toss old items. "A good rule of thumb is to throw things away that are over a year old," says Kathy Cameron, Executive Director of the American Society of Consultant Pharmacists Foundation. Prescriptions usually have a sale date on the label, and over-the-counter medications an expiration date.

"Medication that a doctor has discontinued or is no longer needed because the condition is not a problem anymore should also be discarded," Cameron explains.

In addition, many first-aid items lose their strength over time. "If it's old, it probably doesn't have a lot of potency left in it anyway and it won't do much good, but may irritate the area," says Cameron.

She advises you to replace makeup and facial lotions periodically, too. "Some have active ingredients, like salicylic acid, that probably lose potency. But the real issue is that bacteria can grow in makeup over time. There's always a risk of infection."

Stock some pain relief. According to Cameron every medicine cabinet should contain Tylenol. "It is a safe analgesic (pain reliever). It doesn't have as many side effects or interact with as many medications as some other analgesics." It might be helpful to have both an adult and child formula on hand if grandchildren are frequent visitors.

Replace outdated gadgets. Cameron recommends you take your old mercury thermometer to your pharmacist so he can dispose of it safely. Buy one of the new digital thermometers instead. "They are a lot safer and easier to use," she says. "They're very quick, and you don't have to try to read the mercury."

Again, if you expect younger guests, there are temperature gauges that go in the ear and skin patches that work well on little ones.

Relocate everything. Where you store your medicine is almost as important as what you stock. "It's actually not good practice to keep prescription and over-the-counter medicines in a cabinet located in a bathroom — because of the moisture and the heat," warns Cameron. Keep items together in a cooler — but childproof — place, like in a bedroom. And don't forget to store medicines that require cooling in a sealed plastic bag in the fridge.

Risky business: separate fact from fiction

Only eight cases of SARS were reported in the U.S. during an eight-month period. In that same amount of time about 30,000 people became ill from the foodborne bacteria *Salmonella*.

Risk is a funny thing. It doesn't seem to be related at all to what makes the big news stories. Here are the facts, and they will surprise you. It turns out real risks aren't exotic and deadly, but all too familiar — and a few simple steps can protect you even from these.

Take to the skies. If the events of Sept. 11 left you afraid to fly, consider these statistics. In 2002, the FAA says not one single person died on a passenger flight in the United States. That same year, nearly 2 million people were injured and close to 40,000 were killed in vehicle-related accidents. Though you can't avoid driving, wear your seatbelt for protection, and use caution on the roads.

Enjoy your steaks. Don't give up beef just because of those crazy cows on the news. There have been only 153 cases of mad cow disease reported in the world, according to the Centers for Disease Control and Prevention (CDC) and not one of them in the United States.

You are much more likely to get the flu. In fact, influenza and its related diseases claim over 2 million people a year. Go ahead and eat your steak, but get a flu shot on the side to minimize your real risk.

Savor "fake" sweets. The National Cancer Institute says artificial sweeteners are unlikely to give you cancer. The U.S. Food and Drug Administration (FDA) strictly regulates them and all tests on humans show little risk. So don't avoid sugar-free sweets just because they use a man-made sweetener.

Instead, consider that 30 percent of Americans are obese — partly because of a national sweet tooth. Being overweight carries a lot of very real health risks — cancer, diabetes, heart disease, sleep apnea, and osteoarthritis. In fact, losing as little as 10 pounds can significantly reduce your risk of heart disease, diabetes, and other conditions.

Make that call. You may have heard cellular phones emit radio frequencies that can cause cancer. If this is the only reason you won't buy one, head for the nearest store. Studies show there is no scientific proof to support this.

However, speaking on the phone while driving carries its own risk. You raise your chances of being in a car accident by 38 percent. Use common sense, don't talk and drive at the same time.

Next time you hear of the newest scare, examine the real risks — and take steps to protect yourself from those.

Fight panic with preparation

You can't always avoid disaster, but a plan can give you some control over its outcome. Here are a few simple precautionary steps the American Red Cross recommends.

- Store copies of important papers in a safe place outside your home.
- Draft a family communication plan. Ask an out-of-state family member or friend to be your contact person. Give their number and e-mail address to every member of your family so they can communicate through this person should an emergency happen. Pick someone who lives far enough away to be unaffected by whatever event occurs.
- Determine emergency exits from every room in your house.

- Pick meeting places in case you get separated. Choose one near your home, and one outside your area in case you have to evacuate.

- Keep an emergency kit close to an exit door or in your car. Include water, first aid supplies and medicine, a flashlight, a battery powered radio or a cell phone, spare batteries, basic toiletries, a warm blanket, and a change of clothing. Slip a set of spare keys, some cash, a credit card, and copies of critical documents into a waterproof container.

- Make sure all family members know how to turn off the utilities in your home.

- Have a disaster plan for your pets. They are not allowed in emergency shelters.

- Install smoke alarms on every level of your house. Test them monthly and install fresh batteries once or twice a year.

- Keep your fireplace in working order in case the power goes down.

- Repair any worn or frayed electrical wires and faulty gas connections.

- Strap your water heater to the wall studs of your home.

- Fasten heavy bookcases and china cabinets to the wall.

- Store any flammable or poisonous products far away from heat sources.

Finally, the Red Cross says to keep your plan up-to-date, make sure your family works together as a team, and stay calm.

Practice good habits for better sleep

Toss and turn tonight and you increase your risk of being in a car accident tomorrow. In fact, the National Highway Traffic Safety Administration says falling asleep at the wheel causes at least 100,000 automobile crashes every year. If that's not bad enough, without the proper shuteye, you will also be less productive, less energetic, and — well — just plain grumpier.

So what's keeping you awake? Stress, worry, medical problems, and unusual schedules are all likely candidates. But follow these simple sleep tips and you'll enjoy restful nights and feel-good days.

Plan your morning menu. Start your day with an anti-fatigue breakfast that will really wake you up. Go ahead and pour a mug of coffee or hot chocolate, but only drink it in the morning. Eat a cup of high-fiber cereal — one with at least 5 grams of fiber — and, according to research, you could reduce fatigue by about 10 percent.

Rub out tension. Still feeling sluggish? Here's a quick way to renew your vigor. Find the two slightly bony ridges at the base of your skull. Apply gentle pressure to the anti-fatigue points below them until you feel a pulse. Or softly press on the hollow above your eye, where your eyebrow meets the bridge of your nose. With this type of acupressure, you can replenish your energy in no time.

Keep your sugar steady. Fight off those sudden afternoon slumps with this peppy potion from the National Honey Board. In a blender, mix 1 pint of ripe, trimmed strawberries with 1/4 cup of honey and 6 ounces of frozen orange juice concentrate. Blend until smooth, stirring in 2 cups of cooled green tea last. Serve over ice. This nutrient-rich brew will keep all your systems on go, with an extra boost from a bit of caffeine.

Fit in some exercise. Just 30 minutes of moderate activity release energizing, feel-good chemicals in your brain. Try three 10-minute sessions of anti-fatigue exercises — like walking, swimming, and biking — every day, and you'll meet this goal.

The best time to exercise is in the late afternoon, at least three hours before bed. By the time the sheets beckon, your body temperature will be back to normal and you should fall asleep easily.

Wind down. Don't hop into bed all keyed up — you'll spend hours staring at the ceiling. Try these quick strategies from the National Sleep Foundation and you'll not only sleep sounder, but you'll wake refreshed and ready to face the world.

- Take a warm bath.

- Avoid caffeine, alcohol, and nicotine late in the evening.

- Have a light snack that contains tryptophan and carbohydrates. Both of these promote relaxation and sleep. For tryptophan choose a dairy food like milk or a protein source like tuna or nuts. And of course you'll get carbs in grain products like crackers or cereal.

- Don't watch TV, work on the computer, or pay bills right before bed.

- Don't stay in bed if you're not sleepy. Get up and read or listen to music until you're ready to snooze.

Finally, if you're over 60 and it takes you more than half an hour to fall asleep every night, speak to your doctor. This might be a symptom of a more serious condition that can shorten your life.

Sleep soundly despite ailments

- If you snore and wake abruptly, you may have sleep apnea. Sleep on your side and sew a tennis ball to the back of your nightclothes to keep from rolling over.

- For relief from osteoarthritis, sleep on your side in the fetal position, or cushion the painful joints with small pillows.

- Elevate your head at night if you suffer from atherosclerosis. This forces blood to your legs.

- Varicose veins feel better when you sleep with your legs propped up on pillows.

- Sleep on your left side or with your upper body propped up if you have acid reflux.

Marvelous mattresses: 5 steps to better sleep

"If you wake up in the morning with aches and pains, it's time to think about replacing your mattress," says Nancy Blass, Executive Director of The Better Sleep Council. With so many options on the market, she has some guidelines to help you find the bed that's right for you.

Plan before you shop. Don't wait until springs poke through to start looking for the perfect mattress.

- Test mattresses next time you're out shopping. When it's time to buy, you'll know your options.

- Don't limit your choices. Firm mattresses used to be the only recommendation for back problems, but new research shows a medium firm mattress relieves lower back pain more effectively.

- Decide on a budget and tell the salesperson right off what your price range is. He can narrow the choices down for you. "The more the salesperson knows about your sleeping habits and what you're looking for," says Blass, "the better he can help you find what you need."

Try before you buy. Blass recommends people take the sleep test. "Select a mattress and lie down on it in your sleeping position. Take off your shoes. Now evaluate it for comfort and support. Does it meet your needs? Are you feeling good?"

"It's also important that you bring your partner," she says. "If you're sleeping with somebody, find a bed that you both can feel comfortable on."

Get the whole story. Once you find a comfortable mattress, ask these questions:

- Does it have special features? Extra padding on top will add softness, and extra support on the sides can stabilize the bed while you sit on the edge. Hypoallergenic fabric will resist dust and mold. These — and other — features might be worth the extra expense.

- How many coils does the mattress have and what is the gauge? More coils mean more support. The lower the gauge number, the thicker the springs.

- Can you view a cutaway? A cross section of the mattress can show you how the springs and padding work together. "If they have a cutaway of a mattress, that's a pretty good indication you are looking at a high level of quality," says Blass.

- Will they deliver the new mattress and take away the old one?

- Is there a comfort guarantee? Make sure you know about any return policies before you spend the cash.

Budget for a box spring. Many companies will void your warranty if you buy their mattress without the box spring. Buy them together. "It's important," says Blass, "because they are engineered and built to work together."

Select the perfect pillow. While you're shopping, complete your sleep environment by choosing a pillow that supports your head without straining your neck. "If you sleep on your stomach, you're going to want a softer pillow." Blass says. "If you sleep on your back, get the medium. If you sleep on your side, you'll want a firmer pillow to support the curve in your neck."

Finally, don't scrimp on this buy. "It's important simply to invest in rest," she concludes. "You spend a third of your life on a mattress — this is not the place to cut back."

Breathe easier with clean technology

The air in your home may be making your asthma or allergies worse. Experts say the best way to remedy that is by removing the source of the problem — whether it's mold, dust, smoke, or a pet. But often that's just not possible. So you are left to choose among the many gadgets that claim to purify the air.

Filter out allergens. "Cleaning devices can help," says Janice Nolen, Director of National Policy for the American Lung Association. "We recommend you get one that is a mechanical filter."

This type of air purifier pulls the air in a room through a filter, removing allergens. Nolen says a room-size unit is most effective. "Little ones, like table-top fans, are usually not useful, because they don't move enough air."

To find a size that's right for you, calculate your space in cubic feet, then read the specifications on the box. Even though they can be large, many purifiers have wheels so you can move them from room to room. Nolen believes they are most productive in the bedroom since people spend so much time there.

You'll also need to be diligent about checking and changing the filter for your purifier. If yours uses HEPA (high-efficiency particulate air) filters, you'll find they are a little more expensive, but are the industry darling. Developed during WWII to cut down on radioactive particles, they will filter out practically everything.

Zap away particles. Electronic air cleaners, or ionizers, are quiet machines that charge the particles in a room then pull them into a filter. "Ionizers," Nolen says, "aren't a problem as long as they don't produce ozone, a known air pollutant."

Get rid of moisture. "Lower humidity has been shown as a way of keeping down dust mites," says Nolen. "And having less humidity in the house makes it less likely you will have mold buildup." That makes a great argument for a dehumidifier. "And they can be helpful as long as they are well maintained," Nolen states. Remember though, their only purpose is to draw moisture out of the air, so they won't clean up particles.

Take care of your ducts. "If your air ducts are dirty," says Nolen, "then it might be a good thing to get them cleaned out. But make sure you know what they are cleaned with." Some products can cause more problems than they solve.

Service your AC. Your heating and cooling system relies on clean filters to run properly, so you should replace them on a regular basis anyway. "This also helps make sure all the particles get filtered as effectively as possible," says Nolen. And that means cleaner air.

She believes the accordion filters are generally better because they have a larger surface area to trap particles.

Safe and simple ways to a brighter smile

It's time to show off your smile again. New technology can make your teeth whiter and brighter faster than you can say toothpaste.

"Whitening will work for the majority of people who have discolored or dark teeth as long as they are not covered by restorations," says Mike Malone, D.D.S., President of the American Academy of Cosmetic Dentistry. "It's common to get extremely good results, especially in people who had whiter teeth in their youth."

There are basically three ways to get your teeth whitened.

- Buy an over-the-counter home whitening kit.
- Get fitted with custom trays at the dentist office and bleach your teeth at home.
- Have your teeth "power bleached" by your dentist.

Be wary of low-cost options. Although whitening kits you can buy at the drugstore are inexpensive, Malone says these are typically the least effective. "None of the trays will be custom fitted, so it's kind of like going to sleep wearing a football mouth guard," he says. "They are big and bulky, and don't fit very well."

He feels a major concern is that you don't know anything about the quality of the product. "Sometimes you get results; sometimes you get no results or poor results."

Get satisfaction from the pros. "Custom trays the dentist makes for a patient to wear at home are fitted exactly to their teeth," says Malone. "They are very thin, comfortable, and easy to wear."

You simply squeeze a small amount of bleaching solution into each tray and slip them on. The peroxide bleach may cause some temporary tingling or sensitivity, but Malone says, "All the products the dentists use are safe. They don't damage your gums, the enamel, or the tooth structure at all. After the bleaching process has been completed, the sensitivity goes away."

"If someone wants excellent results with the lowest cost," Malone says, "the best option is the home bleaching system that is custom fitted at the dental office."

Go for speed with a power bleach. This process involves one or more sessions under a laser in the dentist's office. The main advantage to this option is speed. By the end of an hour you should see a marked improvement in the color of your smile.

"The drawback to the power bleaching," says Malone, "is it costs more money." He recommends combining one power bleach session with a custom whitening kit. "It gets you started off with quite a bit of whitening on the first day and then continues the bleaching process at home."

Although he feels it's best to have your dentist individually evaluate your case and help you decide what will work for you,

Malone recommends teeth whitening to anyone who needs a reason to smile. "It makes people feel really good about themselves."

For more information on whitening and other cosmetic dental treatments, visit the American Academy of Cosmetic Dentistry's Web site at *www.aacd.com.*

Go electric for cleaner teeth

"If you use a manual toothbrush properly it will do as fine a job as an electric brush," says Dr. Richard H. Price, spokesperson for the American Dental Association (ADA). And that's precisely the issue.

Many seniors have problems with their hands — like arthritis — and can no longer grip and manipulate a regular toothbrush as they used to. Electric toothbrushes can make your bathroom routine fun and easy again.

Look for ADA approval. Don't be confused by all the technical descriptions says Price. "Electric toothbrushes now go under the heading of plaque removers. They vibrate; they are ultrasonic; they are subsonic; they do all kinds of things."

The bottom line he says is if it carries the ADA seal on the box. "That means the product will do what it says it will do. It will effectively remove the plaque on your teeth, and do it without harming your teeth or gums."

Read the directions. Most electric toothbrushes will do the job as long as you carefully follow the directions. Some brushes need gentle pressure to activate the rotating head, while others lie against your gums and clean the plaque with sound waves.

"Turn to your dentist or hygienist," suggests Price. "They love to spend time showing you how to use the new brushes."

Invest more time. "There is a disadvantage to an electric tooth-brush," warns Price. "It takes more time." You may get away with giving your teeth a few sweeping passes with a manual brush, but many electric brushes have an alarm that goes off only when you've brushed for two minutes. "You can't fake it with an electric brush," he says. "You've got to take the time to use it. But for those who do use it and use it properly, there are rewards — they're keeping their teeth."

Keep it sanitary. Electric brushes don't require a complicated cleaning regimen. "I think the biggest problem is when you drop it behind the toilet," jokes Price. Otherwise, just make sure the bristles dry out between uses to kill water-loving microbes. Your own immune system and the antibacterial action of your toothpaste will take care of the rest.

"If you're really worried about it, you can put it in the dishwasher," suggests Price. "Don't microwave it though — it has too many metal parts."

Finally, use common sense about replacing the head. "If you look down at your toothbrush and it's splayed all over the place like it's been mashed, then it's time to change it," says Price. Otherwise, dentists generally recommend that you replace the head every three months.

Nuke germs to keep dentures clean

Simple cleaning solutions will not kill all the bacteria on your dentures. For out-and-out germ warfare, nothing beats a microwave.

Follow these directions to the letter, says Dr. Tom Glass, Professor of Pathology and Microbiology at the Oklahoma State University Center for Health Sciences, and you'll leave your dentures virtually germ-free.

- First, ask your dentist if your dentures can be microwaved. They must have no metal parts.

- Dissolve one Polident tablet according to the manufacturer's directions.

- Place your dentures in a microwave-safe bowl with a vented lid and cover them with this cleaning solution. Leave two inches of airspace between the solution and the lid.

- Put on the lid, open the vent, and lay a paper towel on top.

- Set the microwave (1100 watts) for two minutes on high.

- Cool your dentures in the microwave for five to 10 minutes, and then rinse under cold water.

Choose sunglasses for health and safety

Protecting your eyes from cataracts and macular degeneration doesn't have to cost an arm and a leg — just the price of the right pair of sunglasses.

"Ultraviolet (UV) protection is not necessarily expensive," says Dr. Ivan Schwab, a representative of the American Academy of Ophthalmology. "You don't have to rely on sunglasses that are designer specials."

In fact, according to Schwab, many pairs sold at drugstores and department stores can protect your eyes. You just need to know what to look for.

UV comes first. Make sure the glasses reduce over 95 percent of UV rays. If the label says "UV absorption up to 400nm," that means they block 100 percent.

Pick your color. "Tint is a matter of personal selection," says Schwab. "As long as it protects against the UV rays, it doesn't make much difference." Although, he adds, an orange tint may reduce the glare that seems to bother people with macular degeneration.

Skip your reflection. Mirrored glasses do not protect your eyes more than average and may actually allow more UV rays in since they are so dark your pupils dilate to absorb more light.

No Rx is needed. If you wear prescription glasses just to see objects up close, don't bother with the expense of prescription sunglasses, which usually sharpen your distance vision.

Go for the wrap. If you're buying sunglasses to protect your eyes — and not just for style — Schwab says, "You need to have sunglasses that block out as much of the rays as possible." Wraparound sunglasses protect your eyes from all angles and are especially good at blocking UV light.

Consider shatterproof. If your balance is not as good as it once was, or your eyesight is fading in one eye, Schwab says you should consider safety glasses because of your increased risk of falling. "Safety glasses are a little like your windshield. It tends to fragment instead of breaking into sharp shards. So," he says, "it's harder to damage an eye behind safety

---

⚠ **Prevent top vision dangers**

Eye damage is easily avoided. Use common sense and safety gear, and you won't become a statistic.

- Almost 40 percent of all accidents happen around the home. Tools, lawnmowers, light bulbs, and cleaning products are potential hazards.

- Car accidents — while not wearing seat belts — are the leading source of damage to both eyes.

- One in 20 severe eye injuries happen while shooting off or watching fireworks.

- Careless gun handling causes a full 10 percent of all eye injuries.

- Almost 20 percent of all sports-related injuries happen while fishing.

Data provided by the United States Eye Injury Registry, through funding by the Helen Keller Foundation, Birmingham, Alabama, USA.

glass." Ask your optometrist for a prescription, or see if your optician can make a pair for you.

Avoid scratches. "When you aren't using your sunglasses they should go into some kind of case," Schwab warns. Scratched lenses don't necessarily damage your eyes, but they can make it harder to see. "Scratches are going to increase your glare," he says, "and your lenses are going to admit more UV rays if you've scratched away the protective coating. But be careful what you clean them with because many cloths will scratch them." If you can afford it, Schwab advises replacing a badly scratched pair.

Finally, regarding eye diseases like cataracts and macular degeneration, Schwab says, "Don't assume that by wearing UV sunglasses you are going to be able to stop this. But you will reduce the speed of progression."

Make health top priority at nail salons

Manicures and pedicures can make you feel well-groomed and attractive. Just make sure you leave a salon healthy, as well as looking good. Dr. Phoebe Rich, an Oregon dermatologist with special expertise in nail disorders, says to follow these simple tips.

- Ask about cleanliness. "Most reputable salons like to talk about the measures they take to protect their clients," says Rich. "Use common sense. If it doesn't look clean, it probably is not clean." Experts consider infections the most serious health risk related to nail cosmetics.

- Ask if your technician and the salon are both licensed by the state board.

- Watch your technician to see if she washes her hands between clients.

- Tools must be sterilized between each use. Look around for jars with instruments soaking in a blue liquid called Barbicide.

- Bring your own files, emery boards, and foam toe separators. These cannot be sterilized.

- Don't let your technician clip your cuticles. "The cuticle seals the nails from environmental pathogens," explains Rich. "If that cuticle seal is broken, there is a risk of infections."

- "A strong odor could mean that the salon is using Methymethacrylate, which is banned for use in acrylic nails," warns Rich. It can cause allergies so severe you could lose your nail. If your fingers itch, burn, or feel tender, you may be having a reaction. See a dermatologist immediately.

- Keep your acrylic nails short. "The natural nail bends or breaks when stressed," says Rich, "but an acrylic nail is so strong that it won't break. Instead it pulls away from the nail bed and causes damage."

Outsmart the IRS

5 secrets to slashing your taxes

"Your objective should be to pay all of the taxes that are due, but not one penny more than the law requires," writes Jeff A. Schnepper, in his book *How to Pay Zero Taxes*.

As a financial, tax, and legal advisor, Schnepper acknowledges if you don't know the rules, you can't win the game. That's why he outlines these top tax-saving strategies in detail. Just remember, read your instruction booklet carefully or consult your tax professional every year, because laws and threshold amounts are constantly changing.

Itemize deductions. You can subtract certain expenses from your taxable income. The law allows either a standard deduction, or you can itemize them. The standard deduction for married filing jointly in 2004 is $9,700 — up from $9,500 in 2003. You get more if you're over 65, blind, or both.

Schnepper says to first determine your medical expenses — less 7.5 percent of your adjusted gross income (AGI). Add to that all the money you actually spent for home mortgage interest, state and local taxes, charitable contributions, and other expenses allowed on Schedule A of the 1040 form. If the total is more than your standard deduction, then you can save by itemizing. If it's less, you get a bonus and it's a lot less trouble.

Because of our progressive tax structure, the higher your tax bracket, the more money you save with every deduction. Don't forget if your income is more than $139,500 (2003, married filing jointly), there may be a limit on your itemized deductions.

Schedule expense payments. If your expenses are on the borderline with the standard deduction, Schnepper advises you to look for items you can pay early or late. Load up on expenses one year, he says, go light the next. That way you can alternate — take the standard deduction one year and itemize the next.

Double your savings. Contribute to an individual retirement account (IRA) or a 401k plan and cut your taxes while you build a nest egg. Those funds are deducted from the amount you pay tax on. If you're self-employed, use a simplified employee pension (SEP) or Keogh plan to save untaxed dollars.

Flex your medical spending. The IRS allows most employers to withhold pre-tax money from your paycheck, which you can then use to pay medical expenses. They're called medical savings accounts, cafeteria plans, Health Savings Accounts (HSAs), or flexible spending plans. According to Schnepper, it's a better deal than itemizing on your tax return, since you don't have to deduct 7.5 percent of your income from your expenses. Talk to your employer for details.

Drive a gas-saver. Purchase a new electric car and earn a $3,000 tax credit in 2004. Hybrid vehicles that use a combination of electric and gasoline power qualify for a clean-fuel taxable income deduction up to $1,500. Cars that use other clean-burning fuel — like propane, natural gas, and hydrogen — also give you a tax break. If your business owns and operates clean-fuel vehicles, like trucks or vans, you're allowed an even higher deduction. Act now, because these rewards are scheduled to decrease each year after 2004.

Your home is money in the bank

Home ownership is one of the best tax breaks around — especially if you have a mortgage. Chances are, you can get paid simply for owning and living in your own home.

Here's how it works. When your itemized deductions are more than the standard deduction, you can subtract the extra from your taxable income. You pay less tax, which is money in your pocket. Read on to learn how your home is a source of many itemized deductions.

Cash in on interest and taxes. Your biggest deductions usually come from first mortgage interest payments and real estate taxes. If these two items total more than $800 a month, you're probably over the annual standard deduction already. By adding on medical expenses, charitable contributions, and other itemized deductions, you'll get an even bigger tax bonus.

There's more you can deduct. In fact, Gerald J. Robinson has written an entire book — *J.K. Lasser's Homeowner's Tax Breaks* — on the subject. Here are some things he suggests.

Convert to home equity. Interest on home equity loans counts against taxable income. These loans are based on the value of your home less the amount of your mortgage and other liens. You must use your home as collateral and can only deduct interest on the first $100,000.

You can use the money to pay off your credit cards, buy a new car, take a vacation, or whatever else you want. As long as the loan is secured by your home, the interest you pay is a tax deduction.

Earn more with a home office. If you work at home, the portion of the house — office, workroom, storage — that you use for business is deductible. You can also add a percentage of utility bills, insurance, and depreciation to your business expenses. Remember, though, if you claim any depreciation on your home

115

as a result of your business, when you sell, that portion of the gain will be taxable.

When your home is your principle place of business, you can deduct transportation costs when you leave to call on clients. You can also write off the full cost of home office equipment.

Buy a second home. Mortgage interest and real estate taxes on second or vacation homes get the same deduction as your main residence. If you rent it out for less than 15 days a year, all the income is tax-free. More than that is subject to formulas and computations.

Your vacation home becomes income property if you rent it out and don't use it yourself. It still can be a valuable tax shelter, but there are different rules. Rental property can be your old home, your future second home, or just a house you buy for an investment.

Trade down for retirement funds. Your home can even be a source of income for your retirement if you trade down — sell the house and buy something smaller and less expensive. The old capital gains rules have changed so that, for married couples, up to $500,000 profit on your house is not taxable at all, as long as you have lived in it at least two years.

Or you can take out a reverse mortgage — which is like a home equity loan — and use the money for retirement. Read more about reverse mortgages in *Gain extra cash from your home* on page 152.

This new capital gains rule is also helpful for homeowners who buy in a rapidly appreciating neighborhood, stay for two years, and then cash out at a higher price. The same goes for you if you're a handyman. Buy a fixer-upper, improve it to increase its value, and sell.

Seniors earn extra tax breaks

One advantage of getting older is that Uncle Sam gives you extra federal income tax breaks — some just because you're a senior and some because your situation changes. Don't overlook these loopholes.

Enjoy your retirement. When you retire you get built-in tax relief because your retirement income is usually less than when you were working. With less income, you pay less tax. Tax-deferred retirement plans like an IRA or 401k, and qualified annuities are good deals because you don't pay taxes on them until you are in a lower tax bracket.

Social Security payments are usually part of retirement income. They are not taxable so long as half your Social Security plus the rest of your income isn't more than $32,000 if you're married and filing a joint return. Even if it's more, only a portion of it is taxed, depending on your total income.

Itemize health expenses. It's a good idea for seniors to consider itemizing medical expenses instead of taking the standard deduction. The 7.5 percent of your income you have to subtract from medical deductions gets smaller as your income goes down. You're also likely to have more medical expenses as you get older.

- Most payroll deduction health insurance premiums are already tax-free, but when you start paying them yourself, you can deduct them on your tax return.

- Qualified long-term care insurance expense is deductible, and so is the cost of medical care in a nursing home or similar facility.

- If you drive yourself to doctors, you can deduct mileage, parking, and toll booth fees. The same goes for bus, taxi, train, or plane fares. You can also deduct ambulance service fees.

- Itemize the cost of weight-loss programs prescribed to treat a disease and stop-smoking plans.

- Sometimes overlooked expenses include eyeglasses and hearing aids; special equipment like wheelchairs, braces, and crutches; and the cost of remodeling your home to accommodate a disability.

Cash in on your birthday. Once you hit 65, there are some automatic benefits on your tax return. First off, the minimum amount for filing a return increases at 65, as does the amount of the standard deduction. And, depending on your income, you may also get an extra tax credit just for being that age.

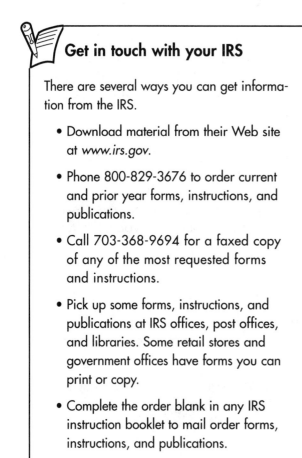

Get in touch with your IRS

There are several ways you can get information from the IRS.

- Download material from their Web site at *www.irs.gov*.

- Phone 800-829-3676 to order current and prior year forms, instructions, and publications.

- Call 703-368-9694 for a faxed copy of any of the most requested forms and instructions.

- Pick up some forms, instructions, and publications at IRS offices, post offices, and libraries. Some retail stores and government offices have forms you can print or copy.

- Complete the order blank in any IRS instruction booklet to mail order forms, instructions, and publications.

If you want benefits before 65, there's an advantage you get when you're 59-1/2. That's the age you can withdraw from IRA and 401k plans without penalty. Before then, it costs you an extra 10 percent.

Look for personalized benefits. Pre-death life insurance payments to the chronically ill are not taxed. Neither are expense paybacks from volunteer organizations like the Retired Senior Volunteer Program, Foster Grandparent Program, and Service Corps of Retired Executives.

Learn more about these and other senior benefits by talking to your tax professional or reading the Internal Revenue Service Publication 554, *Older Americans' Tax Guide.*

14 payments the IRS can't touch

Not all the cash you get is taxable income. According to Jeff A. Schnepper's *How to Pay Zero Taxes*, you don't have to pay federal income tax on:

- part of the profit from selling your home.
- most social security payments.
- a portion of annuities income.
- interest on state and municipal bonds.
- life insurance proceeds.
- inheritances and other gifts.
- many alimony and support payments.
- court-awarded damages.
- some scholarships and grants.
- "cafeteria" or flexible benefit plans.
- employer expense reimbursements.
- workers' compensation.
- employer-paid medical insurance premiums.
- public assistance/welfare payments.

Like most IRS rules, there are loopholes and exceptions, so check with your tax professional for specifics.

Save taxes while you pay for school

It's pretty easy to get tax credits and deductions for college expenses if you're a student or a parent of a student. But what if you're a grandparent and you want to help out a student — whether it's your grandchild or someone else — and beat the tax man at the same time.

You can do it, but you must start early, because the advantage comes from tax-free earnings on investments.

Establish an ESA. The Coverdell Education Savings Account (ESA), formerly called an Education IRA, is an account set up while the child is still young. Money that goes into an ESA is after-tax cash, but the earnings are tax-free.

It may not sound like much, but over a period of time, it adds up. For instance, if you put in $1,000 a year for five years and it earns 8 percent a year, it will grow to more than $17,000 in 18 years. And neither you nor your grandchild will pay tax on $12,000 of it!

Here are some of the rules for a Coverdell ESA.

- Set up the account in the name of a beneficiary — who must be under age 18.
- You cannot contribute more than $2,000 per year for each beneficiary.
- You, as a contributor, cannot earn more than $110,000 — $220,000 for joint returns — per year.
- When the beneficiary draws out money for qualified education expenses, no tax is due. You can use the money for college, high school, or elementary school.

Seek out other plans. You get the same type of benefit from special education U.S. savings bonds and from Qualified Tuition

Programs (QTPs) run by state governments or eligible schools. QTPs used to be called 529 plans.

If you claim your grandchild as a dependent on your tax return, you can subtract college expenses from your total taxes through the Hope Credit or the Lifetime Learning Credit. Most scholarships and grants are not taxed and you can deduct certain educational expenses from taxable income. You can also deduct the interest on student loans.

It's best to keep your tax returns — and the records that back them up — for six years, says Scott Estill in his book *Tax This! An Insider's Guide to Standing Up to the IRS.*

The IRS has three years to audit most tax returns, he writes. If it can prove you omitted at least 25 percent from your gross income, it can go back six years.

Estill points out that you should keep some records forever, including those that relate to investments and real property.

Remember, you can get many of these tax benefits if you go back to school yourself. You're never too old to learn — or to save money.

As with all tax matters, make sure you understand the program thoroughly before you start. Read IRS Publication 970, *Tax Benefits for Education*, or see a tax professional.

File a confident tax return

It's pretty easy to do your own taxes when all you need is a W2 form and the standard deduction. But how complicated does it have to get before you ask for help?

"The most important thing is that you feel comfortable filling out your own return," says Eric Erickson, a spokesman for the

Internal Revenue Service in Atlanta. He feels that if you are confident, you should do it.

File your taxes online. There are several things the IRS does to help give you that confidence. One is IRS e-file, a paperless transaction you can complete on your computer.

"Electronic filing has really made it easier for a lot of taxpayers to do their own returns," Erickson says. "You just go online, enter the amounts in the proper boxes, click, and you're done. It figures it out for you and boom, you get your refund."

In some states, or if you meet certain income requirements, e-filing is free. You can also pay a tax professional to send it in for you.

Call on the IRS. Every year there are lots of new books written about how to do your taxes. But the basic information comes from the IRS — at no cost.

"There are dozens and dozens of publications," Erickson points out, "and instructions that coordinate with every form. Our publications cover every bit of the tax code."

The IRS also has a TeleTax phone line — 800-829-4477 — that gives recorded messages on about 150 topics. For more detailed questions or to talk to a person, call 800-829-1040 and follow the prompts.

Use volunteer counselors. Volunteers trained by the IRS give free person-to-person assistance through the Volunteer Income Tax Assistance (VITA) and Tax Counseling for the Elderly (TCE) programs. VITA will help you fill out basic tax returns if your income is under $35,000. TCE offers tax counseling and help preparing returns if you're over 60. To find out where to go for these programs, call the IRS at 800-829-1040.

The AARP's Tax-Aide counseling program is part of TCE and is also free. Call 888-227-7669 or visit *www.aarp.org*.

Consult a pro. "Sometimes you feel better with a preparer who knows more about the ins and outs of current tax law," says Erickson.

That's when you need to find a professional tax preparer. These pros keep up with tax law changes and can spot overlooked deductions. They also know more about tax shelters, special credits, and other advantages that may not apply to everybody.

The National Association of Tax Professionals (NATP), a nonprofit professional organization, says hiring a tax preparer will often pay for itself, and at the same time teach you how to save on future taxes.

There's a wide range of fees and levels of expertise for tax services, so shop around. Think about what you need, look for someone who has the qualifications that fit your situation, and don't base your decision on cost alone. Here are some of the kinds of preparers you will find.

- Certified public accountants (CPAs) are also qualified to do business books.

- Certified financial planners (CFPs) can advise you on investments.

- Enrolled agents (EAs) are required to pass an extensive IRS tax exam and can represent you in the case of an audit.

- Individual practitioners and regular accountants have various backgrounds. The NATP says most of these are qualified and reputable, but cautions it is more important to ask questions and check references when using them.

Make sure it's done right. Remember, you are ultimately responsible for the information on your return, so be sure you trust your preparer and have faith in his abilities.

"Even though a preparer has done it for you, it's your signature," emphasizes Erickson. "If there's a mistake or something's not correct, we come to you, not the preparer."

Here's how long the IRS estimates it takes to research and prepare certain portions of your tax return.	
Form 1040 (Individual Return)	13 ½ hours
Schedule A (Itemized Deductions)	5 ½ hours
Schedule B (Interest & Dividends)	1 ½ hours
Schedule C (Business Profit or Loss)	11 hours
Schedule D (Capital Gains & Losses)	8 hours
Schedule E (Supplemental Income & Loss)	6 hours

Cut your odds of an audit

The Internal Revenue Service uses the threat of an audit to make sure you tell the truth when you fill out your tax return. Although they actually audit only about 1 percent of all tax returns, most people would like to reduce their odds of being in that select group.

The IRS randomly chooses a few returns for audit — but only a few. Most are picked because IRS employees and computers spot various red flags, says Scott Estill in his book *Tax This! An Insider's Guide to Standing Up to the IRS.*

Just because your return raises a flag, it doesn't mean you'll be audited, Estill, a tax attorney and former IRS senior trial attorney, explains. A human being will review the return manually and decide who gets a letter from an auditor. Here are some of the things he says you can do to keep from getting picked.

Know your score. The IRS uses a computer-generated score called the Discriminant Index Formula (DIF) to compare your numbers with national statistics. The IRS uses the DIF to pick the majority of audited returns, so be aware that lopsided numbers attract attention.

For instance, if the average amount of charitable contributions for your income group is $1,000 and you claim $3,000, the computer will flag this entry. According to Estill, Schedule C (sole proprietorship business) losses are also known to boost the DIF score — and your chances of an audit.

Report everything. Unreported income is the main target of most audits. Since the IRS matches information it gets from other sources with your return, you're asking for trouble if you don't list the income from every W2 and 1099 you receive.

Use exact numbers. The IRS knows rounded numbers are probably estimates you can't support in an audit. Estill does not recommend using approximate numbers but precise amounts — like $1,988 or $511 instead of $2,000 or $500.

Check the math. Computers screen your return and make automatic corrections if you add it up wrong, but errors give the IRS a reason to look closer. To slide through without calling undue attention, Estill advises you make sure your arithmetic is accurate.

File with the crowd. Most tax practitioners believe you reduce your chances for an audit if you file as close to April 15 as possible. Estill says they believe that variations in your DIF score will not stick out as much when so many returns are coming in.

File late. Estill also says if you file late, the IRS will already have chosen most of the returns to audit. But he cautions, you must file an extension and pay at least 90 percent of the tax due before April 15 to avoid late payment penalties.

Be neat and organized. Don't risk getting picked for an audit because the IRS has trouble reading or understanding your return. Inexpensive software is available to help you print it from your computer.

Use Cohan rule as last resort

In an IRS audit, you must justify your tax deductions with receipts or other adequate records. But sometimes, they're just not available. Under the Cohan rule, estimates are sometimes allowed if the taxpayer can prove he is entitled to a deduction for the expense.

It comes from a tax court ruling won by entertainer George M. Cohan in 1930, and was used for years to avoid keeping travel and entertainment receipts. Those loopholes have since been closed, but the Cohan rule still occasionally stops auditors from throwing out all undocumented deductions.

Document unusual deductions. If you have a casualty loss, theft, or other extraordinary deduction, attach police reports or similar explanations to the return. When the IRS looks at it, maybe they'll decide you have enough proof and an audit isn't necessary.

On the other hand, Estill does not recommend attaching an explanation for any deduction that you might question yourself.

Be extra careful. Estill says the IRS targets specific occupations and professions, like lawyers, nurses, ministers, construction workers, and mechanics; and likes follow-up audits for taxpayers who were audited in the past and had to pay extra taxes. If you fall into these categories, it's best to have everything in order so the auditors won't find anything.

Foolproof finances

Spring-clean your credit report

The most important financial move you can make this year is to check your credit report.

It's the key to qualifying for a loan, and the secret to lower interest rates and better deals on insurance. It can be the pebble that tips the scales in your favor when you're looking for a job.

The information in your credit report is gathered and sold by Consumer Reporting Agencies (CRAs). The best-known are the national credit bureaus, Equifax, Experian, and Trans Union — "the Big Three."

These credit bureaus keep four kinds of information:

- personal identification and employment
- credit payment history
- requests for your credit report in the last one to two years
- matters of public record, like bankruptcies and foreclosures

Check your report. No one should be more interested in your credit report than you. Check up on it once a year, or before you seek a loan or make a major purchase — and make sure it's accurate and up-to-date.

Thankfully, the Fair Credit Reporting Act (FCRA) is there to help. It makes sure you have easy access to your report and provides you with a way to correct any mistakes you may find.

Order one. Each CRA can charge up to $9 for your credit report, although some states require they give you a free copy or two every year. Calls to the national credit bureaus are automated, so if you live in a state whose laws allow a free report, there won't be any mention of a fee. Otherwise, be ready with your credit card.

Equifax	www.equifax.com	800-685-1111
Experian	www.experian.com	888-397-3742
Trans Union	www.transunion.com	800-916-8800

You're entitled to a free copy regardless of where you live if, for instance, you're denied credit, insurance, or a job because of information on your credit report. But you must make your request for the report within 60 days of receiving notice of the denial.

CRAs will also send you a free credit report if you can prove

- you're unemployed and plan to be job hunting within 60 days.
- you're receiving government assistance.
- your report is wrong because of fraud.

Repair your credit report from home. With reports in hand, study carefully. Be sure everything is accurate and complete. If there is a mistake, don't panic. The CRAs and companies that provide information used in your report have to correct errors. The CRAs even send a dispute form with your report.

- Circle disputed items on your report.

- Explain what you believe is wrong, and ask them to correct or delete those items.

- Attach copies — not originals — of documents that support your claim.

- Make two copies of the entire package. Mail one set to the CRA and one to the company that provided the incorrect information. Save a copy for your files.

- Send everything by certified mail, return receipt requested, and keep the receipts.

- Expect a fix. The CRA will send you the results of their investigation and a new, improved credit report.

The final step is to ask the CRAs to notify anyone who has received your old, incorrect report in the past six months. Now your financial spring-cleaning is done!

Best bets for budgeting success

Don't let financial chaos keep you from getting ahead. Instead, take your cue from Judy Lawrence's book, *The Budge Kit*.

It's a workbook chock-full of pages to record expenses, income, debt, and other financial transactions as well as worksheets to help you with the nuts and bolts of setting up a budget. In addition, she helps you understand how to take charge of your money. Here are just a few of the principles behind her strategy.

Set goals for your gold. Decide what specific financial goals you want to reach, Lawrence advises. Think about long-term goals like retirement. Also decide what to achieve in the next few years, what to accomplish this year, and what you can do in the next month.

Write these all down, rank them by importance, and assign due dates. Next, estimate how much you must save to meet each goal. Figure how much to put aside each week to reach your total savings goal and then write down specifically how you'll make that happen.

Brace for Murphy's law. Open an extra account at a bank or credit union to store money for emergencies like car repair or a layoff. Lawrence says to accumulate about three months' worth of take-home pay.

End monthly mistakes. Lawrence says a monthly budget sheet coordinates your monthly bills and expenses with your take-home pay. But there's probably no such thing as an average month, so outline each month individually. Be sure to include planned savings — treat these like required expenses.

Track credit purchases. Don't get ambushed by high credit card bills. Every time you use a card, write down the date, what you bought, and the amount charged. If you use several cards, keep separate sheets or columns for each.

Plan a fiscal year. Lawrence strongly recommends laying out a yearly budget of planned expenses that aren't part of your regular monthly bills — things like new glasses or contacts, firewood, insurance premiums, vacations, or annual club fees. Review a previous year's spending and estimate what costs are likely to be this year.

Decide where you might cut back, then total the remainder and divide by twelve. Now you can see how much to put aside monthly for these expenses.

Work together. Make budgeting a family affair says Lawrence. By sharing the information, you also share the burden.

Dealing with debt is best solution

Contrary to what many people hope, debt doesn't just go away. And winning the lottery isn't a solution you can count on. So what should you do when you fall behind and debt threatens your financial health?

First, let your lender know you're having problems. If you've been reliable in the past, they usually understand a temporary setback. Then follow the advice Rich and Kathi Mintzer offer in *The Everything Money Book*.

Find funds to pay off debt. The first thing, of course, is to change your spending habits. Discipline yourself to give up unnecessary expenses so you'll have funds to pay off the debt. Then, go to work to get your head back above water.

- Sell off investments. If you catch it soon enough, you may be able to cash in some of your assets and get rid of the debt before it gets the best of you.

- Rearrange your debt by paying it off with a home equity loan. You'll lower your overall monthly payments, the interest rate on a home equity loan will be lower than interest on credit card debt, and you'll reduce your tax bill since the interest on a home equity loan is tax deductible.

- Create extra income. Mintzer suggests you find ways — from part-time to full-time work — to earn additional money and use it exclusively to bring down your debt.

Get a credit counselor. If you need outside help, Mintzer recommends contacting the National Foundation for Credit Counseling (NFCC) at 800-388-2227 or via the Internet at *www.nfcc.org*. They provide credit education, counseling, and help you get better terms with your lenders.

In severe cases, they can set you up on a Debt Management Plan (DMP) — you pay them monthly and they distribute the funds to your creditors.

File bankruptcy as last resort. With a few exceptions, personal bankruptcy basically takes all you own, applies it to your debt, and lets you off the hook for what's left. Bankruptcy is not pleasant and it takes years to get a credit rating back, but it will get you out of debt.

Mintzer advises bankruptcy only when your debt exceeds your annual income and is multiplying faster than you expect your income to grow. Consider it also if your creditors sue.

Write letter to defeat credit collectors

Sometimes a lender turns a debt over to a collection agency. If you don't want these third-party collectors to call you, the Fair Debt Collection Practices Act — a federal law — says they have to stop. You'll still owe the debt, however. Use the letter on page 133 as a guide.

Pick a credit card that suits your finances

Television ads entice you with carefree lifestyles. Mailers flatter you with "pre-approved applications." Zoo animals, sports teams, tropical islands, or patriotic figures can peek from your wallet. But is this really how you should choose a credit card?

Consider your budgeting habits first. "Someone who pays the balance in full every month is looking for entirely different features than someone who carries a balance and is looking to reduce their interest charges," says Greg McBride, Senior

Third-party collector letter

```
(Date)
(Your name)
(Your address)
(Your city, state, and zip code)

(Name of the contact person, if you have one)
(Company name)
(Company street address)
(Company city, state, and zip code)

Dear (contact person) or To Whom It May
Concern:

(Company name) has contacted me regarding a
debt you say I owe to (name of original
lender). I do not want you to call me again
regarding this debt.

As you should know, The Fair Debt Collection
Practices Act, a federal law, says you may now
contact me only to say there will be no further
contact or to notify me that you or the credi-
tor intend to take some specific action.

Sincerely,


(Your name)

(Your account number, if applicable)
```

Financial Analyst for Bankrate.com, a leading provider of consumer financial information.

If you carry a balance, interest rates and fees are most important. "Find a card with a low interest rate," says McBride, "and keep in mind that an annual fee is not automatically a deterrent."

Read the small print. Then, look beyond the big bold letters advertising the interest rate and study the disclosure agreement. Be especially alert for policies that punish certain actions. Will one late payment throw you into a much higher rate cycle? These differ among both card issuers and the various cards they offer.

"The disclosure agreement is more important than the annual percentage rate (APR)," he warns. "The smaller the print, the more important the words."

McBride says to look at the day-to-day procedures. "What kind of billing cycle do they have? How much of a grace period do you have to get the payment in? And if you are doing a cash advance or balance transfer, how do those policies differ from that of purchases?"

⚠ Women need a credit history

Credit cards are not all bad. Have one and you have a credit history.

If you are a woman, a senior, and a widow, all the credit history might have been in your husband's name. And now you could have a hard time qualifying for loans, getting overdraft protection, or even renting a car.

Although it's against the law, this kind of credit discrimination happens. Don't wait until you need a credit history. Establish your own now with a credit card in your name.

Compare the perks. "Rewards and rebates really only benefit those who pay the balance in full every month," says McBride. "If you're carrying a balance, you should not be looking at these cards." Remember that rewards are not confined to frequent flyer miles or cash back anymore, so shop around.

Other differences in credit card features include insurance and warranties. Again, check the fine print for protection against rental car damage and flawed merchandise.

"It varies from card to card," McBride says. "If there's something of value to you, make it a point to investigate the specifics of it."

Look beyond brand names. According to McBride, as long as the other terms are similar, the name on the card doesn't make a difference. MasterCard and Visa are credit card networks that license individual banks to issue cards. Discover is both a network and a card issuer. American Express and Diners Club are basically charge cards — you have to pay your bill in full every month — although they are beginning to add some credit options.

"It's the terms that really matter when you're comparison shopping," McBride says. "Things such as the interest rate, the fees, the grace period, the perks earned on rebate or reward cards."

Credit or debit — clear up the confusion

All the plastic in your wallet is not the same. Even though debit and credit cards look alike, the differences between them affect your budgeting and cash flow.

"A debit card deducts money directly from your checking account, just like withdrawing cash or writing a check," explains Ken Kavanagh, Debit Card Executive for Bank of America. "You do not pay interest because you are accessing your own money."

On the other hand, he says a credit card accesses a line of credit issued by a bank. "Cardholders are given a period of time to pay off the purchase amount. If they do not pay in full by the end of this period, they will be charged interest."

Each type of card has certain advantages and disadvantages you should consider carefully.

Choose a debit card for convenience. Kavanagh lists the following benefits for Bank of America's Visa Check Card, its version of a debit card:

- Budgeting. You're more likely to spend within your means and avoid debt.

- Speed. Purchases are fast and easy. You swipe, authorize, and go.

- Simplicity. You don't have to carry bulky checkbooks, multiple identification cards, and large amounts of cash.

In addition, there's no annual fee and, unlike a credit card, if your debit card gets lost or stolen, no one else can use it without your pin number. Remember though, since debit card transactions come out of your checking account immediately, you must keep track of your withdrawals to avoid embarrassing shortfalls. And you can't stop payment on debit card purchases.

Get protection with a credit card. Besides the added benefits of rebates and bonus points you get with many cards, Kavanagh says these are good reasons to use traditional credit:

- Purchase protection. Some card issuers will replace, repair, or reimburse you for eligible items purchased with your card. Check your cardholder agreement for damage guarantees and warranties.

- Universal acceptance. Many consumer credit counselors recommend credit cards for purchases online or during overseas travel.

Still, credit cards can be costly if you don't pay attention to extra fees, penalties, and interest rates.

Take charge of credit card debt

The first thing to do when you're in a hole is stop digging. So, when credit card debt has you down, stop spending.

Keep a rein on your wallet. "Only carry the cards you're going to use," advises Scott Bilker, author of *Credit Card and Debt Management*. "Otherwise, you could lose them and it's going to be tempting to spend."

Bilker emphasizes, however, that cutting up your credit cards and closing out all your accounts isn't necessarily the answer to debt. "If you don't have spending discipline, it doesn't matter," he explains. "Anyone who's not disciplined with credit cards isn't going to be any more disciplined with cash. It's not so much having debt, it's improperly using your debt — wrong priorities and bad spending decisions."

Cut the cost of your debt. Once you have your spending under control, Bilker says you've got to become efficient with your debt. This means setting it up so it costs you as little as possible.

Consider a new credit card so you can consolidate your other debt into a single lower-interest account. Check the terms, interest rates, fees, and other charges carefully.

"The only catch," Bilker cautions, "is that you must be disciplined enough not to spend that new line of credit. Use it solely for the purpose of reducing your debt."

Jumping from card to card isn't a bad thing, Bilker believes, as long as you make sure the deal is good. "There's no penalty for jumping around," he says. "You're going to save money as long as you do it the right way. Compare all your options and then pick the least expensive one."

Improve your credit. "If you don't have the availability of lines of credit, work every day at getting them," Bilker says. Clean up your credit report — get errors removed and start paying on time.

"In a few months, you'll be able to get new lines of credit." he explains. "They may not be at great rates, but they'll be new.

Once you have them — and if you use them just for reducing your debt — you'll have a bargaining tool to negotiate with your current creditors."

Pay on time. "Being a late payer is the most expensive action to take when repaying debt," Bilker says. "When you're late, the fees are stiff — not just the late fee, but the increase in interest rates that most banks will penalize you for being late."

Pay as much as you can. That means making more than the minimum payment each month. The more you pay down the principal, the less there is to charge interest on and the quicker the debt melts away. Use all your resources to do this.

Bilker explains, "Someone who has $3,000 in a savings account and doesn't use it to pay off his $3,000 credit card bill is paying $45 a month just to have money in the bank. That's a terrible move."

Bank on the right financial institution

You need somewhere to put your money. And under the mattress just won't do. So how do you choose between the thousands of banks out there clamoring for your business?

Identify your banking personality. Figure out what you want from your bank first, advises the American Bankers Association (ABA). Here are some questions to ask.

- What's the reason you need a bank? Possibilities include saving money, having a checking account, and getting a loan.

- How much money will you normally keep in an account and how many checks will you write? These are the biggest factors in determining service charges.

- Are large purchases, like a car or a house, on your horizon? If so, you'll be interested in what kind of loans they offer.

- Do you have a big expense, like college education, retirement, or an RV, in the future? Then savings options — including uninsured investments — are important.

- How do you like to do your banking? If you use ATMs and online banking a lot, then look for electronic capability. If you like going into the bank and talking to someone in person, look for convenient hours and locations, and pleasant, knowledgeable employees.

Compare your options. Now call or visit several banks in the neighborhood where you live or work. Look for information online, too, and include your current bank in the search, the ABA says.

Examine services and the range of products closely. Today's financial institutions go far beyond the simple checking account, saving account, loans menu of the past. Look at fees and service charges just as closely as you do interest rates. Can you qualify for a package that will give you the services you want at no charge?

Think about how comfortable you feel with the bank. Most people say price is not the only — or even the most important — factor in choosing a bank.

Insure safety with FDIC, NCUA. Make sure the bank you choose is federally insured. The Federal Deposit Insurance Corporation (FDIC) insures banks and savings and loans, and the National Credit Union Administration (NCUA) insures credit unions. Both guarantee the safety of your deposits up to $100,000.

Many insurance companies and brokerage houses now offer banking services, too, but their products and services are not federally insured. The Securities Investor Protection Corporation (SIPC) — a nonprofit corporation not a government agency — attempts to replace securities when a brokerage firm fails. But it won't protect you against fraud or market risk.

Simple rules offer investor success

Most financial advice is more complex than it has to be, says Burton G. Malkiel, author of *The Random Walk Guide to Investing, Ten Rules for Financial Success.* Instead, Malkiel offers simple guidelines that he promises are all the investment advice you will ever need. Besides investing early and regularly, here are a few of his investor tips.

Figure out your investment personality. Think about your age, your financial circumstances, and your willingness to accept risk when deciding how to divide up your funds between cash, stocks, bonds, and real estate.

Spread out the risk. If you don't put all your eggs in one basket, you won't lose so much when the basket takes a tumble.

Investing wisdom for the ages

As you get older, your priorities change. So should your investment strategy. *The Wall Street Journal Lifetime Guide to Money* offers this blueprint for success.

- 20-39 — Save at least 10 percent of your income. Invest heavily in stocks. Set up an IRA or contribute to your company's 401(k) plan. Invest a fixed amount every month.

- 40-59 — Stay the course on savings. Reduce your stock holdings and buy more bonds. Good rule of thumb: subtract your age from 100. That's the percentage of your portfolio to put in stocks.

- 60+ — Balance your stocks and bonds to generate security plus income. Put three years of spending money, or about 15 percent of your portfolio, into super-safe investments — like CDs, short-term Treasury securities, or a money market mutual fund.

Don't try to beat the market. Malkiel insists that following the latest financial trend — even those touted by so-called experts — can destroy a savings plan. The stock market works so quickly and efficiently that no one can know in advance who the winners will be.

Avoid common blunders. Watch out for overconfidence, don't speculate on hot tips or past successes, and know when to get out.

Low-risk investments protect retirement security

Will Rogers is remembered for saying, "I'm more concerned about the return of my money than the return on my money."

His words are especially true as you approach retirement — not the time to take chances with your hard-earned funds. Ted Miller, author of *Kiplinger's Guide to Investing Success*, presents five types of investments considered low-risk.

Federal insurance offers best protection. About the safest place you can keep your money is in a checking, savings, or money market deposit account (MMDA) with a federally insured financial institution. The Federal Deposit Insurance Corporation (FDIC) and the National Credit Union Administration (NCUA) guarantee the return of all your money up to $100,000.

The return on your money probably won't be enough to keep up with inflation, but it will be safe. Miller classifies money in these accounts as savings rather than an investment.

Certificates of Deposit (CDs), however, will give you higher rates, depending on how much money you invest and for how long. Miller suggests you can earn an extra one or two percentage points if you shop around for banks with higher rates. Just make sure your CD is FDIC-insured.

When it comes to stocks, nothing is a sure bet. But, according to investing experts, here are 16 stocks that will skyrocket in the 21st century.

- Abbott Laboratories (ABT)
- Allstate Corp. (ALL)
- American International Group (AIG)
- Boston Scientific (BSX)
- Cisco Systems (CSCO)
- Citigroup (C)
- Coca-Cola (KO)
- ConocoPhillips (COP)
- Fidelity National Financial (FNF)
- First Data (FDC)
- General Electric (GE)
- Microsoft (MSFT)
- Nabors Industries (NBR)
- Pfizer (PFE)
- Procter & Gamble (PG)
- Teva Pharmaceuticals (TEVA)

Government backs Treasury investments. Treasury bills (T-bills) are securities issued by the U.S. Treasury for one year or less. They may even be safer than bank CDs, because the federal government backs them. T-bills yield a little less than CDs, but they're exempt from state and local income taxes. You can buy them from banks, brokers, or direct from the government.

Other federal securities are T-notes, which lock up your money from two to 10 years, T-bonds, with maturities over 10 years, and U.S. savings bonds, which Miller rates as an excellent savings vehicle.

Loan money out for steady income. When you buy a bond, you actually loan your money for a certain length of time, at a set interest rate, with a regular payment schedule. Federal agencies — like the Farm Credit System — and the major mortgage-related agencies — like Fannie Mae, Ginnie Mae, and

Freddie Mac — issue bonds. So do state and municipal governments and private companies.

Municipal bonds are attractive because of their tax advantages. Corporate bonds usually pay higher rates because there is a bigger chance of default.

Bonds have several kinds of risks, Miller cautions, and the idea that they are about the safest investment you can find is not always true. Judge your risk using ratings by an investment data company like Standard & Poor's or Moody's Investor Services.

Brokers balance short-term risk. A mutual fund is an arrangement where you pool your money with many investors and get a slice of a wide assortment of investments you could never afford on your own.

Money market mutual funds concentrate on CDs, federal government securities, and other short-term investments — nothing longer than 90 days. Default risk is low and returns stay close to the going rate because there isn't time for major changes to take place.

According to Miller, money market mutual funds have a well-deserved reputation for being about the safest uninsured non-Treasury investments around.

Fund managers limit stock losses. No other investment holds as much promise as stocks over the long run, Miller says, but there are many mistakes you can make. Mutual funds are a good way to get into the stock market while letting the experts make investment decisions.

Professional mutual fund managers put together diversified portfolios that spread the risk and give each individual investor a better chance of coming out ahead. Choose a fund that targets the kind of investment — high or low risk; growth or income; stocks, bonds, or money market — that suits you.

Online trading: fast and cheap for those in the know

Save time and money by using your computer to connect directly to a brokerage house. You trade instantly and usually save on commissions.

Kiplinger's Guide to Investing Success by Ted Miller suggests you'd probably be happiest with an online broker if:

- you like to do your own research instead of paying someone else to do it, and

- you use the Internet a lot to track down information.

But remember, you're on your own when it comes to making decisions. By cutting that full-service stockbroker out of the action, you're losing guidance, detailed reports, and recommendations on how to put together your investment package.

Old stock certificates may still have value

That old bond or stock certificate gathering dust in your attic may still be worth something, says Jane Bryant Quinn in her book *Making the Most of Your Money.*

Use the Internet or your local library to find a current listing of the company that issued the securities. Then call or write them for a value. Or ask your broker to check his sources.

For $75 per company, R.M Smythe & Company, a stock and bond research firm in New York, will also find out market value. Call them at 800-622-1880 or check their Web site at *www.smytheonline.com.*

Match your habits. You can trade online through both full service brokers and discount brokers, so it's especially important to compare services, fees, and what Miller calls "bells and whistles" — free quotes, year-end cost-basis information for tax purposes, etc.

Your choice of an online broker should depend mostly on how often you buy and sell, maintains Miller. Frequent traders are likely to go with the company that charges less per trade, while others will look for more services.

Guard against impulse buying. The danger in online trading is that it can be too easy. Quick trading and easy access can lead to short-term wheeling and dealing. If you're impulsive you can get into real trouble.

Check for online safety. Below are some of the controls online brokers use to safeguard your transactions. Miller says to make sure your company is doing one or more of them.

- Encryption. Data sent over the Internet is encoded. Most online brokerages use high-end encryption featuring a 128-bit algorithm.

- Time-out. The system automatically logs you out if there is no activity after a certain amount of time.

- "Three strikes." If you can't get your PIN number right after three tries, your account is blocked and you have to call in to get it reactivated.

- Cash controls. The broker won't allow funds to be withdrawn online. They only issue checks payable to you or your bank account.

Safeguarding your future

Seniors cash in with free services

Free meals, free transportation, even free minor home repairs. And that's just for starters. The best news — absolutely anyone over 60 can get in on these freebies.

In 1965, the federal government passed the Older Americans Act (OAA), which created a whole network of programs aimed at improving the quality of life for older adults. Their goal is to help people stay independent and live in their own homes longer. Here are just a few of the many services for seniors offered under the OAA.

- Transportation programs offer rides for essential trips like doctor appointments, business errands, shopping, and senior activities. Door-to-door service is even available in some areas.

- Volunteers provide escort service if you have trouble getting around. They might pick you up at your home, take you to appointments, and help you run errands.

- If you want to recuperate at home instead of in a hospital or nursing home, OAA's home health care services provide in-home care under a doctor's supervision. This is not for people who need round-the-clock medical care, however.

- Homemaker services lend a hand with basic housekeeping duties for people who can't physically manage these chores and have no one to help. A volunteer might do laundry, go grocery shopping, and even prepare meals.

- Chore services perform heavier duties — including yard work, minor home repairs, and house cleaning.

- Home meal delivery brings hot, balanced meals five days a week to people who cannot prepare their own food and don't have anyone to help them.

- Community home repair and renovation programs help seniors fix minor problems around the house before the damage becomes serious. Volunteers may come over and patch holes in the roof, insulate walls, or repair leaky plumbing.

The OAA also sponsors programs like these around the country, all available to seniors over 60.

- legal assistance
- senior centers
- adult day care
- housing assistance
- state energy assistance
- exercise programs
- employment
- nutrition education
- visitors and telephone reassurance
- crime prevention and victim assistance

The Area Agencies on Aging coordinate many of these services and can put you in touch with those in your community. Just dial the Eldercare Locator toll-free at 800-677-1116, or visit their Web site at *www.ElderCare.gov*.

Age is the only criteria, not income. Still, some agencies will assess your needs first so they can provide services to the people who need them most. Others work on a first come, first served basis. And some programs provide services up to a set dollar limit.

Get a financial physical

Just like going to the doctor for a yearly checkup, you need to check up on your retirement finances, too. After all, the plan you set up 10 years ago may no longer suit you.

"Things change in people's lives," explains Alan McKnight, a Certified Financial Planner (CFP) and Vice-President of Kays Financial Advisory Corporation. "We encourage clients to come in at least once a year for a financial physical."

When McKnight meets with his clients, he looks at four major issues. Use these as a guide for your own financial physical — and make sure you discuss each area with your advisor.

Evaluate cash flow. Compare your monthly expenses to your monthly income. Find out if you are spending more than you receive each month from pensions, social security, or other retirement savings.

McKnight says he would ask, What are your monthly needs? Have they changed since we last met? "Because," he says, "we don't want to overspend in retirement and run out of money before the end of our lives."

Manage your risk. This includes all the insurance you carry — home, auto, life,

---

Get set for retirement with online help

If retirement planning makes your head spin, let your fingers do the walking. Quicken, the company that makes tax and financial software for your computer, offers a Web site on the ABC's of retirement planning. In fact, it's a favorite with Alan McKnight, CFP and Vice-President of Kays Financial Advisory Corporation. "It's very simple, and very easy to use," he says.

Just hop on the Internet and go to *www.quicken.com/planning/*. You'll find articles on tax, retirement, and estate planning, as well as calculators and other tools. Use it as a guide, but be sure to discuss your plans and concerns with your financial advisor.

personal liability, health, disability, and others. Your advisor will look at how much insurance you have and propose adjustments. He may also help you decide if you should purchase long-term care insurance, and whether you need and can afford to buy private health insurance.

Count your pennies. Ask yourself if you are meeting your goals for retirement, says McKnight. You and your advisor should look at how you've invested your money, then discuss any changes you need to make to stay on track.

But investments aren't everything. He should talk to you about accumulating enough wealth to pay for things like setting up a college fund for grandchildren, or buying another house.

Plan your estate. A financial advisor should make sure you have legal documents in place to protect your estate and your health. "We just want to make sure you have a simple will, a living will, and some type of power of attorney for healthcare and financial circumstances," McKnight says.

In addition, he looks at how his clients plan to pass their estate on to their heirs. Make sure, he says, your assets will be passed on efficiently — free of taxes — to the people you choose.

This may sound like a lot, but a good advisor will cover all these bases and more. Think of your retirement and estate plan like a lifeboat. According to McKnight, a good planner should be able to spot the holes and help you plug them. That way, if anything catastrophic happens — a serious illness, or the death of a loved one, for example — your whole ship won't sink.

"It's also important to let your advisor know if anything in your life has changed," explains McKnight. A good planner won't just tell you how much money your investments earned. He will want to know what curve balls life has thrown your way recently, since it may affect financial decisions.

Compare retirement accounts

	Traditional non-deductible IRA	Traditional deductible IRA	Roth IRA	401k
Who funds it?	You	You	You	You, plus employer's match
When does money go in?	after taxes	before taxes	after taxes	before taxes
Are contributions tax deductible?	No	Yes	No	Yes
After age 50, how much can you contribute every year?	up to $3,500	up to $3,500	up to $3,500	up to $16,000
How long can you contribute?	to age 70 ½	to age 70 ½	to any age	to any age, if working full-time
When do you have to start taking withdrawals?	after age 70 ½	after age 70 ½	never	after age 70 ½
When do early withdrawal penalties apply?	before age 59 ½	before age 59 ½	before age 59 ½	before age 59 ½
When you withdraw after 59 ½, what do you pay taxes on?	only the interest earned	the entire amount withdrawn	nothing, if the IRA is at least 5 years old	the entire amount withdrawn

You can only fund these retirement accounts with earned income. Check with your tax and financial advisors. These rules are accurate as of 2004 but have exceptions and may change.

Live well on a fixed income

Many people have to get by just on Social Security, says John Howells, author of *Retirement on a Shoestring*. But even if your budget is more than "bare-bones," Howells has tips that could help you retire in style.

- Cut housing costs by either moving to a less expensive home or to a low-tax area.

- Get experts at the power company to help you "weatherize" your home. Contact the Department of Energy, Division of Weatherization Assistance, at 1000 Independence Avenue S.W., Washington, D.C. 20585 or call them at 202-586-2207.

- Share a home or apartment with a housemate or two if you're single. You'll save when you split rent, utilities, and other costs each month.

- Earn extra money with a part-time position, seasonal job, or temporary work. Just be sure your pay isn't high enough to cut your Social Security benefits.

- Fun hobbies like woodworking, crafts, or painting can add to your funds. Hire out or sell your creations at arts and crafts shows to boost your budget.

- Take advantage of senior services. Call the Eldercare Locator at 800-677-1116 to discover what's available near you.

- Find out if your community has a senior citizen newspaper. It might help you uncover valuable discounts, opportunities, and benefits you never thought of.

Maximize social security benefits

You've earned your social security — but don't expect the government to tell you how to get all you're entitled to. It's up to you to be the watchdog.

Here's how the process works. Each year, your employer tells the Internal Revenue Service (IRS) and the Social Security Administration (SSA) how much money you made. The SSA records these numbers and uses them to estimate your social security benefits.

But what if your employer gets your name or social security number wrong, or doesn't report all of your earnings? If you don't catch the mistakes, there's a chance no one will.

The government sends out regular statements showing the earnings your employers reported alongside your estimated social security benefits. This earnings record is your best tool for finding errors, says Mary Jane Yarrington, a Senior Policy Analyst at the National Committee to Preserve Social Security and Medicare. Here's her advice for getting the social security you're due.

Double-check the statement. Compare the amount the earnings record says you made to your W2 earnings statements. Make sure the numbers match up, especially if you worked more than one job in a given year. The SSA admits mistakes are more likely if you had more than one job or changed jobs often. Check this record every two years.

Report any errors to the SSA. Call them at 800-772-1213, or visit your local Social Security office. Take copies of your W2 forms for the year in question. If you are

---

Gain extra cash from your home

A reverse mortgage is a special type of home loan that lets you take the value built up in your home over the years — the equity — and turn it into a monthly income check.

Only homeowners 62 and older can get a reverse mortgage. When you sell the home, move out, or the last borrower dies, someone must repay the loan with interest.

Reverse mortgages can be full of tricks and traps. So talk with your family and an attorney first. Also, call the Federal Housing Administration at 800-569-4287 for reverse mortgage information and referrals.

---

self-employed, bring copies of your federal tax return, plus a certified copy of your cancelled check showing the amount of tax you paid.

Order a statement. If you haven't checked yours lately, ask the SSA for your recent earnings record. Call and have them send you an application. Fill it out, mail it in, and expect to receive your statement in about a month.

If you have specific issues, ask Yarrington. This expert answers questions about social security in her column "Ask Mary Jane." Go to the Web site *www.ncpssm.org*, and click on the link *Ask Mary Jane*. From here, you can e-mail her with your questions and read past answers.

5 simple steps to organize your estate

Will your loved ones know where to find important papers after you pass away? The most carefully laid plans can fall apart if no one knows where your will, insurance policies, or financial information is filed. Ease their burden and help yourself get organized by following these simple, clear suggestions. All you need is a notebook, a pencil, and a little bit of time.

Begin with a "people list." On the first page of your notebook write your date of birth, social security number, and your legal state of residence. On the next page write down the name and address of:

- your attorney.

- anyone you have given power of attorney.

- all the people who are dependent on you for care or financial support.

- anyone you want notified if something happens to you.

Record important papers. Next, create a page to list your vital documents. You'll add information to each entry as you go along. Include:

- medical records

- will

- power of attorney

- funeral arrangements

- insurance policies — life, accident, home, auto, medical, and others

- birth certificate or citizenship papers

- passport

- marriage certificates

- divorce information

- titles, deeds, and registrations for your home, your car, and any property you own

When appropriate, list next to each one a policy number, company, contact name, phone number, and beneficiary.

Catalog your funds. Turn to a new page in your notebook and list your financial accounts — loans, credit cards, checking, savings, investments, retirement, and mortgage.

- Begin by writing down the name on each account and the account number. Include any beneficiaries you have for these.

- Next, list contact information for each. Give the name, phone number, and address for the institutions that manage these accounts, such as the bank or mortgage company, and an agent's name if you have one.

- If you have created any trusts, write the names, phone numbers, and addresses of the trustees.

- Tell where your tax records are located and the name of your tax accountant if you have one.

Stash everything safely. Now it's time to put all this information in a secure place.

- Make copies of all the important documents you have listed, and place them in a binder along with your logbook.

- Store the originals in a fireproof safe or safe deposit box. Give an extra key to your spouse or someone else you absolutely trust. If you get a safe deposit box, you also need to give this person the authority to open it without you.

- Don't store the original copies of power of attorney documents. In general, the person you name as your agent should keep these. Also, don't place your final arrangement papers in a safe deposit box.

- Return to the list of important papers in your notebook and write down where you put each document.

Let people know. Make a last entry in the notebook, giving instructions on how to locate your safe deposit box or home safe and who is authorized to open it.

Experts say you should have these important documents in place. They can ease your family's burden and protect your estate when you pass on.

- will

- living will, also known as a medical or healthcare directive

- durable power of attorney for finances

- durable power of attorney for healthcare also known as a medical or healthcare power of attorney

- revocable trust or living trust

Tell your executor, attorney, adult children, or someone else you trust where you put the binder and notebook. If no one can find them, none of this organizing will do any good.

Find your retirement paradise

Everyone has a unique vision of the perfect retirement. That's why you must do your own sleuthing, and pinpoint the exact place that will make your golden years truly golden.

Choose a community that fits. What sort of place are you looking for — a college town, a rural neighborhood, or somewhere you can find big city excitement. The Chamber of Commerce is a good place to get information on local goings-on.

Or take a peek in the newspapers to get a feel for areas you are considering. Your library may carry papers from larger cities, while the Internet offers an excellent resource for viewing small-town papers. Just check *www.NewspaperLinks.com* to see the online versions of newspapers around the country.

Consider housing costs. The same house that goes for $250,000 in one city may only cost $100,000 in another. Decide how much you want to spend, then check prices. Contact real estate agents in that area or do your own research online. The Web site *www.realtor.com* lists over 2 million properties for sale around the country. You can search a city by price, or specify a number of bedrooms, acreage, and amenities.

Look into local healthcare. Everyone needs a doctor at some point, but if you have a serious health condition, it's especially important to live near high-quality medical facilities. Start by visiting the American Medical Association's Web site at *www.ama-assn.org*. Here, you can search for doctors by location. Your current doctors might have advice, too, on where to go for good hospitals and specialty centers.

Watch out for the weather. Climate can have a huge impact on your health, quality of life, and the size of your utility bills. Track the weather trends through local newspapers, or watch a national news station like the Weather Channel. Weather Web sites like *www.weather.com* and *www.WeatherBase.com* offer a wealth of information on locales around the nation — or the world.

Track those taxes. State income tax, county property tax, local sales tax — how big a bite will your new home take out of your income? The Internet can quickly put you in touch with the tax division in each state. Go to *www.taxsites.com*, and click on *State & Local Tax*. Or call the state's tax division for their latest rates.

Check up on crime. Everyone wants to feel safe. Find out ahead of time how your would-be retirement community stacks up. Read the headlines in its local newspaper. If a small crime makes big news, it may be a safe city. On the other hand, if a murder gets buried on page 15, it could be a sign of a high crime rate.

You can also check crime rates in the latest *Federal Bureau of Investigation (FBI) Uniform Crime Report*. Go to your library and ask for a copy, or view it online at *www.fbi.gov* under *Reports & Publications*.

These are just a few slices of life to think about before settling in a new place. You should also consider the convenience of local transportation and airports, theater and music offerings, local churches, outdoor activities, and even educational opportunities. These Web sites can lead you to more information.

Airports	www.fly.faa.gov
Churches	www.BeliefNet.org
National parks	www.recreation.gov
Theater	www.aact.org
Music	www.symphony.org
Festivals	www.festivals.com
Education	www.petersons.com

Judge nursing homes with a clear eye

Putting yourself or a loved one in a nursing home can be a painful choice. "It's a tremendously large decision," says Dr. Marilyn Rantz, Professor of Nursing at the University of Missouri-Columbia.

Rantz knows firsthand. She worked as a nursing home administrator for many years, and then had to find a good home for her own mother. "It's really tough," she says. "But there are times you need a nursing home. There are people who need that care."

The key is finding the right place. That's why Rantz co-authored *The New Nursing Homes*, voted Book of the Year by the American Journal of Nursing. It's an easy-to-read guide that tells families where to start, what to look for, who to talk to, and what to ask to find the best facilities. Her philosophy is you can make a good choice if you know what to look for.

Ask around. When Rantz and her sister started their own search, they began within their community. They checked first with neighbors who were familiar with different facilities. "There were some places where they had had terrible experiences," she says. "We didn't bother to even visit those."

Volunteer. Rantz recommends volunteering at local nursing homes ahead of time. "You'll find the good ones before you need them," she says. Plus you'll build a social support system with staff and residents.

Walk through. Visiting a nursing home in person is crucial, says Rantz. Schedule a tour with the admissions staff and take 20 or 30 minutes to walk through the facility, talk to people, and get a feel for it. While you're there, ask yourself these questions.

- How does it smell? "If you walk in and are overwhelmed with unpleasant odors, turn around and walk out," Rantz advises.

- Is it clean? While it doesn't have to be spick-and-span, she says, "People should not be living in a dirty environment."

- Do the residents seem comfortable, happy, and well cared for? If not, go someplace else.

- How does the staff interact with residents? Rantz asks, "Do they talk to each other? Do they seem happy with each other? Do they smile at each other?"

- Are residents walking around? Nursing homes should encourage people to maintain or regain their mobility. "You should see people walking," Rantz says. "Not everyone should be rolling around in a wheelchair."

Talk to visitors. Question family members or friends visiting a resident. Ask how long they have been coming to the facility, and what they think. "You'll get an earful real quick if it's good or if it's bad," says Rantz.

Question the staff. Introduce yourself, then ask how long they've worked there. Look for longevity. "If everybody you talk to was hired this year," warns Rantz, "you have to think there is something wrong." Get a sense of how much personal care residents receive. Find out how many staff members serve on each shift, and about how many patients a nurse handles per shift.

Pick the best over the closest. Rantz believes the biggest mistake people make is choosing a nursing home because it's close, not because it's the best quality. It's better to drive, she says, if it means better quality of care.

Medicare offers a tool on the Internet called Nursing Home Compare. With it, you can compare Medicare and Medicaid certified nursing homes in your area, look up their violations, and check staffing information. Just go to *www.medicare.gov* and click on the link for *Nursing Home Compare*.

Choosing a nursing home will never be easy, but *The New Nursing Homes* can help ease some of the pain. Ask for it at your local bookstore, or order it directly from the publisher, Fairview Press, by calling 800-544-8207.

Don't get buried by funeral scams

Paying for funerals in advance is a hot trend, but one that could get you burned.

There are two ways to pay a funeral company up front to handle the arrangements after your death. Buy burial insurance through the funeral home, or pay into a trust fund.

"At first blush, it sounds so sensible," says Joshua Slocum, Executive Director of the nonprofit, educational organization Funeral Consumers Alliance. "Lock in today's prices. Take care of this now."

See the shortcomings. But in Slocum's opinion, prepaying has four major drawbacks.

- Not all states make funeral homes guarantee their locked-in rates, and changing your plan later may void any price guarantees.

- With burial insurance, you could pay more in premiums than the actual cost of your services.

- In some states, the mortician may keep up to 30 percent of your money as a commission.

- Prepaid plans don't change with your needs. Many are irrevocable, meaning once you buy them you're stuck with them. You can't cash out if you change your mind, and you could lose money if you need to change your policy.

Get the details. "Unless you know what to ask for," Slocum warns, "you could be getting into a lot of trouble." So, if you're still sold on prepaying your funeral, ask the funeral home these questions before signing on the dotted line.

- Is the contract revocable or irrevocable? "Medicare only allows you to shelter money in irrevocable prepaid funerals," says Slocum.

- Is the plan transferable? "Large chains tell you since they have funeral homes all over the country, your plan will move with you wherever you go," Slocum says. But what if you move to a state or city where they don't have a branch nearby? Slocum says to make sure it's legally transferable.

- How much of your money will the funeral home refund if you cancel or transfer your policy? They may only have to return a fraction of what you paid.

- What if the goods you choose and pay for now aren't available when you die? Will your family have to buy more expensive versions?

- What goods and services are not covered by the plan? "No prepaid contract can include everything," warns Slocum. Flowers, monuments, and opening and closing the grave, for instance, generally come out-of-pocket. "Your family could face hundreds if not thousands of dollars in extra charges."

- Does the funeral company let the interest grow in your account to offset inflation, or do they skim it every year to pay their operating costs?

Ask for help. According to Slocum, states regulate prepaid contracts. "But," he says, "each state regulates them differently." Try contacting your state's attorney general's office to learn more about how their prepaid — also called pre-need — funeral laws protect you.

Still have questions? You can find your local branch of the Funeral Consumers Alliance by visiting them on the Internet at *www.funerals.org*, or calling their national office at 800-765-0107.

Put your funeral plans in order

Preplanning — not prepaying — is the key to settling your final arrangements, according to Joshua Slocum, Executive Director of the nonprofit Funeral Consumers Alliance (FCA). "People need to look at funeral purchases in the same way they do any other major purchase," he says, "with the same level of skepticism and basic shopper's savvy."

Comparison shop. "The prices for comparable goods and services can vary by thousands of dollars in the same city," Slocum says. He advises everyone to call several funeral homes or stop by and ask for itemized price lists. Look them over at home so you won't feel pressured into spending more than you planned.

Find a society. Make use of memorial or funeral societies and nonprofit groups like the Funeral Consumers Alliance. FCA chapters, for instance, offer educational pamphlets, do price surveys on local funeral homes, negotiate discounts for their members, and fight back against funeral scams. They also offer an end-of-life planning kit to help you organize papers and personal information. Order this kit and find your local FCA chapter by visiting their Web site at *www.funerals.org*, or calling their national office at 800-765-0107.

Try a Totten. You have several options for putting aside funeral money, but Slocum favors a Totten Trust, which you can set up with your bank or credit union. The money stays in your control — you can cash it out if you change your mind — and it becomes available to a beneficiary for funeral expenses upon your death. "You don't have to wait for a probate judge," says Slocum, "and that is a real advantage."

Put your plans in writing. Record your wishes and detail any final arrangements you have made in a document separate from your will — and don't put it in your safe deposit box. "The will usually isn't discovered and read until after you're buried," explains Slocum. And if your family has to make plans over a weekend or holiday, they may not have access to a safe deposit box. Give copies to your lawyer and family members, and keep another in an easy-to-find place.

Review them regularly. Look over your final arrangements every few years and each time you go through a major life change — like moving to another city or state, entering a nursing home, or marrying.

Know your rights. The Federal Trade Commission (FTC) regulates how funeral homes sell goods and services and what they charge, among other things. Their pamphlet, *Funerals: A Consumer Guide*, answers common questions about planning funerals and your legal rights. Order it from the Federal Citizen Information Center by calling 888-878-3256, or visiting them on the Internet at *www.pueblo.gsa.gov*.

If you feel a funeral home has taken advantage of you, it's best to try and work out your problem with them first. However, either the FCA or the Funeral Service Consumer Assistance Program may help. You can reach them at 800-662-7666. Finally, you can file a complaint with the FTC by calling their Consumer Response Center at 877-FTC-HELP. Or visit their Web site at *www.ftc.gov*.

Slocum's organization believes everyone is entitled to a meaningful, dignified, affordable funeral. "We think planning ahead is the most important thing you can do."

Money tricks and traps

12 tips to thwart identity theft

Almost 10 million Americans had their identity stolen, at a cost of about 50 billion dollars, estimates the Federal Trade Commission. And that's in just one year.

When someone uses your social security number, takes out loans or opens credit cards in your name, steals your bank account number and makes withdrawals, racks up charges on your credit card, or writes fraudulent checks on your account — that's identity theft.

How does this happen? A thief may steal paid bills or pre-approved credit offers from your mailbox, or simply snatch your wallet. Some thieves, known as "dumpster divers," go through your trash looking for discarded bills and receipts. Telephone and e-mail scams are on the rise, too.

Don't be a victim. Learn what you need to do to protect yourself with savvy advice from Johnny R. May, a Certified Protection Professional, independent security consultant, and author of *The Guide to Identity Theft Prevention.*

- Buy a crosscut shredder — the kind that turns paper into confetti — and feed financial statements, pre-approved credit offers, canceled checks, and other sensitive paperwork through it.

- Set your garbage on the curb the day of trash pickup, not the night before. Thieves have less time — and less darkness — to dig through your garbage.

- Drop paid bills and other money-filled mail at the post office or in an official U.S. Postal Service mailbox.

- Pick up new checks at the bank instead of having them mailed to your home. Or get them sent by registered mail so you have to sign for them.

- Limit the amount of personal information on your checks. Only add your telephone or driver's license number if the merchant requires it, and never give them your social security number. A legitimate retailer won't need it.

- Only carry the credit and bank cards you need, not every one you own. And don't keep your social security card in your wallet. Store it in a safe place. If a thief steals your wallet, it's one less piece of information they have.

- Cancel credit cards you rarely use. Having fewer open accounts makes you less vulnerable to identity theft.

- Write down all your credit card account numbers and expiration dates, as well as the names, phone numbers, and addresses of each creditor so you can call them if the cards get stolen. Store this information in a safe place.

- Pay attention to when you usually receive bills and statements, and be on the lookout for them. If one hasn't arrived within a few days of its normal date, call the company who sent it and let them know it may have been stolen.

- Carefully check each statement and bill as soon as you receive it. Look for charges you didn't make, and report them immediately to the company billing you.

- Request copies of your credit report every year. Read *Spring-clean your credit report* on page 127 for information on ordering and reviewing your credit reports.

• Opt out of pre-approved credit card offers, and give thieves less to steal. You'll find out how to do this later in this chapter.

Fight back against identity theft

Identity theft is serious business. You could be denied credit, mortgages, jobs, educational opportunities, and even arrested for crimes committed in your name. Even though you must spend your own time and money repairing the damage, it's essential you do so.

The international non-profit network Call for Action urges you to watch out for these warning signs that someone has stolen your identity.

• You suddenly stop receiving monthly bank statements or credit card bills.

• You start getting bills from companies you don't recognize.

• You are denied loans or credit for no reason you can think of.

• Collection agencies begin contacting you about debts you didn't create.

Acting fast is key in limiting the damage. Take these emergency steps set out by the Federal Trade Commission (FTC) as soon as you suspect your identity has been stolen.

Call in fraud alerts. Notify the fraud department of one of the three major credit bureaus and ask them to place a fraud alert on your credit file. They will notify the other two bureaus and have them do the same. This alert flags your file so creditors will contact you before they open any new accounts in your name or make changes to your existing accounts.

This initial alert will expire after a certain amount of time, and you must call each bureau to renew it. Contact them at these numbers to report the fraud.

Equifax	800-525-6285
Trans Union	800-680-7289
Experian	888-397-3742

Review your credit reports. As soon as you have placed fraud alerts, each bureau will send you a free copy of your credit report. Look it over carefully for suspicious activity — like accounts you didn't open or unexplained debts.

Order your reports periodically the first year following the crime, then at least once a year after. Use the sample letter, on page 171, from the FTC to dispute fraudulent activity on your report, and send it to the bureaus at these addresses.

See *Spring-clean your credit report* on page 127 to learn more about ordering your report and fixing errors in it.

```
Contact   Equifax
          P.O. Box 740241
          Atlanta, GA 30374-0241

          Experian
          P.O. Box 9530
          Allen, TX 75013

          Trans Union
          Fraud Victim Assistance
          Division
          P.O. Box 6790
          Fullerton, CA 92634
```

Close your accounts. Contact credit card companies, utility companies, banks, lenders, and other creditors, and ask to speak with someone in their security or fraud department. First, close any existing accounts you know the thief tampered with, as well as any new accounts he opened. Next, open new accounts with different passwords and PINs (personal identification numbers). Don't go for the obvious — like your mother's maiden name, your birthday, phone number, or the last four digits of your social security number. These are too easy to guess.

Dispute debts in writing. Phone calls aren't enough. It's crucial to tell your creditors about the fraud in writing. Otherwise, they could still hold you liable for the bad debts.

- To challenge charges made to one of your existing accounts, mail a dispute letter to the creditor telling them which charges are fraudulent. Use the sample letter later in this chapter from the FTC.

- To dispute new accounts a thief opened in your name, fill out an ID Theft Affidavit — a form put out by the FTC — and mail it to the creditor. You can print the Affidavit off the Internet at *www.consumer.gov/IDTheft/recovering_idt.html*. Or order a copy by calling toll-free 877-FTC-HELP.

  Some creditors may require you to fill out one of their own fraud forms. Ask which they prefer when you call.

- Insist the creditor send you a letter saying they have forgiven the fraudulent debts and closed the unauthorized accounts. You may need this information in writing if these same bad debts reappear on your credit report.

File a police report. An official police report builds your case and may protect you from creditors collecting on fraudulent debts. Give the police as much information as you can, then get a copy of the report. Your creditors may need proof of the crime to forgive the debts. Plus, the credit bureaus will automatically block or erase any fraudulent activity from your credit report if you send them a police report.

Complain to the FTC. File a complaint about the crime with the FTC. This government agency tracks trends in identity theft and gathers information to help solve future cases. Filing a complaint also helps government officials understand how widespread this crime is. Call the FTC's Identity Theft Hotline toll-free at 877-438-4338, or file a complaint through their Web site at *www.consumer.gov/idtheft*.

Stay organized. You could spend weeks or even months undoing the damage from ID theft. The FTC offers these tips to help keep you organized.

- Keep a notebook. Write down the name and company of everyone you speak to, what they told you, and the date of the conversation.

- Follow up all phone conversations in writing.

- Make copies of every piece of correspondence you mail regarding your case.

- Only mail copies — not originals — of police reports, sales slips, or other supporting documents. Keep the originals in your own files.

- Send all correspondence by certified mail, and request a return receipt. This way you can prove the date a creditor received your letter.

- Save your files, even after you think the case is closed. Problems could crop up later on.

You are never alone when dealing with identity theft. Many consumer groups offer counseling and step-by-step help.

```
Contact   Call for Action
          301-657-7490
          www.CallForAction.org

          National Fraud
          Information Center
          800-876-7060
          www.fraud.org

          Identity Theft Resource
          Center
          858-693-7935
          www.IDTheftCenter.org
```

Dispute debts from ID theft

Customize this letter and send it to your creditors to dispute fraudulent charges racked up in your good name.

```
(Date)
(Your name)
(Your address)
(Your city, state, and zip code)
(The account number you are writing about)

(Creditor's name)
Billing Inquiries
(Their address)
(Their city, state, and zip code)

Dear Sir or Madam:

I am writing to dispute a fraudulent (charge or
debit) attributed to my account in the amount of
$_____. I am a victim of identity theft, and I
did not make this (charge or debit). I am
requesting that the (charge be removed, or the
debit reinstated), that any finance and other
charges related to the fraudulent amount be cred-
ited as well, and that I receive an accurate
statement.

Enclosed are copies of (mention copies of any
documents you are including, such as a police
report or sales slip) supporting my position.
Please investigate this matter and correct the
fraudulent (charge or debit) as soon as possible.

Sincerely,


(Your name)

Enclosures: (List the documents you are
enclosing.)
```

Fix fraud damage to credit reports

Circle the mistakes on a copy of your credit report and mail it, along with a dispute letter, to each major credit bureau. Fill in the details and use the addresses given in *Fight back against identity theft* on page 167.

```
(Date)
(Your name)
(Your address)
(Your city, state, and zip code)

Complaint Department
(Name of credit bureau)
(Their address)
(Their city, state, and zip code)

Dear Sir or Madam:

I am writing to dispute the following informa-
tion in my file. The items I dispute also are
circled on the attached copy of the report I
received. (Identify which items you are disput-
ing by the name of the source — such as
creditors or tax court — and the type of item —
such as credit account, judgment, etc.)

I am a victim of identity theft, and did not
make the charge(s). I am requesting that the
item be blocked to correct my credit report.

Enclosed are copies of (mention any documenta-
tion you are including — such as a police
report) supporting my position. Please investi-
gate this matter and block the disputed item(s)
as soon as possible.

Sincerely,


(Your name)

Enclosures: (List the documents you are
enclosing.)
```

Just say no to pre-approved credit

You're pre-approved for dozens of credit cards with limits of thousands of dollars. So is your spouse, your son, your daughter, even your grandchildren. This is dangerous in two ways. Not only can the temptation of easy credit spell disaster to anyone's budget and financial security, but the risk of identity theft rises with every credit card offer drifting through the postal system. And all that clutter of junk mail is simply annoying.

Your answer is to "opt out." This means you stop the offers of pre-approved credit cards at the source — the credit bureaus. You have the choice of getting your name removed from the mailing list for two years or permanently.

You can opt out by calling toll-free 888-567-8688. You will be asked for personal information including your name, telephone number, and social security number. Don't get nervous — these details remain confidential and are only used to process your request.

```
Contact   Equifax, Inc.
          Options
          P.O. Box 740123
          Atlanta, GA 30374-0123

          Experian
          Consumer Opt-Out
          701 Experian Parkway
          Allen, TX 75013

          Trans Union
          Marketing List Opt Out
          P.O. Box 97328
          Jackson, MS 39288-7328
```

Or opt out in writing. The Federal Trade Commission has even developed a sample letter you can use (see opposite page). Send it to each major credit bureau at these addresses.

You can cut back on much of your other junk mail for five years by registering with the Direct Marketing Association's Mail Preference Service.

Sample opt-out letter

(Date)
(Your name)
(Your address)
(Your city, state, and zip code)

(Creditor's name)
(Their address)
(Their city, state, and zip code)

To whom it may concern:

I request to have my name removed from your marketing lists. Here is the information you have asked me to include in my request:

FIRST, MIDDLE, & LAST NAME: (List all name variations, including Jr., Sr., etc.)

_____

CURRENT MAILING ADDRESS:

_____

PREVIOUS MAILING ADDRESS: (Fill in your previous mailing address if you have moved in the last 6 months.)

_____

SOCIAL SECURITY NUMBER:

_____

DATE OF BIRTH:

_____

Thank you for your prompt handling of my request.

_____
(Your signature)

```
Contact   Direct Marketing
          Association
          Mail Preference Service
          P.O. Box 643
          Carmel, NY 10512
```

Just send the same opt-out letter to the Direct Marketing Association at this address. You may still receive some unsolicited mail, but you should get less of it.

Put the brakes on phony fund-raising

You want to give generously, but do you know who you're really giving to? Thousands of people contribute to "charities" each year only to learn their donations didn't go to a children's hospital or police fund but instead filled the pockets of a scam artist.

Bone up on these tips to make sure your money helps those who need it most.

Learn more about the charity. The Firefighters' Assistance Foundation sounds like a worthy cause but may not even be a real charity. Phony fund-raisers often use names that sound legitimate so people will donate. Find out more before you give.

- Tell the solicitor to mail you information about the charity before you make a donation, says the Better Business Bureau's (BBB) Wise Giving Alliance. You can ask for the group's latest financial statements or for literature about the programs your donation would sponsor.

- Ask the solicitor how much of each donation goes to the charity, and how much goes to pay the fund-raising company. The Wise Giving Alliance says that, in general, no more than 35 percent of your donation should pay fund-raising costs. That means 65 percent should go directly to the charity.

- Call the local group the solicitor claims to represent and ask if they are having a fund-raising drive. A scam artist could be using their name to con people out of money.

- Verify national charities through the Wise Giving Alliance, or call your local BBB about local nonprofit groups. Check out these Internet Web sites for more information on charities and giving.

Better Business Bureau	www.bbb.org
BBB Wise Giving Alliance	www.give.org
American Institute of Philanthropy	www.charitywatch.org
GuideStar	www.guidestar.org
Federal Trade Commission Charity Fraud	www.ftc.gov/charityfraud

- When giving to a faith-based organization, ask to see an official listing in its denomination's directory.

Pay wisely. How you pay is just as important as who you pay. Try these tips from the Wise Giving Alliance to protect yourself when making donations.

- Mail a check to the charity rather than paying by cash or credit card.

- Make the check out to the charity, not the company they hired to do the fundraising.

- Never give your credit card or bank account information to unknown solicitors, even if the charity sounds legitimate.

- Don't feel pressured to give on the spot. A real charity will be just as happy to get your money next week as today.

Just say no. The experts at GuideStar, a national database of charities, say you should walk away or hang up if a solicitor:

175

- tries to pressure you into giving.

- won't take no for an answer.

- refuses to send you more information about the charity.

If you think you've been the target of a charity scam, report it to your state attorney general. You can also file a complaint with the Federal Trade Commission by calling 877-FTC-HELP.

Take charge of charitable requests

Each time you give to a charity, they add your name to a donor list, which they may sell to other groups. The American Institute of Philanthropy, a charity watchdog service, suggests sending the letter on page 177 with your donation to limit unwelcome fund-raising mail and phone calls.

6 sure tip-offs to telephone fraud

Thousands of people lose money to telephone fraud every year. It could be just a few bucks or your entire life's savings. Seniors, especially, are targeted by con artists and their phone scams.

Prepare yourself before the phone rings again! Hang up if you hear lines like these.

- "You've won a fabulous prize!" If you haven't entered a contest, be suspicious.

- "You only have to pay taxes, shipping, and handling fees!" Real prizes shouldn't cost you anything.

- "You can't afford to miss this high-profit, no-risk offer!" Not likely. Every investment carries some risk. Discuss big investments with a trusted friend or financial advisor first.

Charitable requests letter

Dear (name of charity):

I am sending this note to reduce the waste and invasion of privacy caused by unwanted mail solicitations and telemarketing calls. If you would like me to consider contributing to your organization in the future, please agree to the following checked items:

___ Remove my name and address from your mailing list.

___ Do not sell, rent, exchange, or give my name or contribution history to any other organization or business without first receiving my approval.

___ Do not send me direct mail solicitations more than ___ times a year.

___ Do not telephone me to ask for money, or…

___ Phone me no more than ___ times a year, and only on the following day(s) and times:

Name and address labels from your solicitation(s) to me are enclosed.

Thank you for respecting a donor's wishes.

Sincerely,

(Your name)

(Your mailing address)

Fundraising Reduction Notice

Reprinted with permission from the American Institute of Philanthropy and www.charitywatch.org ©2001

- "It's a brand new offer and printed material isn't available yet." Or maybe they say, "There isn't time to mail information." Either way, beware. A legitimate organization will happily send you literature about their program. Con artists will find any excuse to avoid it.

- "You must act now!" Scammers may tell you "this offer is about to expire," or "there are only a few left." Nonsense. An offer should be just as good tomorrow — after you have checked them out with the Better Business Bureau — as it is today.

- "All we need is some personal information." They might ask for a credit card, calling card, bank account, or social security number to verify your identity or secure your prize. You should never have to give this information over the phone for identification, especially to someone who calls you unsolicited.

Fight back against fraudulent telemarketers. Show them you're not easy pickings for a scam.

⚠ Sidestep computer scams

Identity thieves now attack electronically, too. They may send scam e-mails, lead you to phony Web sites, or trick you into buying fake products. The goal — to steal your bank account, credit card, or social security numbers; or gain access to other sensitive personal information. Don't be fooled by computer fraud. Learn how to protect yourself in *Protect your privacy online* on page 294.

Double-check area codes. To call the Caribbean, for instance, you dial a country code that looks a lot like an area code in the United States. Dialing an 809 code then the phone number connects you to the Dominican Republic. The code 758 dials St. Lucia, while 664 reaches Montserrat. You could rack up serious international charges by calling these numbers.

Check area codes you don't recognize before you dial them. Ask the operator where the code would call, or visit the Directory Assistance link at *www.consumer.att.com* to look it up on the Internet.

Scan your phone bill. Look it over each month for long distance charges you don't remember making. If you find any, contact both your local and long distance telephone companies to discuss the charges.

Join the "Do-Not-Call" list. Register your phone number for free with the Federal Trade Commission's national Do-Not-Call list. To join by phone, dial 888-382-1222 from the telephone you wish to register. Or join online at *www.DoNotCall.gov*. You will stay on this list for five years — you can renew after this time — or until your phone gets disconnected. Your state may also run its own "do-not-call" list. Check with your state attorney general or consumer protection program.

If you think you've been the target of a phone scam, call the National Fraud Information Center at 800-876-7060, or visit their Web site at *www.fraud.org*. They can help you file complaints with the Federal Trade Commission (FTC), Federal Bureau of Investigation (FBI), your state attorney general, and local consumer protection programs.

Don't get played by fake sweepstakes

You've just won $10,000… A trip to Jamaica… The Australian lottery… ! You may get lines like these every day from telemarketers and in junk mail. Just remember, if it sounds too good to be true, it probably is. You could lose your savings, your house, and your good credit by falling for phony sweepstakes.

Dodge the shams. Learn to tell a legitimate sweepstakes from a corrupt contest with this winning information.

Don't fall for false promises. The Federal Citizen Information Center (FCIC) says to be suspicious of phrases like these.

- "You have been specially selected..."

- "You have won..."

- "Yours, absolutely free! Take a look at our..."

- "Your special claim number lets you join our sweepstakes..."

- "All you pay is postage, handling, taxes..."

Pull the plug. Hang up if a solicitor says you've won but must pay fees to claim your prize. Free is free. According to Federal Trade Commission (FTC) rules, valid sweepstakes must tell you that you don't have to buy anything to enter or win a prize.

Watch for copycats. Scam companies may use names that sound like well-known sweepstakes, and ask for a deposit or other fees. The Direct Marketing Association suggests calling the real sweepstakes company to verify the offer.

Never pay up front. Con artists may ask you to send a refundable deposit or money for taxes or fees. Don't do it. If you win a real

> ⚠️ **Steer clear of top scams**
>
> The Federal Trade Commission (FTC) received over half a million consumer fraud complaints last year. Not counting ID theft — which made up over 40 percent of those complaints — here are the top 10 categories of fraud.
>
> - Internet auctions
>
> - Shop-at-home or catalog sales
>
> - Internet services and computer complaints
>
> - Prizes, sweepstakes, and lotteries
>
> - Foreign money offers
>
> - Advance fee loans and credit protection
>
> - Telephone services
>
> - Work-at-home plans
>
> - Magazine buyers clubs
>
> - Office supplies and services

sweepstakes, you pay taxes to the Internal Revenue Service (IRS), not the company awarding the prize. And if you send money overnight or by wire, the crooks could have your cash in hand before you realize you've been duped.

Protect personal information. Never give an unknown solicitor your social security, bank account, or credit card numbers — especially over the phone. The Federal Trade Commission says legitimate sweepstakes will not ask for this financial information.

Keep an eye on others. Loved ones are not immune to phony sweepstakes. You may need to help them watch out for sham contests, especially if they receive a lot of junk mail or ask about sending money overseas.

Blow the whistle. Report suspicious phone calls or mail offers to your state attorney general or office of consumer protection, as well as the Better Business Bureau in the sweepstake company's home state.

You should also notify the National Fraud Information Center at 800-876-7060 or online at *www.fraud.org*. To file a complaint with the Federal Trade Commission, call them toll-free at 877-FTC-HELP or visit them on the Internet at *www.ftc.gov*.

Win big with sweepstakes secrets

Not every sweepstakes is a scam. Plenty of real people win fabulous prizes every day. In fact, Carol Shaffer has made a hobby — and a name — from winning sweepstakes. In her book *Contest Queen,* she reveals her secrets to success. Here are just a few of her tips to help tip the odds in your favor.

Be selective. Shaffer admits there are more contests and sweepstakes out there than any one person could possibly enter. She advises you pick ones you'll enjoy the most and you have the best chances of winning. That means contests with short deadlines, those going on during the holidays or summer vacations, and those restricted to certain states or regions — fewer people will enter, thereby increasing your odds of winning.

Create eye-catching entries. Paste pictures on the backside of the entry form, submit a picture postcard instead of a plain white index card, or simply fill out entries with colored markers. Bright stationery and envelopes really get the attention of judges. So do drawings. Break out the magic markers and sparkly stickers to create your own designs.

Pick a theme. Decorate your entry to match the contest and boost your odds even more — for instance, a Statue of Liberty postcard to win a trip to New York.

Follow the rules. Be sure to check the fine print before you get too creative. Some sweepstakes prohibit postcards or multiple entries.

Make yours easy to pull. Crumpling your entry, making it stiff with paint or water, or folding it like a fan may mean a judge will draw it from the box first.

Be neat. A judge won't look twice if she pulls your entry but can't read it. Print legibly or someone else could win your prize.

Spread the winning around. Send in one for yourself, and then enter all your family and friends — especially in contests that only allow one entry per person.

Track your progress. Keep a log of all the sweepstakes you enter and which techniques you used to see what helps you win.

Join a contest club. These groups gather to talk about sweepstakes and share advice for winning. You can also sign up for newsletters or visit Internet contesting sites for the latest news.

In *Contest Queen,* Shaffer offers more tips and techniques that have helped her "win big" over the years. You'll find pages of Internet contesting sites, newsletters, and clubs to help you with your new hobby.

Order *Contest Queen* from Truman Publishing by calling 800-786-6785, or visit their Web site at *www.trumanpublishing.com.*

Don't get nailed on home improvements

"I was just in the neighborhood... ." These words are often the beginning of a very common scam. If your house has been damaged in a fire, flood, or other natural disaster, you could be a prime target. Phony contractors make big claims and charge big bucks to repair your home. They may demand a large deposit up front, then start the job and never finish it. They may use poor quality material, perform shoddy work, or fail to meet building codes.

"People are often so consumed with the devastation that has occurred in their lives that they are more vulnerable to disaster fraud," explains Robert Bryant, President of the National Insurance Crime Bureau (NICB).

Learn the signs of fraud. "If you educate yourself against dishonest contractors now, you can avoid becoming a victim of disaster fraud," Bryant says. Beware of contractors who:

- go door-to-door looking for customers, drive an unmarked van, or have out-of-state license plates.
- ask you to pay the entire cost of a job up front.
- encourage you to spend a lot of money on temporary repairs.
- ask you to obtain the permit for any work. It could mean the contractor does not have a license.

- you can only reach through an answering service.

- quote you a price that's vastly different from estimates from other contractors.

- make outrageous promises and pressure you for a quick decision.

Know who to trust. Follow these tips for protecting yourself and hiring an honest, reliable contractor.

- Ask your insurance agent, friends, and neighbors who they recommend.

- Write down the salesperson's license plate and driver's license numbers.

- Ask the contractor for proof of his insurance coverage and any licenses he needs to perform the repairs.

- Ask for a list of recent customers, then call them and find out if they were satisfied with the work.

- Call your local Better Business Bureau or Home Builders Association to find out if a contractor has complaints against him.

- Get estimates in writing from at least three contractors. These should include all the labor, materials, and verbal promises the contractor made.

- When you are ready to sign a contract, make sure it includes all work details, warranties, time schedule, the quality of building materials, and cost.

- Fill in all the blanks in the contract. Never leave empty spaces for someone to fill out later.

- Pay by credit card or check — never cash. Credit cards offer the most protection, because you can stop payment if you have a dispute with the contractor.

- Pay in installments. Put as little money down as you can, and only make the last payment when you are completely happy with the work.

- Tell your insurance agent if an unlicensed or fraudulent contractor approaches you. Or call the NICB Hotline at 800-TEL-NICB.

Disaster fraud doesn't have to ruin your life. Report repair rip-offs to the consumer division of your state attorney general. To file a complaint and learn more about fraud prevention, you can also call the Federal Trade Commission toll-free at 877-FTC-HELP. Or visit them on the Internet at *www.ftc.gov.*

Credit card insurance: safeguard or scam?

The sales pitch for credit insurance sounds good. It may claim to pay off your credit card debt if you die, or cover your payments if you become disabled or unemployed. But do you really need it?

The Federal Deposit Insurance Corporation (FDIC) wants you to think twice before signing up. "Review your financial situation and weigh the costs and benefits before deciding if this type of coverage makes sense for you," advises Deirdre Foley, a senior policy analyst with the FDIC. Keep in mind these suggestions from the FDIC Consumer News.

Understand the coverage. "We're all prone to focus on the benefits of an offer, written in bold, without evaluating the conditions and exclusions," says Foley. Generally speaking, credit card insurance is akin to life, health, disability, accident, or unemployment insurance. It may pay off your debt if you die, or make the minimum payments if you become unemployed or can't work. But find out if the policy covers only accidental death. Most people die from illness or natural causes, and the policy may not pay out benefits in these cases.

Review your other insurance. You may already have enough insurance to cover your debts should something happen. Talk to your insurance agent or financial advisor about your situation and whether you really need credit insurance.

Consider the cost. According to the FDIC, credit insurance typically costs more in the long run than term life insurance. Although it could offer a better deal if you are older or ill, and can't qualify for life insurance.

Compare the cost of credit insurance to term life insurance given your age and health. Don't like either option? Simply stash the money you'd spend on insurance in a savings account and use it to pay off debts in an emergency.

Bone up on the benefits. Most life insurance policies give your family money to spend as they need upon your death. Credit insurance only pays off one debt — the specific credit card it covers. Your family would still have to worry about other bills.

Read the fine print. Make sure you can use the card while drawing the insurance benefits. Some policies freeze your credit line while the insurance is making the payments. If you lose your job or become sick, you may need that credit line to buy groceries and pay bills.

Also, find out whether the credit insurance will make monthly payments on your debt, or whether it simply freezes the debt until you can pay on it again.

Watch out for fraud. Don't fall for a credit protection scam. Con artists may try to pressure you into buying fake credit card protection. Really they are fishing for your credit card and bank account numbers.Be wary, and never give out this sort of personal information through unsolicited phone calls, e-mails, or unknown Internet sites.

Credit insurance is usually optional. If you sign up for it and change your mind, you may be able to cancel it and get a refund. Contact the credit card or insurance company with questions and problems. If that doesn't work, call your state insurance commissioner. They enforce the state laws and regulations governing prices, benefits, and how much information consumers are given.

Insurance essentials

Choose best health coverage

You always knew you were a million-dollar baby, and now experts agree — you need a health insurance policy that covers at least $1 million in medical bills over your lifetime.

While this may sound like a lot, Carrie Schwab-Pomerantz and Charles R. Schwab, authors of *It Pays to Talk: How to Have the Essential Conversations with Your Family About Money and Investing*, point out a chronic or terminal illness can burn through the entire million in no time.

And yet a simple dollar figure doesn't guarantee the right health coverage. Before you buy, insurance experts say to get the facts on issues like these.

Know the dollar limits.

- How low is the lifetime cap — the maximum amount your insurance will pay for medical expenses over your lifetime?
- What's the maximum amount you'd ever have to pay each year — also called the annual cap?

Estimate your real costs.

- How high are the monthly premiums?
- What are the copayments?
- How high is the deductible?

Check the services covered.

- Are things like prescription drugs, preventive screenings, dental care, eyeglasses, mental health care, or physical therapy included?

- How complete is the coverage for hospitalization and visits to the emergency room?

Understand the restrictions.

- What health expenses are not covered by this insurance?

- Which pre-existing conditions get no coverage or restricted coverage?

- Who decides if a treatment is "medically necessary" and therefore covered by the policy?

Finally, you'll want to review the list of approved providers. Is your choice of doctors wide-open or restricted? Find out if you need a referral before you can visit a specialist.

With questions like these answered, you're better equipped to evaluate health insurance choices and buy the right coverage to protect you and your family.

Do you have as much insurance as you need?

- Health — Purchase at least $1 million in lifetime benefits.

- Home — Get full replacement cost on both your house and personal property, and maximum personal liability coverage.

- Life — You will want sufficient funds to provide for your dependents, about six to 12 times your annual income.

- Disability — Look for one with an income replacement option.

- Auto — Buy as much liability as possible. Include maximum protection against uninsured motorists.

- Long-Term Care — If you can afford the premiums without affecting your normal lifestyle buy enough to give you peace of mind.

Compare federal health programs

Government health insurance programs are hard to keep straight. Discover basic differences between Medicare and Medicaid and learn about your federal health plan options.

	Medicare	Medicaid
Who can use it?	People 65 or older and people of any age who have selected disabilities or end-stage renal disease (kidney failure) are eligible.	Requirements vary by state, but depend on income, age, and if you are disabled or pregnant.
Who is in charge?	The Federal government manages Medicare.	Generally, each state decides who is eligible, which benefits to offer, and how much services cost.
How does it help you?	Medicare Part A (Hospital Insurance) helps cover inpatient hospital care. Medicare Part B (Medical Insurance) helps with outpatient care, doctors' services, and possibly some items not covered by Part A.	Although coverage varies by state, certain services must be covered in order to receive federal funds. Other services — many items that fall between the Medicare cracks — are optional and decided upon by each state.
What do you pay?	Part A: no premiums, but a deductible and copayments; Part B: premiums, a deductible, and copayments	You may pay a small copayment or have a small deductible, depending on your state and status.

Although Medicare won't cover all your medical expenses, you don't have to qualify for Medicaid to fill those gaps. As long as you have both Medicare Part A and Part B, either Medicare + Choice or Medigap policies may help with out-of-pocket medical expenses.

- Medicare + Choice Plans are offered by private companies with Medicare's approval. They include the same coverage and protections as Medicare — but often with more choices or more benefits.

- Medigap policies — also called Medicare Supplement Insurance — are not part of Medicare. Private insurance companies sell these heavily regulated policies to cover such Medicare costs as copayments. If you already have Medicare + Choice, you don't need a Medigap policy, and in fact it is illegal for anyone to sell you one.

Call 800-MEDICARE or go online to *www.medicare.gov* to find out more about Medicare or to get details on Medigap and Medicare + Choice plans available in your area.

Retire early — but stay insured

Retiring early may be the American dream — but not when saying good-bye to your job means good-bye to its benefits, too. If Medicare coverage is months or years away, and your employer doesn't offer retiree health benefits, you need insurance from somewhere.

You could keep your previous employer's group health coverage temporarily, thanks to COBRA (Consolidated Omnibus Budget Reconciliation Act). If your company says you qualify, you can retain your insurance for 18 months — and sometimes longer. Just be ready to pay up to 102 percent of the full premium and be sure to apply for COBRA within 60 days.

For more information about Medicaid, check entries under "United States Government" or "Community Services" in your local phone book or visit them on the Internet at *www.cms.hhs.gov/medicaid.*

LTC insurance can solve health care dilemma

More than 6 million people over 65 need long-term care (LTC), and with nursing home costs approaching $200 a day, many wonder how they will pay for it without going bankrupt.

The three most obvious answers to this predicament all have their drawbacks.

- Pay for long-term care yourself. Consider this option if you have plenty of liquid assets and are not concerned about keeping them or passing them on to your heirs.

- Depend on Medicaid. This state/federal program pays for nearly half of all nursing home bills. However, its choices are limited and you generally have to use up all your own money first.

- Purchase LTC insurance. It's expensive, but you can choose where and how you receive care.

Private Long-Term Care Insurance: To Buy or Not to Buy? is a special report from the United Seniors Health Council (USHC), a program of the National Council on the Aging. It explores these options and pays special attention to the question of whether or not to buy LTC insurance.

Gain peace of mind. According to the report, a major reason people buy LTC insurance is to maintain emotional and financial independence. If you don't want any other person or organization making decisions about and paying for your health care later on, then LTC insurance may be for you.

Reject Medicaid restrictions. Not only do you have to "spend down" all or most of your income and assets before Medicaid will kick in, but then you are limited to the specific services Medicaid will pay for.

Rules vary from state to state, but nursing homes are usually the only type of long-term care that Medicaid will pay for. So, without LTC insurance, you may be forced into a nursing home when you could get along with home health care, an assisted living facility, or other less restrictive alternative.

And not all nursing homes accept Medicaid clients. Those that do usually have only a certain number of Medicaid beds available. With LTC insurance, you have more choices.

Qualify financially. The USHC says before you sign up for LTC insurance, evaluate your finances. You should:

- be able to afford the premiums without it affecting your normal lifestyle.

- be able to handle possible premium increases.

- have, as a couple, an annual retirement income of at least $35,000 to $50,000.

- own assets of at least $75,000, not counting homes and automobiles.

These are national averages, and may be high or low depending on where you live and your individual circumstances.

Remember also, a major benefit of LTC insurance is that it helps preserve your assets and income for your spouse or other heirs. If you don't have a lot of property and no one in particular to leave anything to, this type of insurance may not be appropriate.

Understand the limitations. The Consumer Federation of America, an association of non-profit, pro-consumer groups, warns that LTC insurance has some drawbacks.

- If you have to drop the policy, you get nothing for all you have paid into it.

- Because of inflation and rising costs, the policy benefits you purchase today may be inadequate by the time you need them.

- Premiums are not guaranteed to stay the same.

LTC insurance is a complex, emotional issue. Get advice and recommendations from several reputable sources before you buy.

Smart choices for LTC policies

Don't rush into a decision to buy long-term care insurance. It's too important and often too complex to hurry. Here are just a few of the steps you should take and issues you should consider before buying.

Become well-informed. Begin by reading *A Shopper's Guide to Long-Term Care Insurance*, a booklet written by the National Association of Insurance Commissioners. Although you can get it from your state insurance department, by law, insurance companies and agents must give it to you before you buy. Along with good explanations, it has worksheets to help you keep track of information you gather as you shop.

Compare coverage. Next, be prepared to talk to several companies and agents so you can compare benefits, limits on coverage, and premiums. Long-term care means more than just going to a nursing home. There's also assisted living, home health care, and others. Learn what kinds of facilities and what types of care your policy will cover.

Pick a financially strong company that has a better chance of still being around when you need it. You may get a better deal with a group plan where you work, or through an association you belong to, but make sure you can keep the policy if you no longer belong to the group.

Figure the costs. There are two basic ways you receive benefits through your long-term care insurance policy — the expense-incurred method or the indemnity method. Read the literature on policies you're considering to understand the difference.

The bottom line, however, is that you will probably buy a policy with a dollar limit. When you reach that limit, your coverage runs out. What your dollar will buy can vary greatly depending on where you live — or will end up living.

According to The MetLife Market Survey of Nursing Home & Home Care Costs, the average cost of a semi-private nursing home room in 2003 was $158.26. But that number ranged from $88.19 in Shreveport, to $333.20 in New York City, and $419.80 in Alaska. The average hourly rate for home health aides went from $12.20 in New Orleans to $26.54 in Fort Worth.

Decide how much you might be able to afford from your own sources and how much you want to get from insurance. Then factor in inflation. The MetLife survey says semi-private nursing home costs rose 11 percent from 2002 to 2003. Inflation protection will increase your premiums, but it can be one of the most important parts of your policy.

Learn the triggers. You're only eligible for benefits when the insurance company says you are — usually based on benefit triggers, or your inability

---

Pay for long-term care with alternate funds

Experts from the Consumer Federation of America and the National Council on the Aging suggest you consider financing your health care in different ways.

- Use a reverse mortgage on your home.

- Sell your home and use some or all of the proceeds for an annuity or other income-producing investment.

- Purchase or continue whole life insurance policies beyond retirement. Borrow against them to pay nursing home expenses.

---

to perform certain activities of daily living (ADLs). Normally these include bathing, dressing, eating, toileting, transferring, and continence.

Make sure you understand your policy's requirements. The more clearly it describes these benefit triggers, the less confusion there will be when you file a claim.

Pick a waiting period. You can save premium dollars if you choose to pay your own costs for, say, the first 20 or 100 days you need care. The longer you're willing to pay out-of-pocket, the lower your premiums.

Disability insurance: a cushion of secure income

Fall off the roof and your financial plan may crash with you, says Jane Bryant Quinn in her acclaimed book *Making the Most of Your Money*. A bout of disability can quickly sap your savings and investments, while disability insurance means a dependable source of income.

Insurers usually offer policies that cover only a portion of your income — often anywhere from 40 to 70 percent. That's why you need to look for the best value. Quinn says to forgo the bells and whistles. Your objective is a policy that meets your reasonable needs.

Think long term. Many policies pay benefits only for a year or two. These are not too expensive and Quinn says only about 10 percent of disabilities last longer than that. However, the best — and more expensive — insurance policies will provide for you until you turn 65, when you are eligible for Medicare and Social Security.

Lock in security. A "noncancellable" policy guarantees the same premiums and benefits over your lifetime, so it's expensive.

"Guaranteed-renewable" coverage is more common. Your benefits won't change — but your rates might.

Pay now, less later. If you can afford to pay higher premiums now, choose a fixed rate that lasts the life of the policy. On the other hand, an annually renewable disability-income (ARDI) policy starts low and gradually increases every year. If your income also increases, Quinn says that's not too bad a deal.

Consider your occupation. You'll come across terms like Own Occ (own occupation) and Any Occ (any occupation) when researching policy payouts. But Quinn says the best choice is an income replacement option. This covers you for a certain level of income regardless of the job you get after an injury.

Collect enough to work less. Sign up for Residual Benefits if you choose an Any-Occ or Own-Occ policy and you'll receive the difference between your previous and your current benefits.

Don't pay after pain. Make sure your insurer will waive your premium once you're disabled. Otherwise, factor this cost into the income you need to insure.

Cut costs with details. All the choices may seem intimidating, but Quinn says some of them can save you money.

In *Making the Most of Your Money*, author Jane Bryant Quinn lists three places to look for disability policies.

- Many employers offer affordable short- or long-term disability insurance. Just make sure it's an individual policy that can go with you if you leave the company.

- Professional associations offer rock bottom rates — often screening out only the most serious illnesses. If you're self-employed, this may be your best option.

- Independent insurers also sell disability insurance to individuals. These policies are usually more expensive, but offer better benefits. They may, however, reject you because of your age, health, or occupation.

- Buy into a unisex plan if you are a woman. This can save you up to 50 percent, since women usually pay higher premiums than men.

- Ask for the non-smoker discount.

- Choose the longest elimination period you can afford. If you can wait six months to receive benefits, your policy may cost 30 percent less.

- Skip add-ons that don't increase the value of your policy – such as presumptive disability, accidental death and dismemberment, hospital income, and premium refunds.

Life insurance: security for loved ones

Sixty percent of all Americans either have no life insurance or are underinsured, say Carrie Schwab-Pomerantz and Charles R. Schwab, authors of *It Pays to Talk: How to Have the Essential Conversations with Your Family About Money and Investing*.

Although you're spending money on something you hope you'll never use, life insurance, they say, is vital for protecting the people you care about.

Know when to buy. Consider life insurance coverage for yourself and your spouse if:

- you have dependent children.

- you support your parents.

- your spouse depends on your income.

On the other hand, if you have no dependents and are single, or are married with substantial assets, you probably don't need life insurance.

Find the right amount. Here are three possible ways to determine how much life insurance you need.

- A very general "rule of thumb" in the insurance industry is to figure six to 12 times your annual income and purchase that amount of insurance. Take into account your number of dependents, your current financial obligations, and any special needs to help gauge if you're at the low or high end of that range.

- Count on replacing your lost income with annual dividends. For example, you would need $750,000 of coverage to replace a $45,000 a year income, at a conservative 6 percent average annual return.

- Many companies have financial calculators on the Internet to help you determine the exact amount of coverage you need. For instance, go to *https://schwab.inslogic.com*. Select *Needs Assessment* on that Web page and you can fill in specific numbers to get an insurance estimate.

Choose the best plan. There are two basic types of life insurance.

- Term insurance lets you specify the amount of coverage you want for a given time — in 5-, 10-, 15-, 20-, 25-, and 30-year periods. Experts say to buy guaranteed renewable full-term insurance. Your premiums won't change, and your beneficiary receives the full value anytime during the term of the policy.

- Cash value insurance has higher premiums because you're buying an investment that offers lifelong coverage. As long as you pay your premiums, a percentage is set aside and invested. As your policy grows tax-deferred, you can make withdrawals from or borrow against it. If you cancel the policy, you can receive some or all of the cash value back.

Know where to buy. Don't choose life insurance based on price alone. Buy from a company that is financially sound.

- Sign up with your employer's group plan if possible. The coverage, however, will probably be less than you need.

- Buy additional insurance from an independent agent or company, and lock it in at your current age.

- Shop for term insurance quotes online. Remember though, all quotes apply to someone in excellent health. Your actual cost will depend on things like weight, health and genetic history, and cholesterol levels.

Get recommendations from family and friends. Compare quotes from several insurance agents, then settle on one that fits you best.

Find an insurance agent you trust

There are many splendid life insurance agents in this country, says Jane Bryant Quinn in her book *Making the Most of Your Money.* But there are also some who either don't understand what they're doing or are motivated more by commission income than your best interests.

Quinn admits it isn't easy to find one of the smart, straightforward agents. These are the ones who search out the policies and strategies that are best for you, encourage you to buy only what you need, and help you squeeze the most out of every dollar you invest.

Reject cold callers. The first step, Quinn says, is to find an agent by yourself. Don't take someone who comes to you from a cold call, a reference by an acquaintance who just bought a policy, or a chance meeting at a party or on the street. It's not likely these prospecting agents will be the smartest ones.

A better way is to ask your business associates, accountant, banker, or lawyer who they think are the best agents in your community. Then ask why. Tell them your priorities are competence and experience.

Interview your prospects. After you have some names, make a short list of agents to interview. Quinn recommends the following basic qualifications:

- full-time agents in business for at least five years
- chartered life underwriter (CLU) designation — younger agents should at least be working on their CLU and have already taken some of the exams
- representatives of large, high-quality companies

Make appointments with the most promising candidates and ask them about their personal histories as well as their business practices. Find out how they are paid (fees, commissions, bonuses, rewards for high sales, etc.), what kind of policies they like, and how they take care of clients after the sale. Ask if they attend or teach continuing education seminars and what they think about placing policies with different companies.

If the agent appears to resent any of your questions, move to the next candidate. Check out their answers by talking to other clients and then call your state securities regulator for their file information.

Notice if your prospect asks about you and your insurance needs. This should be a two-way interview. In the end, you'll probably rely on gut feelings, but going through the process will do a lot to help your intuition.

Find an independent adviser. Typical insurance agents charge an up-front commission, plus fees that are wrapped into — and sometimes hidden by — your premium. A rare treasure, Quinn says, is an independent insurance adviser. They charge only by the hour for evaluating your needs and setting you up with the right kind of policy.

You'll pay more up front to an adviser, but you pay more in the long run to an agent.

Some insurance agents have business cards that say "financial planner," "insurance adviser," and "actuarial consultant," Quinn warns. These agents may present themselves as fee-based, even though they get additional income from commissions.

Look at a cash-value schedule for the policy you intend to buy. An agent-sold policy will have little or no cash value in the first and second year, as the agent takes fees out. An adviser-sold policy should be worth almost its full value the first year and increase dramatically after that.

Adequate home insurance = peace of mind

You want the best coverage for where you live and what you own. Don't risk everything just to save a few extra dollars in premiums. Here are top tips from the National Association of Insurance Commissioners.

- Insure your home for 100 percent of its replacement cost — not its actual cash value. Get guaranteed replacement cost coverage or an inflation guard endorsement. Insure detached structures and their contents.

- Buy the personal property replacement cost option. Add floaters to cover costly items like jewelry, furs, or antiques.

- Get coverage for additional living expenses to cover motels, restaurants, and storage if you're displaced from your home.

- Purchase personal liability to protect you from a lawsuit. Ask for the maximum amount of the most comprehensive type of coverage — an umbrella liability policy or comprehensive personal liability policy.

- Maximize the coverage on medical payments for guests injured on your property.

- You'll have to purchase flood or earthquake insurance separately, but if you live in a high-risk area, do it.

6 clues to cut car insurance costs

Don't pay big bucks for your auto insurance. Follow these tips from the National Association of Insurance Commissioners and the Insurance Information Institute and start saving money today.

Tweak your policy. If you're willing to pay the first $500 of collision or comprehensive losses instead of just $200, for instance, you could save 15 to 30 percent of the premium. If you can afford more, ask about a $1,000 deductible.

Even better, think about dropping physical damage coverage altogether on older vehicles. It may not be worth it to insure cars worth less than 10 times the cost of the coverage. Figure how much you'd get on a claim — minus the deductible — and compare it to the amount of the premiums.

Of course, if you have a loan on the car, the bank may require a certain amount of coverage. Review your coverage at renewal time to see if you want to change things.

Live with lower premiums

Lowering your risk can also help lower your home insurance premiums. Often, insurers will provide discounts if you:

- install dead-bolt locks or alarm systems.

- install smoke detectors, carbon monoxide detectors, and fire extinguishers.

- don't smoke.

- participate in a neighborhood watch program.

- use fire resistant building materials.

Some insurance companies offer discounts if you're a long-term policyholder or if you buy your auto insurance from them as well. Look for senior discounts if you're over 55.

If all else fails, you can always raise your deductible to lower your premiums.

Ask for discounts. These vary in different states and with different companies. Ask your agent or customer service representative about discounts for:

- insuring more than one car or combining your auto and homeowner's policies.

- being a longtime customer.

- anti-theft devices and safety equipment like airbags or anti-lock brakes.

- mature drivers, good students, or college students away from home.

- driving fewer miles or carpooling.

Remember, it's possible a company with fewer discounts can have a lower overall price.

Be a safe driver. Don't get traffic tickets and avoid accidents, and you'll receive better insurance rates. Sometimes a defensive driving class will count.

Keep good credit. Insurance companies

You can't always avoid an accident. But you can always be prepared for one. Here are some things you should keep in your glove box just in case.

- instant or disposable camera to document the scene, damage, vehicles, and people involved

- pens or pencils

- paper or small notepad so you can record names, license plate numbers, insurance and contact information, and details about the accident

- registration and insurance cards

- phone number of your insurance company, which often provides a checklist of what to do after an accident

- flashlight

find that drivers with long, stable credit histories have fewer accidents. That means a favorable credit report can assure you better rates.

Buy the right car. Companies charge more to insure cars that cost more to repair, offer less protection or cause more damage in accidents, or are more likely to be stolen. When shopping for a new or used car, check to see what the insurance rates are before you buy and avoid an expensive surprise.

Shop around. Rates can vary a great deal between insurance companies, so get quotes from several. Talk to friends, relatives, or your state insurance department for recommendations. Take into consideration the financial stability of the company, how well it takes care of its customers, and how fairly and efficiently it settles claims.

Some companies have agents that provide exclusive representation, some work through independent agents, and others sell directly over the phone or on the Internet. Make sure you're comfortable with this arrangement.

Insure yourself against insurance fraud

From out of nowhere, a car swoops in front of you and slams on its brakes. You stop as quickly as possible, but still bump the other car. An accident like this could happen to anyone — unless it's not an accident.

The "swoop and squat" is a common type of staged accident used to commit insurance fraud — and older drivers are favorite targets of this scam.

"Seniors are maneuvered into staged car crashes so con artists can make fake injury claims against auto insurance companies," explains James Quiggle, Director of Communications for the Coalition Against Insurance Fraud (CAIF). "They are perceived to be less attentive drivers, easily intimidated, and less likely to recall incriminating details."

Document the evidence. The CAIF suggests you carry a disposable camera in your glove box to counter scams like this. Then if you're in an accident, take pictures of the other car, the damage it received, and the passengers. Insurance cheats will make up fake damage claims and report injuries to people who weren't even there.

Call the cops. Be sure and notify the police, even for minor damage. It's hard for crooks to claim serious injuries or car damage when a police report notes just a small dent. Get names and addresses of everyone in the car and note their behavior. Notice if they suddenly act hurt when the police arrive.

Drive defensively. Allow plenty of space between your car and the car in front of you so you have time to stop suddenly. Look beyond the first car and use your brakes if you see traffic ahead slowing down.

The "swoop and squat" isn't the only maneuver scheming drivers use. Watch out for someone who slows down and waves you into traffic. He may then crash into you, deny waving, and say it's your fault. Crooks will also deliberately sideswipe you if you drift out of your lane on highways or multiple turn lanes at busy intersections.

Stay away from quacks. When you or your vehicle need professional treatment as a result of an accident, use only providers you know and trust. A common scam is to convince people to use doctors or body shops that give shoddy or no service, and then bill the insurance company for thousands of dollars. A dishonest lawyer may want you to sue when you're not really hurt.

Have friends or relatives recommend a doctor, lawyer, or body shop if necessary. Check with your state medical board, the American Bar Association, or the Better Business Bureau to see if complaints have been filed.

Report shady characters. "Call your state insurance department and the National Insurance Crime Bureau (NICB) for any staged-accident suspicion," urges Quiggle, "whether it's strangers, body shops, shady doctors, lawyers, or your overall suspicion of a staged accident."

Contact the NICB hotline at 800-835-6422. Give them the license plate number, location of the accident, why you think it was fraud, and as many details as possible.

Steer clear of useless insurance

Proper insurance coverage is a godsend when you need it, but there are some types of policies you'll probably never use. Here are eight insurance plans experts say you should stay away from.

Life insurance if you're single. Life insurance provides money to live on if the breadwinner dies. If you have no dependents, your death won't create a financial hardship. The same is true if both spouses have ample individual income or an adequate retirement plan. A rule of thumb is if your income won't be needed, then don't buy life insurance.

Air travel insurance. If you die suddenly, it doesn't matter if it's from an airplane crash or a heart attack. Your family will still need financial support, so get regular life insurance with full coverage. Besides, most credit cards offer free coverage anyway if you charge the tickets.

Mortgage-life insurance. These policies protect your lender if you die, since proceeds can only be used to pay off your loan. A better — and cheaper — choice is straight term insurance, which can be used for anything.

Private mortgage insurance. PMI is a special case, because you usually have to get it when you buy a home with less than a

20 percent down payment. The cost of PMI simply becomes part of your loan payment. However, once you owe less than 80 percent of the value of your home, you can — and should — ask to cancel PMI.

Credit-life insurance. These are policies attached to bank and credit card loans. They pay your loan off if you die, or make your payment if you are sick, hurt, or out of work. It is very expensive insurance and sometimes you don't even know you're getting it. Buy term life insurance instead and forget about the disability or unemployment policies, because their payouts are so low.

Life insurance on children. The death of a child is an emotional catastrophe, not an economic one. When no one depends on them financially, life insurance is little consolation.

Cancer insurance. Unless you're pretty sure you're going to get hit by a particular disease, spend your money on more comprehensive health coverage. In any case, read the fine print closely. Many of these, and other one-disease policies, are cheap because they don't cover a lot.

Rental car insurance. This really isn't even insurance — rental car companies call it a "collision damage waiver." It's very expensive and your own car insurance or your credit card company probably covers you. Check to be sure, especially if you'll be renting in a foreign country.

Low-cost legal aid

Simple strategies resolve consumer complaints

Stop settling for excuses about bad service and broken products. Follow these steps from the Federal Trade Commission and other organizations, and say goodbye to consumer problems.

Go to the seller. Start with the store where you bought the product, or the company that sold you the service. If the first person you talk to is not helpful, ask to speak with the manager. Keep moving up the chain of command until you find someone who will help you.

Can't get anywhere with the local retailer? Speak to someone in the consumer affairs department of the company's headquarters.

Call the manufacturer. Complain to the company that made the product if you have a warranty or can't get the seller to cooperate. Get the manufacturer's name and a phone number for customer service from the label, warranty, or other paperwork you received with the item.

Whether you contact the seller or the manufacturer, have this information handy.

- the product's name and serial number
- date of the purchase
- the history of the problem and how you have tried to solve it

Stay calm when you call and be polite — but firm. Insist on a resolution to your problem.

File a written complaint. Still not satisfied? Write a complaint letter. Include all the facts of your case, and keep it clear, short, and sweet. Use the sample consumer complaint letter on page 210 as a guide.

- Include your name, phone number, and address so the company can contact you, as well as the product's name and serial number.

- Explain the steps you have already taken to resolve the issue, and what you would like the company to do now.

- Enclose copies — never originals — of sales receipts, work contracts, warranties, cancelled checks, repair orders, and any letters you and the company have sent each other.

- Send everything certified mail and request a return receipt. It costs a little more, but you'll have proof down the road that the company received your letter.

Call in the big guns. These agencies offer different types of assistance. They'll even fight on your behalf. Contact them if your letter doesn't work, and explain the situation.

- your state attorney general

- the Better Business Bureau in the state where the seller or manufacturer is located

- your local consumer protection office

- the consumer action department of a local newspaper, television, or radio station

- the legal clinic at a local law school

Document everything. Finally, keep a log of all your dealings with the seller or manufacturer. Write down the names of everyone you speak to, the date and time, and what they told you.

Sample consumer complaint letter

(Date)
(Your name)
(Your address)
(Your city, state, and zip code)

(Name of the contact person, if you have one)
(Their title)
(Company name)
Consumer Complaint Division (if you don't have
a contact)
(Their address)
(Their city, state, and zip code)

Dear (Contact Person):

On (date), I (bought, leased, rented, or had
repaired) a (name of the product, with serial or
model number, or service performed) at (location
and other important transaction details).

Unfortunately, your product (or service) has not
performed well (or the service was inadequate)
because (state the problem).

To resolve the problem, I would appreciate
(state the specific action you want — refund,
credit, repair, exchange, etc.). Enclosed are
copies of my records.

I look forward to your reply and a resolution to
my problem, and will wait until (set a time
limit) before seeking third-party assistance.
Please contact me at the above address or by
phone at (home or office number with area code).

Sincerely,

(Your name)

(Your account number, if applicable)

Enclosure(s): (List receipts, guarantees, warranties, canceled checks, contracts, model and
serial numbers, and any other documents you are
including.)

Make copies of all the letters or e-mails you and the company exchange as well as any documents related to the complaint. You may need this information if you go to court.

Visit these Web sites for further advice.

National Consumers League	www.nclnet.org
Consumer Federation of America	www.consumerfed.org
Consumer Resource Handbook	www.pueblo.gsa.gov/crh

Expert tips for winning in small claims court

Going to court? Don't lose your cool. Small claims court is made for people like you who want to represent themselves. Here's how to tip the scales of justice in your favor.

- Go to the courthouse and watch a few small claims hearings to learn how the system works.

- Ask the local small claims court advisor to help you prepare for the hearing.

- You can always seek an attorney's advice before a hearing even though in most cases you can not bring a lawyer to small claims court.

- Talk to potential witnesses before the hearing. Get all the facts straight and make sure their testimony supports your case.

- Ask your witnesses or experts to come to court with you to testify. The judge may not accept their testimony unless they give it in person.

- Rehearse what you want to say in front of friends or a mirror. In two or three sentences you want to clearly and unemotionally state the most important facts of your case.

- Write down the main points you want to tell the judge if you think you might forget them.

- Give yourself plenty of time to arrive on the day of your hearing so you can relax and think about your case.

- Bring all the evidence you need to support your case — sales receipts, letters, contracts, leases, deeds, estimates, canceled checks, advertisements, photographs, or other documents. You need two copies of each original document, one for the judge and one for your opponent.

- If you are asking for money, be prepared to explain the amount and back it up. You may even want to itemize the costs for the judge.

- Don't speak to your opponent during the hearing. Talk directly to the judge.

- Listen to the judge, and answer his questions carefully and honestly. They may not seem relevant to your case, but he could be applying a law you aren't familiar with.

- Do not interrupt when the other party tells his side of the story, even if you think he is lying. The judge should give you time to reply later.

- Never trade insults or argue with your opponent in the courtroom. Stay calm.

The judge may issue a decision at the end of the hearing, or he may want time to think it over. In that case, you will get his decision in writing later.

Free legal aid for seniors

Age has its privileges. Whether you cannot afford an attorney, or simply want a little legal advice, these services offer free legal help to older adults.

Area Agencies on Aging (AAA). You can get free legal advice if you're over 60. Best of all, you don't have to be below a certain income level to qualify. Thanks to the Older Americans Act, the state you live in must provide you with legal assistance for financial, insurance, and tax counseling, as well as represent you in matters of guardianship.

To find your local Area Agency on Aging call 800-677-1116, or visit their national Web site at *www.n4a.org*. There are no income limits on receiving services, but seniors with the greatest economic need get preference.

Legal hotlines. Legal hotlines offer another solution for people over 60. The lawyers who staff these hotlines can answer legal questions, mail pamphlets containing the information you need, or refer you to a special, low-cost group of attorneys or to a free legal services program. The one drawback — they can't represent you in court.

Unfortunately, only some areas of the United States have legal hotlines in place. Contact your state's bar association or Area Agency on Aging, or go to this Internet site *www.aoa.gov/eldfam/ Elder_Rights/Legal_Assistance/Legal_Hotline.asp* to find out about legal hotlines in your area.

Pro bono programs. Many states offer free — also called pro bono — legal aid. Usually, the state's bar association sponsors these programs. Private practice lawyers volunteer to handle cases free of charge for people who otherwise could not afford an attorney. Call your state's bar association and ask about pro bono programs in your community. They can put you in contact with these services and may be able to tell you the eligibility requirements.

Legal Services Corporation (LSC). This private, non-profit corporation hires staff attorneys to help clients who cannot afford a lawyer. They specialize in issues such as credit and utility problems, foreclosures, social security, welfare, and unemployment, just to name a few. LSC offices won't handle criminal cases or class action lawsuits, though.

Top sites offer legal counsel

Click onto the Internet for answers to general legal questions. These Web sites provide free articles, book recommendations, and other useful links on a huge variety of legal issues from estate planning and social security to auto injury and small claims court.

FirstGov for Seniors	www.seniors.gov
SeniorLaw	www.SeniorLaw.com
Nolo.com	www.nolo.com
FreeAdvice.com	www.FreeAdvice.com
LawGuru.com	www.LawGuru.com
FindLaw	www.FindLaw.com
National Senior Citizens Law Center	www.nsclc.org
National Consumer Law Center:	www.ConsumerLaw.org
American Bar Association	www.AbaNet.org
The National Elder Law Network	www.keln.org

Check your telephone book for an LSC office near you. You can also visit the LSC Web site at *www.lsc.gov* and click on *Get Legal Assistance,* or call 202-295-1500.

The National Legal Aid & Defender Association (NLADA) is a similar nonprofit organization that provides attorneys to low-income clients. To find a Legal Aid office, go to *www.nlada.org* on the Internet, or call 202-452-0620.

Law school clinics. Many law schools offer legal aid clinics where law students, supervised by professional attorneys, handle cases for people in the community. Some clinics help everyone, while others accept only seniors or low-income adults. Call the law schools near you and ask about their legal aid programs.

AARP Legal Services Network (LSN). AARP offers free and discounted legal services to its members through LSN. AARP screens and interviews each attorney in this program, plus checks their standing with the bar association and malpractice insurance.

You reap the benefit by getting a free 30-minute initial consultation with an approved attorney as well as special flat rates on common legal needs such as drawing up a will or power of attorney. You also receive 20 percent off the lawyer's fees for all other legal matters.

Look for an LSN attorney by calling 888-OUR-AARP, or going online to *www.aarp.org/lsn*. Have your AARP member number ready when you call the attorney to make an appointment.

8 easy ways to lower your legal fees

Wish you could afford a lawyer? Hugo Gerstl, a practicing trial lawyer for more than 33 years, tells you how you can in his book, *How to Cut Your Legal Bills in Half.*

Talk it out. Keep trying to work things out with your foe, especially before you get a lawyer. If you can't get through to them, approach their friends, colleagues, or anyone else who could convince them to sit down with you. It's a lot cheaper and simpler than suing.

Try mediation. Even if you don't go to court, lawyers can still help. Hire an attorney or other neutral person to act as a mediator between you and the other party. Mediation costs a fraction of the price of going to court.

Crack a book. Take a trip to your county's law library to bone up on your case. Law librarians are famous for their helpful attitude. While they can't give you legal advice, they can help you find the books you need and point you in the right direction.

Hire a paralegal. Legal paperwork can be a nightmare, but you may not need a lawyer to fill in all the blanks. Many cases are simple enough, says Gerstl, that you can hire a paralegal to do the paperwork rather than an attorney, and at about a tenth of the cost.

Negotiate fees. If you do get a lawyer to represent you in court, do a little haggling up front. Negotiate a fixed fee for your case, or, if he charges by the hour, agree on a high and low range for the total cost. For some cases, attorneys want a percentage of your settlement. Gerstl suggests you cap that amount at 25 percent if you settle before trial, or at 33.3 percent if your case goes to court.

Get it in writing. Have the lawyer put all the legal fees you agree on in writing, then read the contract carefully. Make changes if you need to, initial them, and have your lawyer do the same.

Question costs. Discuss any concerns you have about the attorney's bills while he is working on your case, not after it's over. Addressing troublesome charges early on will save you money and frustration later.

Keep calls to a minimum. Only call your lawyer when you absolutely must. Your attorney is there to help you, but remember he doesn't run a charity. You'll get the bill for every minute spent talking to him.

Raise the bar when choosing a lawyer

You want a capable, honest lawyer — someone you can trust. After all, you're about to give them a lot of responsibility for your well-being. Before you start flipping through the phone book, follow these tips for finding a good attorney.

Get a good match. You need a lawyer who specializes in solving your type of problem. You wouldn't hire a divorce attorney to handle an auto accident case, would you? Friends, relatives, or organizations with similar experiences can offer good leads. A local senior center, for instance, might know a few good attorneys who specialize in elder law or estate planning.

Check references. Get several names, then investigate their background. Call your local bar association and ask if the attorneys are members of the bar in your state and in good standing. The local public or law library may also have a list of practicing attorneys, with information on what types of law they specialize in and how many years of experience they have.

Cross-examine your choices. Now that you have a short list of names, it's time to interview them by phone or in person. Many attorneys will give you a free initial consultation of 15 to 30 minutes. Use that time to sound out your prospective lawyer, and consider asking these questions.

- How much experience do you have with my kind of case?
- When you have handled cases like mine in the past, how have they turned out?
- How would you handle my case?
- About how long do you think it will last?
- Will you actually be the person working my case? If not, who will?
- Will they bill me separately from your fees?
- How much do you charge?
- What payment options do I have?
- Will I receive an itemized bill?
- Can you give me an estimate of what my case will cost from start to finish, including all the miscellaneous fees?
- Will you put any fees we discuss in a written contract?

• How can I contact you, and how long would you usually take to get back with me?

Their answers should give you a good idea of whether you want them to handle your case. AARP's Legal Services Network suggests you also think about practical issues like the law firm's location. Can you get to the office easily? Is there plenty of parking? If you have a physical disability, can you get in and out of the building?

Go with your gut. No matter how good a lawyer is, you must be comfortable with her. You must be able to trust her with personal details, and feel confident in her abilities. If there is any personal conflict, you need to keep looking.

Going to court is a serious business, so spend a little extra time choosing the attorney that's right for you.

Shopping solutions

Beat the prescription blues

Don't expect your pharmacist to tell you this, but here are seven great ways to get prescription drugs for less — or even for free.

Save with free samples. Ask your doctor for free samples of the medicines he prescribes. Not only does this buy you time to comparison shop for the best price, but you also find out whether the drug will work for you without distressing side effects. Your doctor gets lots of free samples of prescription and nonprescription drugs from pharmaceutical companies, so don't hesitate to ask.

Tap into Medicare tips. Medicare offers a *Prescription Drug and Other Assistance Programs* section to help you find drug discounts. Visit them online at *www.medicare.gov* or call 800-633-4227 to discover which discounts you may be eligible for. To find out more about prescription drug assistance programs, surf to *www.benefitscheckup.org* or *www.needymeds.com*.

Go to the source. Through the Together Rx program, a group of drug companies discounts their products for folks on Medicare. Visit *www.togetherrx.com* for more information. Individual drug companies, such as Pfizer and Eli Lilly also have assistance programs. Visit *www.pfizerforliving.com* or *www.lillyanswers.com* to find out more.

Split drug costs. Ask your doctor to prescribe the larger tablets you can cut in half. A 10-milligram pill, for example, may cost little more than the 5-milligram size. Some pills are even scored so you can divide them easily. Look for an inexpensive pill splitter at the drugstore.

Just remember, never split some pills, such as extended release tablets or those shiny enteric-coated tablets. Splitting pills like these won't save you money and could endanger your health or even your life.

Research suggests medications like sertraline (Zoloft) and sildenafil (Viagra) are safe and cost-effective to split. Here are some others:

clonazepam (Klonopin)	doxazosin (Cardura)	citalopram (Celexa)
atorvastatin (Lipitor)	paroxetine (Paxil)	pravastatin (Pravachol)
nefazodone (Serzone)	olanzapine (Zyprexa)	lisinopril (Zestril)

Yet, even these medications may be unsafe to split if you have certain health conditions. So be sure to talk to your doctor before you try to split any pill.

Ask for alternatives. Your doctor may be able to replace a name-brand drug with a lower-priced generic equivalent. The two may not have exactly the same content, but it's usually bases and fillers that are different — not the active ingredients.

Buy more, pay less. For any medication you take for a chronic condition — once you are sure you will continue it long-term — try to buy a three- to six-month supply at a time. The price per pill is usually lower when you buy in bulk. And since the pharmacist charges a fee each time he fills a prescription, you'll save by avoiding refills.

Bring your own drugs. Before a stay in the hospital, ask your doctor if you can bring your prescription and non-prescription drugs from home. If the hospital supplies them, they're likely to be a lot more expensive.

Discover deep drug discounts at Internet pharmacies

Going online certainly beats waiting in line to fill a prescription. You don't have to fight traffic, juggle paperwork, or even change out of your pajamas.

But besides being convenient, many Internet pharmacies — or e-pharmacies — also offer discounted deals on the prescriptions you regularly take. And with drug prices on the rise, shopping online could save you a bundle. Here's how.

- Internet pharmacies have lower overhead costs, so their prices may beat your local drugstore on prescription drugs.

- It's easier to compare costs sitting at your computer than it would be to drive store-to-store, or to call and wait for a druggist to look up your prescription.

- Even online, prescription prices can vary a lot. But one group of researchers discovered that you tend to get the best deals when you buy more than one item.

- Certain Web sites can quickly compare drug prices from a number of Internet pharmacies, so you can see in an instant which offers the most savings. Visit *www.PillBot.com* and *www.DestinationRx.com* to check the prices on your medications.

Understand the risks. If you have access to a computer, shopping for drugs online may be a good option for you. But be careful. Buying medicines on the Internet can save you cash, but in some cases it's still risky business.

Save money on over-the-counter drugs

The Flexible Spending Account your employer offers can now save you big money on over-the-counter (OTC) drugs. According to the Internal Revenue Service, you can claim these and many other OTC products under Flex plans.

- aspirin
- anti-itch creams
- cough remedies
- cold medicines
- laxatives
- adhesive bandages
- hot/cold packs
- hearing aids
- glasses

Items used for general good health or cosmetic reasons may not be eligible. Your doctor must recommend a certain dosage for a specific medical condition to get reimbursed for these:

- vitamins
- herbal supplements
- sunscreen
- skin moisturizers

A recent medical study found that most e-pharmacies don't do enough to educate customers about their medications or protect them from dangerous drug interactions. And while every Internet pharmacy in the study seemed to have a pharmacist on hand, researchers could not tell if qualified staff had actually handled their order.

Shop only the best. Your safest bet when shopping for drugs online is to look for the VIPPS (Verified Internet Pharmacy Practice Sites) seal on an Internet pharmacy's Web site. This seal means a pharmacy is licensed by the states in which it operates and has passed the National Association of Boards of Pharmacy (NABP) requirements for quality and security. VIPPS-certified pharmacies are also required to offer free phone consultations with a pharmacist.

These online pharmacies have received VIPPS certification:

Accurate Pharmacy	www.accuratepharmacy.com
Caremark, Inc.	www.rxrequest.com
CIGNA Tel-Drug	www.teldrug.com
Clickpharmacy.com	www.clickpharmacy.com
CVS Washington, Inc.	www.cvs.com
Drugstore.com	www.drugstore.com
Eckerd Pharmacy Services	www.eckerd.com
Familymeds.com	www.familymeds.com
Medco Health	www.medcohealth.com
Care For Life	www.careforlife.com
Walgreens	www.walgreens.com

To find out if others have been added to the VIPPS certified list, you can go directly to the NABP Web site at *www.nabp.net*.

Many of these online pharmacies offer free health and nutrition advice as well as information about the drugs you order, so you can check side effects and possible drug interactions.

Rely on the experts. Just remember, no safeguard is as good as talking to your doctor. Check with her first before taking any supplement, prescription drug, or over-the-counter medication. Only a real expert can warn you about possible dangers such as side effects and drug interactions.

Canadian pharmacies: help or hazard?

Getting medications from Canada is a hot topic and a major source of savings for people living on fixed incomes.

"Many Americans are putting their health at risk by not taking prescribed medicines simply because they cannot afford to purchase them," says William D. Novelli, the CEO of AARP. "It is a national embarrassment that in a country with the most advanced medical system in the world, so many of our citizens can obtain affordable prescription drugs only by seeking them in foreign countries."

AARP and other groups argue that if the United States and Canadian governments can make the process safer, then people should be allowed to order their drugs from Canada. This may not put a permanent stop to soaring drug costs, admits AARP, but importing Canadian medicines will help until the government can offer seniors affordable drug coverage.

On the other hand, the Food and Drug Administration (FDA) and the American Pharmacists Association worry that the health hazards of buying imported drugs outweigh the benefits of saving money.

- Foreign pharmacies may sell customers counterfeit medications, the wrong doses, contaminated drugs, or even the wrong drug.

- Medications shipped from other countries may not be manufactured, packaged, or stored under safe conditions.

- Internet pharmacies may claim to operate out of Canada to make people think their products are safe, while they sell drugs from an unsafe source.

- People often don't tell their local doctor and pharmacist about their imported medicines. These health professionals might prescribe duplicate medications, or miss important drug interactions.

- People ordering from online pharmacies or foreign doctors may not get the information they need on how to take medications and possible side effects.

These are real concerns, but critics of the FDA argue that buying medicine in the United States can be just as dangerous. For instance, the FDA has uncovered counterfeit drug rings in the United States selling fake and contaminated drugs to pharmacies around the country.

The state of Illinois recently studied the safety and savings of importing drugs from Canada. The researchers found that drug quality and pharmacy practices in the Canadian provinces of Manitoba and Ontario were just as safe — sometimes safer — as those in Illinois.

- The United States and Canada have similar rules and regulations to ensure the safety and effectiveness of prescription drugs.
- Canadian drugs may actually have a lower risk of being fake or contaminated.
- Both countries have virtually the same laws on storing drugs under safe conditions in warehouses.
- Educational requirements and regulations for pharmacists are as strict in Manitoba and Ontario as they are in Illinois.

According to this study, Illinois could save almost $35 million by getting certain medications over the border, and could lower drug copayments enough to save people over $20 million.

Other states have also considered importing drugs. Some have even listed specific Canadian pharmacies on their states' Web sites to make sure that people ordering Canadian drugs get them from safe, reliable sources.

Currently, the FDA limits the import of prescription drugs from Canada and other foreign countries. Some members of

Congress and a growing number of states are trying to change those laws.

In the meantime, play it safe. Follow this advice from the FDA whenever you order from an online pharmacy.

- Only take medications your doctor has prescribed for you.

- Don't order from any pharmacy that offers to fill a prescription drug without a prescription.

- Avoid sites that offer to prescribe a medicine for you for the first time without seeing your doctor.

- Don't buy from a site that sells drugs the FDA has not approved.

- Only buy from Internet pharmacies that give you access to a licensed pharmacist to answer your questions.

- Look for sites that have easy-to-find customer service policies and clear, simple privacy and security policies.

The FDA warns you should never order these prescription drugs on the Internet due to special safety concerns.

- Accutane (isotretinoin)

- Actiq (fentanyl citrate)

- Clozaril (clozapine)

- Lotronex (alosetron hydrochloride)

- Mifeprex (mifepristone or RU-486)

- Thalomid (thalidomide)

- Tikosyn (dofetilide)

- Tracleer (bosentan)

- Trovan (trovafloxacin mesylate or alatrofloxacin mesylate injection)

- Xyrem (sodium oxybate)

Talk to your doctor and pharmacist if you are thinking about getting your medications from Canada, or if you take imported drugs. That way, they can avoid writing or filling a duplicate prescription and can help you watch out for drug interactions and side effects.

16 tips to cut your grocery bill in half

Cynthia Yates has a knack for saving. She has written four books on how to budget, including *1,001 Bright Ideas to Stretch Your Dollars*, and her latest, *Living Well on One Income*. In fact, her thrifty tips could trim your grocery bills by as much as $50 to $150 a month, without cutting back on food. Just follow the advice in this free frugality guide.

- Learn prices so you know a good deal when it comes your way.

- Get to know your grocers. "Talk to produce managers, stocking clerks, butchers, and store managers," Yates says. Ask questions and you may find out about special deals.

- Check the shelf price tag. It usually lists the price per pound or ounce, which can help you compare the cost of similar products.

- Bend and squint to find the best deals. "The less expensive products," she says, "are usually on the lowest shelves."

- Buy items in bags rather than boxes if you have a choice. Bagged foods generally cost less.

- Consider going generic. "Generic or store brands are often just as good as the gourmet brands," Yates says. And they might be cheaper.

- Check the expiration date on dairy products and other perishable foods before you buy.

- Ask the store to break up bunches of produce so you can buy a smaller amount. There's no sense paying for more than you will eat.

- Weigh prepackaged foods like fruits, vegetables, and meat. They sometimes hold more than their label claims. Yates says, "You may find a 5-pound pack of spuds weighing in at 6 pounds."

- "Shop seasonally," she advises. "Prices drop when markets have an abundance of certain foods." Holidays and back-to-school seasons, for instance, have their effect — for better or worse — on store prices.

- Steer clear of the gourmet aisle and processed food. "You can rip your own lettuce, or cut your own cheese, or season your own drumstick," Yates says.

- Skip the junk food. "Back off on the stuff that isn't good for you in the first place," she advises. An occasional treat is OK, but too much can drain your budget and your health.

- Don't give in to impulse buys while shopping — or at least limit them to two or three items per trip.

- Avoid overbuying. "I believe everyone should have enough water and food stashed to get through a week or so, should an emergency come along," says Yates. But she discourages hoarding. One of her rules — buy only what you eat, and eat what you buy.

- Check the prices at checkout. "Mistakes happen," she warns. "Watch the register and check receipts." A checker may scan an item twice, or the sale price may not ring up.

- Don't live with inferior products. "Politely return," she says. "If you have purchased a product that has gone bad, or not held up within reason, take it back."

Grocers sometimes use tricks to sell you more food. "A lot of these things are carrots on a stick," Yates points out. "Don't be a donkey." Watch out for these four grocery store gimmicks.

- Placing staples like milk in the very back of the store forces you to walk past all the tempting aisles.

- Grouping items together encourages you to buy more than one product — like putting salsa next to the chips, or caramel dipping sauce by the apples.

- Setting items on the ends of aisles makes you think they are a special deal. But they may not offer the best price. "Sometimes," Yates says, "a walk down the aisle will find something less expensive."

- Giving away a free item with a minimum purchase, Yates says, only works in your favor if you had planned to spend that much money anyway.

10 tips to save big with coupons

Shopping with coupons can save you cash — if you know what you're doing. Susan Samtur, a contributing editor to Family Circle magazine and co-editor of the rebate magazine Refundle Bundle, offers 10 simple tips for bigger coupon savings.

Get 'em in order. "When you walk into a store, every aisle is by category," Samtur explains. "If I have my coupons arranged that way, it makes it much easier." The flyers are also organized by category, so matching coupons with sale items is easy to do ahead of time.

Make a list. Write the letter "c" next to the items on your grocery list you have coupons for, and include the size or number you have to buy. If it's on sale, write the store name next to it, the size, and the sale price. Arrange your list by the grocery store's categories — paper products, baking supplies, etc. — and you won't have to backtrack looking for items.

Watch expiration dates. "You have to keep in mind that expiration dates are shorter than they ever were before," Samtur says. Pull out old coupons as you come across them so you don't try to use them by mistake.

Read the fine print. More and more coupons are good only on multiple purchases, and many make you buy a certain size or style of product. Samtur says that's where a lot of people get tripped up. If you grab the wrong product and can't use the coupon, don't feel you still have to buy it. Give it back at the register, or go get the right item.

Try new products. Manufacturers work hard to sell new items, and they may issue lots of great coupons for a product around the time it hits the shelves.

Be willing to change brands. In order to get a good deal with coupons Samtur warns, "You have to be a little flexible. You can do very well as long as you don't mind switching brands."

Spot specially marked packages. These may have an instant coupon on the outside or a free sample of another product attached. Or you might discover a surprise coupon on the inside, good on your next purchase. So check before you throw that box away.

Aim for a double play. "One of the most successful ways to be a good coupon shopper is to combine coupons with a store sale," says Samtur. "Sometimes, you almost get the product absolutely free."

Know when to say no. Never buy a product simply because a coupon is about to expire. You may have to let it go if you can't find a good sale or if an item is too expensive, even with a discount. And don't buy something just because you have a coupon. It's not a bargain if you never use it.

Buy wholesale for real savings

Wholesale bulk shopping can really take the bite out of your grocery budget. "Stores like BJ's, Costco, and others can save you up to 26 percent on groceries and usually have screaming deals on non-grocery items," says thrifty author Cynthia Yates.

But don't confuse legitimate low-fee clubs that help you pay wholesale for everything with high-priced frauds. Joining for $300 a year is no bargain if the club only offers a 10 percent discount.

Shop around for the best deal, ask friends for recommendations, and beware if the offer sounds too good to be true. It probably is.

"Even if you saved on it," says Samtur, "it's still costing you money in the end."

Remember your coupons. You can't use them if you don't have them. Take them with you everywhere. You might keep them in your purse, or in the glove box of your car.

"When people begin to use coupons, they get overwhelmed," she admits. "My advice is to get your feet wet and just start couponing slowly." Your savings might not be as spectacular, but you are more likely to stick with it over the long run.

Hang up on hefty phone bills

Don't expect the phone company to tell you how to cut your phone bill without making fewer calls. Whether you'd like to save on local phone service or long distance, shopping around could lead to surprising savings.

Play a match game. The National Consumers League (NCL), a private, nonprofit advocacy group for consumers, suggests you examine how you use your phone. Your habits may determine which calling plan matches your needs. Consider issues like these.

- What time of day do you make most calls? Which days of the week?

- Do you make more local or out-of-state calls?

- Do you use specialty services like call waiting or caller ID?

Run the numbers. Low per-minute rates may not save you money if you rack up a lot of minutes each month. Estimate a per-minute total and compare it to the available flat monthly rates. That could be just as good a bargain as an "all-you-can-eat special."

Give 10-10 the third degree. You've seen the ads that promise you'll save on long distance if you just dial 10-10-something. These are called "dial around" services because they allow you to bypass — or dial around — your basic long-distance provider. These may save you money — or they may not.

To help you find out, the NCL suggests you ask about monthly fees and minimum call times. To decide which dial around service is best for you, check out this Internet site *10-10-phonerates.com.*

Bundle up or pare down. If you use caller ID, call waiting, and other specialty services regularly, the NCL says a discounted package could save you money. But if you'll only use one or two services, purchase just those you need.

Compare carefully. The NCL warns that providers may use different names to describe similar features. As you shop around, check that you are comparing two features — or groups of features — that are genuinely alike.

Trim more fat. Ask plenty of questions as you shop. Here are a few good ones to keep in mind.

- Do you have to talk a minimum number of minutes per month to get the advertised price? Decide whether your calling habits make this a good buy.

- Check whether you'll be charged a connection fee, a flat monthly fee, or a fee per call in addition to the per-minute charge.

- Find out whether calling long distance within your state (intrastate) is more expensive than state-to-state (interstate) calls. Rates vary so check the price in your state with each phone company.

- Most companies charge a fee to switch your plan from one long-distance provider to another. Ask to have this fee waived before you agree to switch.

Surf for answers. Let Web sites help you compare the calling plans available in your area.

SmartPrice.com	www.smartprice.com
SaveOnPhone.com	www.saveonphone.com
Attitude Long Distance	www.attitude-long-distance.com
Long Distance Calling Plans	www.calling-plans.com
TRAC	http://trac.org

Find out more. For more information, visit the Federal Communications Commission Web page at *www.fcc.gov* and click *Consumer Alerts & Factsheets*. Also, see the National Consumers League Web page at *www.nclnet.org/phonebill*.

Shop smart to avoid buyer's remorse

Hold onto your wallet! Do you really know what you're buying, or who you're buying from? Major purchases of household goods like furniture, appliances, and computers have become top sources of consumer complaints. Do your homework before buying a big-ticket item, and save yourself a costly headache afterward.

- Get recommendations from people you trust. Family, friends, and consumer groups are valuable resources when it comes to deciding which product, brand, or service provider will meet your needs.

- Decide ahead of time exactly what you want. Then stick to your guns — and your price. Don't let a salesperson pressure you into buying bigger or spending more than you had planned.

- Shop around. Check with several different companies to get their advice and the best price.

- Find out who you are buying from, particularly when shopping from home. The Better Business Bureau (BBB) says you should never order from a seller whose only mailing address is a P.O. Box, or who doesn't list a phone number. Call your local BBB to learn more about a company before you buy from them.

- Ask about refund and return policies, warns the BBB. Some companies limit returns, especially on sales items. For instance, you may not get a refund on clearance items.

- Get all guarantees and warranties in writing, and look them over carefully. You need to know what's covered if you have problems with the product.

- Take the time to read a sales contract before you sign it. Ask questions about the parts you don't understand. Also, make sure the salesperson puts all his promises in the contract. Never leave blank spaces for him to fill in later.

Catalogs offer easy savings

Nothing beats catalogs for the convenience of at-home shopping. But just four little words can help make sure you're getting the best buy. Before you place an order, the Better Business Bureau recommends asking, "Do you guarantee satisfaction?" Find out how long that guarantee lasts, as well as what the return policy is if you aren't satisfied.

- Pick the safest way to pay. Credit cards often give you some protection. If you end up filing a complaint about the product, you may not have to pay the charge on your card.

• Protect your privacy. A reputable seller won't require personal information — like your social security or bank account numbers — just to complete a purchase. The BBB says before you give out this information, find out who wants it, why, and how they plan to use it.

Should you still have problems with a product or seller, remember you have options. Government agencies and consumer organizations like the Better Business Bureau are on your side. Contact your local BBB for more information, or visit them on the Internet at *www.bbb.org*. Don't be shy. It's your money on the line.

Successful home strategies

Smart ways to sell your home

Do you need a real estate agent to sell your house? The simple answer is no, but selling a home is rarely simple. Here are your options.

Take it easy. Using an agent will certainly make things easier for you. Your agent can screen potential buyers, list your home with other brokers, and handle the negotiations. But you pay for convenience, usually a 6 or 7 percent fee. That could add up to big bucks.

Go solo. If you have the time and don't mind doing it on your own, you can save some money. But selling your own house is hard work. Here are just some of the things you'll have to do.

- File paperwork. Federal and state forms can be complicated and time-consuming.

- Research. Make sure you price your house fairly compared to similar homes in your area that recently sold. Consult the local classifieds and county clerk's office.

- Advertise. Place ads in newspapers and on the Internet. For a fee, you can even list with the multiple-listing service (MLS) available to brokers.

- Schedule appointments. You'll need to arrange times for showing your house to potential buyers. And be prepared to weed out the browsers and deadbeats from the serious, qualified buyers.

- Negotiate. Whether you deal directly with buyers or their representatives, you'll need to know when to make a counteroffer, or simply refuse or accept their offers. You'll probably want to hire a real estate lawyer to look over any contracts.

These Web sites provide valuable information, advice, and services for selling your own home.

Domania	www.domania.com
FiSBO Registry	www.fisbos.com
ForSaleByOwner.com	www.forsalebyowner.com

Whether you decide to go with an agent or not, there are some basic things you can do to make your home more attractive to potential buyers.

- Maintain your lawn. Flowers, trees, and shrubs make a good impression, too.
- Clean and repave your driveway and walkways.
- Power wash your house and give it a coat of paint.
- Clean and repair gutters.
- Fix or replace old door handles.
- Replace or thoroughly clean your carpets.
- Paint rooms a bright, neutral color.
- Open window shades and curtains for more light.
- Replace burned-out lightbulbs.
- Get rid of clutter. Put everything in its proper place.

- Fix leaks or any other plumbing problems.

- Service your heating and air conditioning units and keep your home at a comfortable temperature.

- Eliminate distractions. Don't subject potential buyers to loud music, cooking odors, or pets.

You might also want to get a professional home inspection to uncover any problems that might jeopardize the deal.

No down payment — no problem

You found your dream home. But coming up with the down payment is going to be a nightmare.

Don't worry. If you can't afford to make a down payment, non-profit down payment organizations, like AmeriDream or Neighborhood Gold, can help.

These groups help increase the pool of potential buyers so homes sell quicker and for full market value. The builder or seller pays a fee to the organization, but the buyer never has to pay back the gift. However, you must qualify for a loan that allows down payment assistance.

For more details, go to *www.usadownpaymentassistance.com.*

Simple steps for a smooth move

Whether you're relocating for a new job or to be closer to your grandchildren, moving can be stressful.

Dolores Perlman, a certified moving consultant for Coleman American Moving Services, offers these guidelines for making a smooth move.

Pick the right movers. Your moving company should belong to the American Moving and Storage Association (AMSA). It also helps if it's associated with a major van line. For example, Coleman American is an agent for Allied Van Lines.

"Choose a moving company that has been in business for a long time so you know the company has a record of being honest and dependable," Perlman says.

Compare prices, but don't be fooled by the lowest bid, especially if it comes over the phone.

Make it official. If possible, have a representative of the moving company come to your home so the estimate is as accurate as possible. Then get that estimate in writing to avoid future disputes over prices or services promised.

"Get everything in writing," Perlman stresses.

Check all paperwork for accuracy. Make sure the amount of packing to be done and the dates for packing, loading, and delivery are correct. Also double-check addresses and phone numbers.

Plan ahead. Smart planning can make the difference between a smooth move and a hectic one. Here are some things to do before moving day.

> ### Move quickly to handle moving complaints
>
> Even if you do everything right when planning a move, sometimes things go wrong. You might encounter delays in pickup or delivery, billing discrepancies, and damage or loss.
>
> Here's how to settle a dispute with your moving company.
>
> - Contact the moving company with any problems. Many things can be corrected immediately.
>
> - If necessary, file a claim to resolve the problem.
>
> - If the claim process doesn't work, try an arbitration program developed by the American Moving and Storage Association and the National Arbitration Forum. It's a less costly alternative to the court system.

- Decide as early as possible which items you'll move so you have time to give away things you don't want.

- Use up food and cleaning supplies. Replace only what is necessary.

- Get change of address cards from the post office.

- Make sure you have current appraisals of antiques or other valuable items you'll be moving.

- Call all utility companies in advance so you can have utilities turned on or off as needed. "It is wise to leave the utilities on at your current home through moving day so you have access to phone and other appliances if needed," Perlman points out.

- Get copies of your medical and dental records, including immunization and medication lists.

- Discontinue newspaper delivery and lawn care.

- Transfer bank accounts.

- Arrange for the care and transportation of your pets.

- Gather all items that are not going on the moving van and mark them "DO NOT MOVE."

- Make travel plans and hotel reservations if necessary. "Plan to stay in town the entire day your household is being loaded into the moving van," Perlman says.

- Back up all files on your computer. Insert a blank floppy disk into the drive.

- Disconnect your washer and refrigerator one day before moving to allow time for the water to drain. Also disconnect your dryer.

"Check and double-check all your plans," Perlman says. "Communicate with your moving consultant, driver, and all others who are involved with your move."

For more information, contact Coleman American Moving Services at 800-239-4931.

Renovate rather than relocate

Home sweet home. As you get older, this expression might not apply. Steep stairs, hard-to-reach cabinets, and slippery bathrooms make your home a little less sweet.

Instead of moving, take steps to remain in the home you love. This approach, called aging-in-place, ranges from a few simple changes to major remodeling projects. Here's how to help your home age gracefully.

Consider the cost. First, figure out how much money you can afford to spend on this project. Keep in mind it might make more economical sense to move. Some organizations, like Rebuilding Together, help modify low-income homes.

Find an expert. Consult a Certified Aging-in-Place Specialist (CAPS). These builders or remodelers are qualified to make these types of home improvements. Before deciding on one, get recommendations from friends, check up on the company, and ask for a written estimate.

You can also meet with an occupational therapist or geriatrician for suggestions.

Make some changes. Helpful modifications you can make to your home include the following:

- Install handrails along stairs or add ramps.
- Secure throw and area rugs with double-sided tape.
- Put nonslip surface on steps.
- Replace door knobs with lever handles.
- Enlarge lamp switches.
- Modify windows with easy-to-grip and easy-to-reach handles and locks.

- Adjust kitchen countertop heights.

- Increase access to high cabinets or low storage spaces with adjustable shelving or pull-out units.

- Install bath, shower, and toilet grab bars.

- Get an adjustable-height shower head.

- Elevate toilet with portable seat or pedestal.

- Put nonslip strips in tub or shower.

- Use a side bed rail and chairs with armrests.

- Put lights and adjustable rods and shelves in closets.

- Link a flashing light or sound amplifier to the doorbell if you have vision or hearing problems.

- Move bedroom and bathroom downstairs.

- Install an elevator.

For more information on aging- in-place strategies and programs, contact these organizations.

Contact National Association of Home Builders
1201 15th Street N.W.
Washington, D.C. 20005
800-368-5242
www.nahb.org

Rebuilding Together
1536 16th Street N.W.
Washington, D.C. 20036
800-473-4229
www.rebuildingtogether.org

Give your house a checkup

You go to the dentist twice a year. Those six-month checkups help you save money by detecting problems before they get out of hand.

Give your house the same care you give your teeth. Perform this basic checkup every six months to prevent disasters and save money.

Check emergency equipment. Change the batteries in your smoke and carbon monoxide detectors. Test them to make sure they work.

Help your heating system. Arrange to have your heating and cooling system serviced. Clean or replace the filters. Also clean the vents and make sure they're not blocked by furniture or drapes.

Behold your basement. Inspect your basement floor and walls for cracks and dampness. Make any necessary repairs. Clean your dehumidifier.

Handle your hot water heater. Drain your water heater to get rid of any sediment. Look for leaks and corrosion. If necessary, replace your water heater with a more energy-efficient model.

Reassess your roof. Repair or replace warped or unsound shingles or tiles. Check the area around skylights, vents, or chimneys. Seal any cracks where water might get in. Call a roofing specialist if you find major damage.

Guard your gutters. Unclog and clean your gutters and drain pipes. Repair them if necessary. Make sure to aim runoff away from your house.

Watch windows and doors. Clean the outsides of windows and lubricate door hinges and locks. Seal any cracks that could cause drafts.

Scrutinize your siding. Examine your siding for cracks, holes, and decay. Also look for signs of insect damage. Fix any problems.

You'll also want to check for leaky faucets, toilets, and pipes. Don't hesitate to call an expert to handle anything you can't do on your own.

Silence noisy neighbors

Loud music, barking dogs, late-night hammering — no wonder Robert Frost thought good fences make good neighbors.

"Noise is just audible litter," says Les Blomberg, Director of the non-profit organization Noise Pollution Clearinghouse. "Just as you wouldn't throw your trash on your neighbor's property, you shouldn't throw your aural litter onto your neighbor's property either."

If your neighbor is being a noise litterbug, here's how to handle the situation.

Read all about it. Know the laws. Go to City Hall, and ask for a copy of the noise ordinance and zoning regulations. If your town doesn't have a noise ordinance, noise issues are probably covered in a nuisance ordinance. If the ordinance is based on decibels, buy a sound level meter and determine if the noise in question is in violation. Document how often the problem occurs.

"The person who is suffering the problem should learn more about the noise problem than anybody else," says Blomberg.

"Once you know more about the problem than your neighbor and the police — and possibly the zoning administrator — then we recommend people start working on it."

Seek solutions. Research the problem. Try to find quieter alternatives or ways to quiet the noise. For example, if a noisy air conditioning unit is the problem, solutions might include enclosing it, moving it away from the property line, or replacing it with a newer, quieter model.

Have a chat. Talk to your neighbor about the problem. Don't do this in the heat of the moment, but only after calming down and arming yourself with information. If necessary, inform your neighbor of the ordinance. Perhaps just being aware of the law might help.

"We find that, often, just approaching your neighbor works," Blomberg says.

Call the cops. This shouldn't be done on a whim. Make sure the law is on your side before calling. Your neighbor may be loud but not breaking any laws. Calling the police will only worsen the situation.

Use a middleman. Try taking your problem to a mediator. Perhaps you and your neighbor can settle your dispute without having to go to court. It's a cheaper alternative — and if it doesn't work, you can always sue.

Take them to court. If all else fails, you can sue your neighbor. But don't jump at this step too quickly.

"Suing them is the absolutely last resort," says Blomberg. "It's costly, doesn't guarantee results, and so it should be saved for the end."

In the meantime, learn about the laws, look into solutions, and try to work things out with your neighbor in a peaceful fashion.

"After you solve this problem, you still have to live with the person next to you," Blomberg says. "It does you absolutely no good if every time you see him or her, your blood pressure goes up."

Contact Noise Pollution
         Clearinghouse
         P.O. Box 1137
         Montpelier, VT 05601-1137
         888-200-8332
         www.nonoise.org

Keep burglars at bay

During these uncertain times, you often hear about Homeland Security. But don't forget about your own home security.

Burglars might be eyeing your house right now. Take these simple steps to protect your home.

Install a security system. Alarms work. Not only do they help prevent break-ins, they help limit loss in case a break-in does occur. That's because once an alarm goes off, even the greediest of thieves will cut his crime spree short and run for it. An added benefit of a security system is lower home insurance premiums.

Then again, there are some downsides to security systems. For one, they can be costly. Besides installation fees, you'll probably have to pay a monthly monitoring fee.

There's also the hassle of remembering to set it when you leave and disarm it when you return. Not to mention the risk of setting off false alarms. Too many of those might mean a fine for you — or a less urgent response. You've heard of the boy who cried wolf, haven't you?

Even if you don't have a security system, it's a good idea to post a sign announcing you do. It might be enough to deter a burglar.

Try tricks from experts. Here's how to burglar proof your home without an alarm. Just follow this advice from the American Association of Retired Persons (AARP).

- Put deadbolt locks on all your doors. Door chains break too easily.
- Lock double-hung windows with key locks or pins.
- Use dowels, a broomstick, or locks to keep a sliding glass door from moving on its track.
- Give a spare key to a trusted neighbor instead of hiding it somewhere outside your home.
- Re-key the locks when you move into a new home.
- Install outside lights and leave them on at night.

- Trim any bushes or trees that would allow someone to creep close to your house without being seen — or climb in an upstairs window.

- Leave the TV or radio on so it sounds like someone is home.

- Set timers to turn lights on and off when you're out of town. Or just leave some lights on.

- Leave a car in your driveway or have a friend park there while you're away.

- Join or start a neighborhood watch group.

- Stop your mail and newspaper deliveries while you're on vacation. A pile of papers and mail is a telltale sign of an empty house.

Of course, none of these steps guarantees a burglar won't get in your house — but he'll have to work a lot harder to do it. And, if he liked hard work, he probably wouldn't be a burglar in the first place.

16 super tips for faster cleaning

Cleaning probably doesn't rank high on your list of favorite things. You probably think of it as a necessary evil — and a very time-consuming one. It doesn't have to be.

Don't spend all your free time cleaning. Read these 16 fast, efficient housekeeping tips from speedcleaning guru Jane Lawson. Using the following tips, Lawson is able to clean her four-bedroom, three-bathroom Colonial home in two and one-half hours.

Use two hands. This simple idea can cut the time spent on certain tasks — like dusting or wiping — in half. Just make sure to do similar motions with both hands.

Extend your reach. Use a 25-foot extension cord when vacuuming. This lets you vacuum an entire level of your house without stopping to replug.

Stop dirt at the door. Put door mats inside and outside the front door so no one tracks dirt in your home. You won't have to vacuum as often.

Take advantage of appliances. Don't bother scrubbing the exhaust vent covers above your stove. Just put them in the dishwasher every three or four weeks.

Carry items with you. Lawson designed an efficiency belt, which is similar to a carpenter's belt, to hold her cleaning products and supplies.

"When people don't have a basket or something to keep their tools in, they tend to run miles through the house and waste time," Lawson says. "They exercise, but they don't clean."

Clean from top to bottom. Dust and dirt fall as you clean. If you start at the bottom, you'll end up cleaning some areas twice.

Minimize moving things. When you clean, dust, or polish items in a room, move them away from the wall. Then when you vacuum, just push them back as you go. Same with dusting a cluttered shelf. Move everything to the center, clean the sides of the shelf, wipe down each item, return it to its place, then spray and wipe the middle. "I move things only once," Lawson says.

Eliminate distractions. Focus only on cleaning. Don't watch TV, make phone calls, open your mail, pay your bills, water your plants, or anything else.

"People don't realize that distractions steal your time," Lawson says. "I don't even put the music on. People say, 'Oh, music helps me move.' Yes, you move with the beat, you do aerobic exercises — you do not clean. You have to focus."

249

Plan ahead. Find little ways to save time. Lawson stashes about four empty trash bags in the bottom of each wastebasket. When she takes out the full bag, she just reaches down and grabs a replacement.

Go downhill. Move from the hardest job to the easiest. That way, as you run out of energy, your tasks will get easier. This applies not only to rooms, but also to items within rooms. Lawson usually starts with the kitchen because it's the largest, most time-consuming area, then moves to the bathroom. In the kitchen, the stove requires the most scrubbing. So she'll start there.

Note extra projects. Some things, like the chandelier, refrigerator, or oven, don't need to be cleaned every time you clean your house. But when these extra projects need to be done, start with them. Otherwise, they might never get done.

Never backtrack. Go into each room only once, clean, then leave. "I go through my whole entire huge house, and I never set foot back. It's always forward," Lawson says.

Gang up on dirt. When cleaning the bathroom or kitchen, Lawson uses six sponges at a time. "I will take six sponges and clean my surfaces and when all six are soapy or dirty, I go and rinse them and then I do it again," Lawson says. "So I make six fewer trips to the sink than the average person would."

Squirt with care. Use just a small amount of cleaning products. "The less you put on the surface, the less time it will take you to clean it off," Lawson says. It's easier to add more than to wipe up excess cleanser.

Accept no imitations. Do not buy cheap knockoffs of good cleaning products. You may save money, but the product will not work as well. "That means you will have to scrub harder and longer in order to achieve the same results," Lawson says. "That is not worth it to save a dollar on a cleaning product."

Schedule your housecleaning. Finally, put your home on a schedule, and stick to it. Every two weeks is a good rule of thumb. If you wait too long between cleanings, there will be more soap scum in the bathroom, more burned food on the stove, and much more work for you to do.

Low-cost ways to make your house sparkle

It's easy to be overwhelmed by the wide selection of cleaning products available. It's also easy to shell out way too much money for them. Try a different approach. Here are eight cheap household products that clean almost anything.

- Ammonia. For windows and mirrors, it's hard to beat ammonia. Cleaning expert Jane Lawson likes it because it's cheap, and she can control the consistency by diluting it with water. She recommends one part ammonia to four parts water.

  "Also it has no suds," Lawson says of this top-notch cleaner. "When you spray sudsy liquids on the mirror, you have to wipe it clean and thoroughly because all these little sudsy spots remain, and it will look foggy. Ammonia, with no suds, does not leave that. It evaporates and it's gone like it never happened."

- Baking soda. Another favorite of Lawson's, baking soda works wonders in the kitchen and bathroom. "It's very gentle. It cleans all the surfaces very gently. There's hardly any risk of damaging the surfaces," she says.

- Vinegar. Use this for copper pots, bathtub film, windows, grout stains, and mildew.

- Bleach. Besides whitening clothes, bleach wipes out mildew in the bathtub. It also makes bathrooms and countertops sparkle. Be careful not to mix it with ammonia. The combination can be deadly.

- Liquid dish detergent. This not only cleans your dishes, it can help remove carpet stains and clean bathroom tile.

- Rubbing alcohol. Try rubbing alcohol for countertops, streak-free windows and mirrors, and chrome bathroom fixtures.

- Club soda. Spilled something on your carpet? Club soda should be your first option for stain removal. It also cleans vinyl floors, countertops, and stainless steel sinks.

- Lemon juice. This sour liquid does sweet work on stains and odors. Perfect for wooden cutting boards, mildewed shower curtains, rust stains, and mineral deposits.

In addition to these low-cost household products, you can try these money-saving tips.

Snare free samples. Keep your eye open for free samples. Even if you decide not to buy the product, you'll save some of your own supplies.

Trade riches for rags. Instead of spending money on cleaning rags, use old clothes or dish towels.

Buy in bulk. You may save by buying large containers of cleaning products. Fill your own spray bottles and dilute for long-lasting cleaning power.

Lawson, however, does not recommend this last plan. "If you buy in bulk, even if you save a little money by doing so, you're going to buy years and years worth of supplies. It's incredible how long these things last," she says.

By following her strategy of using only a small amount of cleanser for each job, you'll find even small bottles are enough. "If you are two-thirds through with the bottle, you still have plenty of time to start looking for sales or coupons, and you'll save a nickel. But, really, in the long run, it doesn't even save you that much. It's not worth it to buy ahead of time."

Control clutter the easy way

Just when you thought it was safe to go back in your house — the clutter monster strikes again. Like the Blob or some other movie monster, clutter slowly creeps from room to room until it takes over.

Don't panic. Cleaning consultant Jane Lawson has some surefire solutions for getting your clutter problem under control.

Stick to essentials. Why are our homes so cluttered? "There is only one simple answer to that — we bring home a lot more than we take out," Lawson says. The solution is equally simple. Buy only what you need. Be disciplined. Don't fall for sales or cave in to impulse purchases.

Rethink gifts. Instead of giving — and receiving — space-hogging gifts for every holiday, try something new. Coupons for services, gift certificates to restaurants, gym memberships, or weekend getaways make wonderful gifts. And they don't take up any space.

"My sister and I exchange that type of gift for our wedding anniversaries," Lawson says. "She takes my kids for a weekend and I go away, and I take her kids. There is no money involved."

Follow the "one in, one out" rule. This rule is simple — whenever you bring something into your home, something else has to leave.

"If you bought a suit, an old suit has to go. If you bought a new toaster, the old toaster has to go," Lawson says. "Many people put them downstairs just in case. In case what? When there is no good answer for that question, then get rid of it."

Box it up. You may have bought some fancy plastic bins to store your extra stuff while you sort out your clutter. The problem is these pretty bins often become a permanent part of your house.

"I suggest cardboard boxes instead," Lawson says. "First of all, they're not attractive looking and, secondly, when you empty one, you're more likely to part with it."

Stop stockpiling. The sale sounds so tempting. Why not stock up on shampoo, or pasta, or cans of tuna? Because, in saving a little money, you'll fill up your cupboards, perhaps for years. "That takes up too much space — and don't you think there will be another sale during this time?" Lawson asks.

Lawson also offers the following tips to prevent clutter from getting out of hand.

- If you don't use an item for two years, get rid of it.
- Stay away from yard sales, flea markets, and gift shops.
- Be generous. Learn to give things away.
- Display only items that are worthy. Keep a few items of sentimental value out of sight. Donate the rest.
- Always put things away in the same place.
- Keep mail and papers in a bin. When it starts to fill up, go through it and dispose of every paper one way or another.
- When you start a project, don't start another one until the first one is completed.
- When the new edition of a catalog or magazine arrives, toss the old one in the recycling bin. If you haven't finished reading it yet, let the subscription run out.

Slash your water bill

Do you spend too much money on water? Well, do something about it. By making small, simple changes, you can drastically reduce your water usage and save money.

It's easy. Spend $5 at the hardware store and cut your water use by thousands of gallons a year. Just buy a low-flow faucet aerator. This helpful device uses less water while providing more water pressure.

The Alliance to Save Energy suggests these seven other straightforward, easy steps that will whittle your water bill away.

- Fix leaks. A leaky toilet can waste up to 52,800 gallons a year. Deal with dripping or leaky faucets and check for leaks in pipes, hoses, and couplings.

- Sweep the garage, driveway, and sidewalk instead of hosing them down.

- Recycle water. Connect gutter downspouts to rain barrels or direct them to trees and plants.

- Adjust your sprinklers so they water only your lawn and plants — not sidewalks or passersby.

- Use a hose with a shut-off nozzle while you water plants or wash your car. Better yet, use a bucket of water and a sponge to wash the car.

- Take short showers instead of baths. Use a low-flow showerhead to save up to five gallons a minute.

- Wash full loads of clothes and dishes. Otherwise, you waste water and energy. Wash clothes in cold water for added savings.

> Contact The Alliance to Save Energy
> 1200 18th Street N.W.
> Suite 900
> Washington, D.C. 20036
> 202-857-0666
> www.ase.org

Cooking made easy

Learn to cook like a pro

Pursue your passion for cooking — take classes at a local cooking school. Whether you want to cut carrots like a TV chef, or whip up five-course meals for your family, there's a class out there for you.

Louise Hasson, Director of Bon Vivant School of Cooking in Seattle, offers these suggestions for choosing the best class.

Evaluate your skills. "People are plunged into this fine gourmet realm because it sounds delicious and wonderful, but maybe their skills are not ready for that yet," Hasson explains.

If you're a beginner, start with the basics. Hasson recommends you take a basic knife skills class and buy a set of comfortable knives before moving on to more complex menus. If you're an advanced cook, find a course that's more appropriate for you.

Ask the right questions. Classes don't come cheap. Before you sign up, Hasson suggests keeping these things in mind.

- Goals. Find out what the goals of the class are and what you can expect to gain from taking the class.

- Class size. It's important to know how many students will be in the class. If the class is crowded, you might not get the attention you need.

- Equipment. Ask what equipment you should bring to class. "Cooking schools may ask you to bring an apron, a knife, and a cutting board," says Hasson. But they usually provide a workstation and the food items you will cook with.

- References. Word of mouth is the best way to ensure your skills and personality match up with the class and instructor you eventually choose.

Check out the menu. Alice Thompson, Communications Manager at The Institute of Culinary Education in New York City offers this advice. "Find out the menu beforehand to make sure you are comfortable with it and it's something that's going to excite you," she suggests. There's no sense discovering the French techniques class you just signed up for prepares seafood you're allergic to.

Choose seeing or doing. "Decide whether you want a hands-on cooking class where you actually make the food," Thompson says, "or a demonstration class where somebody stands up in front of the class and makes the food and talks about it."

Each has its advantage. A hands-on experience will give you confidence to try that dish again, but you may only learn to create one part of the menu. In a demonstration class, you watch the whole menu being prepared, from start to finish.

Take more than one. To really master a technique, Hasson recommends taking a series of courses. Most are offered one night a week for several weeks. A little precaution here can also save you lots of time and money later. Start by taking one class from the instructor before signing up for a series. "It will tell you whether that instructor's style is going to work for you," she suggests.

Scale down for an efficient kitchen

Kitchen supply stores sell every gadget under the sun. If you buy them all, you'll find your kitchen so cluttered you won't have any place to work.

Alton Brown, a reformed packrat and author of *Alton Brown's Gear for Your Kitchen*, suggests you pare down to the basics. Here are his recommendations for outfitting the perfect kitchen.

Isolate the useless. First, clear out a drawer and a cabinet in your kitchen. Over the next 60 days, put every kitchen tool you use into that cabinet or drawer. By the end of two months, you should have a relatively accurate idea of what is absolutely necessary in your kitchen.

Clear out clutter. Sort what's left. Label seasonal or rarely used items with the date and return them to your cabinet. Store heirlooms you don't use — but can't part with — in another room or give them to a family member. Get rid of what remains. If you don't use your dated tools within the next six months, consider disposing of them as well.

Decide by design. Now look at the tools you kept. Do they do their jobs well? Do they fit your cooking style? If your vegetable peeler doesn't fit comfortably in your hand, replace it. If the lid on your blender leaks, buy a new seal, or invest in a new blender.

Do your homework. Before you buy an appliance, do some research. Brown suggests consulting *Consumer Reports* and *Cook's Illustrated*. They don't accept advertising so their reviews are unbiased. You might find out your favorite brand ranks low on product ratings, or a cheaper brand makes a comparable or more versatile tool.

Spend wisely. Calculate how long and how often you intend to use that tool. Knives may seem like a minor purchase, but since you use them every day, it's worth buying the best. A fondue pot, on the other hand, may have limited use over your lifetime, so spend less on it.

Win with "multitaskers." Before you buy a new tool, ask yourself if another gadget you already own can do the same job. A good vegetable peeler, for instance, can double as a cheese cutter, potato slicer, and chocolate-curl maker.

Stick to singles. Don't buy sets of tools unless you fully intend to use every member of the group. You will probably save money, and certainly space, buying only the piece you really need.

Keep cleanliness in mind. Make sure a tool can be properly cleaned before you invest in it. Some electric appliances are hard to take apart so you can clean the blades. Other tools have nooks and crannies that can harbor bacteria.

Top 12 tools every kitchen needs

If you're scaling down to the barest essentials, here are some tools you should definitely keep.

- an 8- to 10-inch chef's knife
- separate sets of measuring tools for wet and dry ingredients
- heat- and stain-resistant rubber spatulas
- spring-loaded tongs of various sizes
- an ovenproof thermometer
- a countertop mixer or hand mixer
- a blender with glass carafe
- a food processor
- a toaster or toaster oven
- a 10- or 12-inch stainless steel sauté pan with lid
- a 2- to 3-quart saucepan with lid
- an 8- to 12-quart stockpot with lid

The perfect kitchen only holds essential, well-made tools that excel at their task and don't take up excess room. Stocked with the right tools, your kitchen becomes a fun place to spend your precious time. Just remember, no matter how cool your tools, they won't work well without a competent cook.

Put your microwave to work

A microwave is a waste of space if you only use it to reheat leftovers. Maryann Zepp, author of *Quick Home Cooked Meals: Letting Your Microwave Work for You (in 30 Minutes or Less)*, enthusiastically recommends cooking entire meals in your microwave. It's faster and more energy efficient. And because foods cook faster, they retain more vitamins and minerals.

Here are some of her tips for making the most of your microwave.

Test before you cook. To see if a dish is microwave safe, put it in your microwave beside a glass measure containing a half-cup of water. Cook it on high for a minute. Be careful when you remove the dish. If it's hot, don't use it in your microwave.

Give it a rest. In microwave cooking, heat moves from the outside in. Let your food stand after cooking to give the heat time to reach the center of the dish. You can also stir it halfway to distribute the heat evenly.

Ring light with heavy. The denser your item, the longer it will take to heat all the way through. Arrange heavier items on the outside. If you cook chicken legs, for example, point the bony ends toward the center of the plate and the meaty ends out. The same goes for cauliflower and broccoli — ring the lighter broccoli with the denser cauliflower.

Don't throw out your kettle. Water is very dense, so food cooked in water won't cook faster in a microwave. In fact, you might be better off heating water on the stove, since microwaves tend to overheat liquids.

Pick paper or plastic. Cover your dishes so they don't splatter. Use paper towels or napkins to cover foods you want to cook with dry heat, since it allows steam to escape. Use plastic wrap or glass lids to steam foods.

Keep experimenting. With experimentation, you can adapt a stovetop recipe to the microwave. Start by dividing the cooking time by four. Then gradually increase it until the dish is done. Microwave recipes usually need less liquid than stovetop recipes, so compare your recipe to a similar microwave recipe to gauge approximately how much liquid to cut.

Forget the duds. An egg in its shell will explode, a soufflé won't rise, and potato chips will be limp instead of crisp if you "nuke" them. If you're cooking more than six servings at a time, you won't save time or energy using a microwave. To eliminate frustration, learn the limits of your microwave, and let your conventional stove or oven do what it does best.

Sharp tips for quality knives

When it comes to knives, dull is dangerous. Sharp knives are safer and much easier to use. Chef Rachel Keller, a Professor of Culinary Arts at the Art Institute of Atlanta, recommends investing in good-quality kitchen knives that will last a lifetime.

Start with the basics. You don't need a drawer full. Here are Keller's essentials:

- an 8- to 10-inch chef's knife
- a paring knife
- a bread knife or serrated-edge knife
- a sharpening steel

Try it out. When you shop, experiment with the knife on a cutting board. Mimic the motions you would use at home and pay attention to these things:

- Weight. "You usually want a heavier knife," says Keller, "preferably one that is one solid piece, like a drop-forged knife." Be careful it's not so heavy it hurts your wrist.

- Comfort. The perfect knife should fit snugly in your hand and feel balanced when you cut.

- Support. The best blade runs the full length of the knife — or "full tang." The handle is usually attached with visible rivets. Some cast plastic handles cover the tell-tale silver slice, but it will state in the product specifications that the knife is full tang.

- Process. Forged knives are hammered like Samurai swords and will hold their edge for life. Stamped knives are cut from a flat sheet of metal and aren't as reliable. If the blade ends in a thick bulge of steel before it joins the handle, it's probably forged.

Make it last. A good knife will probably cost around $100, but it will last indefinitely with proper care. Here are easy ways to prolong its life.

- Sharpen it after every use. Keller recommends holding the sharpening steel at arm's length and balancing its tip on a cutting board. With your other hand, run the knife down the steel at a 20-degree angle from hilt, or handle, to tip. "You don't need a lot of pressure," she says. "Focus on maintaining your angle more than pushing the knife into the steel." Always sharpen both sides of the knife to keep the blade straight.

- Wash your knife under warm water as soon as you're finished using it. Never throw it in the dishwasher. "The extremes of temperature affect the sharpness of the blade," Keller says. "The metal will expand and contract, which over time is very bad for the knife."

- Dry it carefully and store it in a knife block. "Don't throw it in a cutlery drawer, and do not drop it," Keller warns. Both will damage the edge.

- Use it only for cutting food. "Don't use it to hack on bones because that will ruin it," Keller says.

Practice good posture. This will protect your hands as well as your knives. "Always stand with your legs shoulder-width apart. You should not lean into the table," Keller says. "Have a good, sturdy, balanced position when you're at the cutting board. That way, your legs support you, and your arms don't have to compensate for any of the weight."

Shop for freshness at farmers' markets

Tasty fresh fruits and vegetables, beautiful cut flowers, and golden sweet honey are just a few of the treasures you'll find at farmers' markets around the country. So skip your supermarket and opt for the freshness, variety, and vitality of the local farmers' market.

"When you buy produce at a major supermarket, you don't know where it came from," says Tommy Irvin, Commissioner of Agriculture for the state of Georgia. You should feel good knowing you bought your fruits and vegetables from the person who grew them and, in some cases, on the same day they were harvested.

Come prepared for the bounty you will find with these simple shopping tips.

- Start early. If you're looking for something unusual, or you want the best quality, get to the market as soon as the sellers do.

- Carry cash in small denominations.

- Bring your own bags or baskets. Local farmers may not have their own supply.

- Don't take a list. Buy what's in season and build your menu around that.

- Sample produce at all the stalls before you buy. Walk around and compare prices and quality. This works especially well if you arrive early and aren't worried about missing your chance to buy rare or high-demand produce.

- Always ask where the produce was grown. Some may come from out of state.

- Taste before you buy. Many vendors are happy to let you sample their wares. Offer to pay for the sample if they hesitate.

- Try something new — especially if you have never seen it before. Ask the farmer for preparation tips or recipes.

- If you like great bargains and don't mind if the produce is a little picked over, wait until the end of the day to buy. Many farmers are anxious to unload their produce at discounted rates so they don't have to haul it back home.

- Only buy what you can realistically process in a day or two — otherwise you're throwing money to the wind.

- Drive straight home and head for the kitchen. Rinse, blanch, and freeze — or eat your bounty while it's fresh.

Seniors at least 60 years old living on a low income may qualify for free fresh produce. Eligible participants receive coupons that can be exchanged for locally grown fruits, vegetables, and herbs at farmers' markets, roadside stands, and community-supported agricultural programs. For more information, contact:

USDA Food and Nutrition Service
3101 Park Center Drive — Room 926
Alexandria, VA 23302
703-305-2281

Find a farmer you like and stick with him. Often sellers keep the best produce for their regular customers. Or they may give you a free piece of produce now and then as a gesture of good faith. Invest in them, and you will gain the best of what farmers' markets have to offer — a personal relationship with the person who grows your food.

Steer clear of deadly trans fat

In the battle between butter and margarine, butter is once again on top. That's because margarine is almost entirely made of trans fatty acids. Recent research shows this man-made fat raises your bad LDL cholesterol and clogs your arteries. Besides heart disease, it also increases your risk for diabetes and, possibly, cancer.

Kim Severson, author of *The Trans Fat Solution: Cooking and Shopping to Eliminate the Deadliest Fat from Your Diet*, has some good suggestions on finding and avoiding this dangerous fat.

Read the label. Check the list of ingredients for partially hydrogenated vegetable oil. Hydrogenation is the process of shooting hydrogen through liquid vegetable oil. This makes it solid at room temperature and increases shelf life. If this ingredient is among the first few on the label, look for a different brand.

Avoid the obvious. Most packaged baked goods, like muffins, doughnuts, cookies, crackers, and cakes, are guaranteed to contain large amounts of trans fats. Brownie mixes, nondairy creamers, whipped dessert toppings, and processed dinners are also obvious targets. Watch out for the unexpected — certain breakfast cereals and bars, microwave popcorn, flour tortillas, processed cheese, and frozen french fries, potpies, and pizzas have hidden trans fats.

Add the numbers. Manufacturers won't have to list how many grams of trans fat are in their products until 2006. Until then, Severson recommends you use simple math to uncover the missing information. The total fat content of one serving is given on the nutritional label. Below it is a breakdown of the saturated and sometimes polyunsaturated and monounsaturated fat. If the breakdown doesn't add up to the total number of fat grams, chances are the missing fats are trans fats.

Cook more often. Because products made with trans fats stay fresher and have a better texture, they're in everything from potato chips to cereals. Learn to prepare as much of your food as possible from fresh ingredients. Shop at whole foods markets. They often have entire lines of trans fat-free products.

Inquire at restaurants. Fast food chains are notorious for using trans fat to fry everything. Upscale restaurants make a bigger effort to use vegetable oils. If a fried entrée catches your interest, ask your waitress to find out what type of oil is used for frying. If it's liquid vegetable oil, you can splurge on the entrée without worrying about trans fats.

But keep this in mind — trans fats aren't the only fats that are bad for you. The U.S. Department of Agriculture recommends you eat less than 20 grams of saturated fat a day on a 2,000 calorie diet. Meat, egg yolks, whole milk, butter, and cheese are high in saturated fat.

Don't just substitute butter for margarine. Find a better way to prepare your food so you don't need either one.

Gardening on a dime

Enjoy a labor-free yard

A low-maintenance yard is the key to simplifying yard work and giving you more time to relax and enjoy the outdoors. It can be yours if you follow these simple guidelines.

Plant with a purpose. Surround your home with hardy, low-maintenance varieties of grasses, flowers, shrubs, and trees. Your choices will depend on the climate, the type of soil, and your tastes.

- Ornamental trees and conifers provide color and shade. When you plant, keep in mind how big they'll grow and the shade they'll provide for whatever grows around them.

- Shrubs provide the next level of landscape variety and allow you to create colorful evergreen borders for every season. Avoid shrubs that demand lots of attention. Some varieties require little or no pruning.

- While perennials are usually the delicate beauties of your yard, plenty of them are tough and self-reliant. Choose those requiring the least amount of care. Don't forget ferns and flowering ground covers.

Use "hard landscaping." When you design your yard with low maintenance, user friendliness, and good looks in mind, don't forget about borders, terraces, paths, patios, and other yard pavements.

"Hard landscaping" refers to these features and the materials used to build them — stone, brick, concrete, railroad ties, pressure-treated lumber, gravel, and mulches. The durability and beauty of these materials make them well worth the investment.

Invest in premium grass. By the time you've done your hard landscaping and planted your gardens, you may not have much room for grass. But whether your lawn is spacious or tiny, you need the right grass if you want a truly low-maintenance yard.

Grass seed is one item where the saying "You get what you pay for" applies. Since you're laying the right foundation for a low-maintenance lawn, be wise and purchase a premium blend of drought-, disease-, and pest-resistant seed.

And take the time to prepare your soil properly. By putting in the effort early on, you'll enjoy the benefits of a labor-free yard for years to come.

De-weed your lawn on a dime

Face it. Weeds aren't going away. So how will you tackle problem weeds in your yard? The key to chemical-free weed control is to grow a lawn so healthy and hardy that weeds won't have a chance to multiply. They will just have to look elsewhere for weed-friendly turf.

That's the advice of environmental gardener Larry Sombke, who provides tips on achieving that goal in his book *Beautiful Easy Lawns and Landscapes*.

Sombke's approach to weed freedom includes:

• aerating the soil

• using natural organic fertilizers

- growing the new disease- and drought-resistant grasses
- watering seldom and slowly

He also recommends allowing the grass to grow tall. When you mow, raise your mower's cutting height to 3 inches. At that height, the grass will create a shade that sun-loving crabgrass (America's most common weed) can't bear. Crabgrass can't germinate and grow without plenty of direct sunlight.

But first, go after the weeds that are already there.

Dig 'em. Some yard keepers love dandelions, but if they're just "weeds" to you, your best bet is to dig them out. This is also the way to get rid of the unsightly plantain. If you don't have a weeding tool, simply use the claw end of a hammer. Your goal is to remove the weed, root and all, like you would a nail from a board. Be persistent, and you'll eventually get it all out.

Mulch 'em. Using the mulch feature on your lawn mower is a potent way to strengthen your lawn and fight weeds. In garden spaces, use a two- to four-inch layer of mulch material — like last fall's leaves, pine straw, hay, pine bark, or even newspaper — to keep weeds from germinating there.

Pull 'em. Use a recent rain as an excuse to get out in the yard and pull up weeds by hand. When the soil is moist, weeds like wild onions come up bulb and all without much tugging or strain.

Make 'em wince. Weeds will wilt — and die — when you pour a cheap solution of white vinegar and salt on them. This is an especially effective remedy for weeds growing in driveway and sidewalk cracks.

Scald 'em. The next time your teakettle whistles, think of the weeds among the flagstones on your walking path. Pour that boiling water on them, and they will disappear.

Squirt 'em. If you have the itch to pull the trigger and shoot those weeds, look for safe, natural herbicides at your area garden center.

When your lawn sports more weeds and bald patches than grass, it may be easier just to start from scratch and reseed the whole yard. If that's the case, aim for weed-freedom by following these tips and cultivating a lawn that will be just plain inhospitable to weeds.

Find the right landscape pro

"If your heart yearns for a landscape above the ordinary, you need a landscape design prepared by a professional," says radio talk-show host and newspaper columnist Walter Reeves.

A 29-year veteran with the University of Georgia Cooperative Extension Service, Reeves has some great advice for finding the right professionals to help create your dream yard.

Decide what you need. "First, decide what your yard needs and what you can afford," recommends Reeves. If you just need guidance or help with routine yard tasks, you may get it free from your county's cooperative extension service. If not, a landscape designer may fit the bill. He may be self-taught or college trained, but he's skilled at matching your dreams with the present realities of your yard.

On the other hand, if you have serious drainage problems, challenging terrain, or plans that include things like berms, gazebos, or ponds, you'll need the services of a landscape architect. They are the big guns of the landscaping realm — college graduates who are trained, licensed professionals. "They know all about landscape planning, drainage, and creating gardens," says Reeves.

Know where to search. Finding professional help is easy. Here are a few places to look.

- Flower shows and garden tours. There is no better place to find the best landscape pros in your region and see examples of their work.

- Garden centers. Local nurseries often have their own landscaping services. Plus, they often offer discounts on plants and planting materials if you contract with them.

- Professional organizations. Get referrals from the American Society of Landscape Architects *(www.asla.org)*, the Association of Professional Landscape Designers *(www.apld.com)*, the Associated Landscape Contractors of America *(www.alca.org)*, the Professional Lawn Care Association of America *(www.plcaa.org)*, or any local landscape association.

- Plant societies. Chances are you'll find skilled landscapers among the members of local plant societies and garden clubs. Attend one of their meetings, and let them know what your needs are.

With so many available resources, you're sure to find expert help that will fit your budget.

Choose the right company. "Landscape companies often focus on one or two specialties. Before you select a company, decide what work you want done — landscape maintenance, drainage problems, yard planning, or planting," Reeves says. Then find a company with a reputation for honesty and quality work in that field.

While you're shopping, look for these credentials.

- Licenses. Your company of choice should have a business license issued by the city or town where it's located and a state pesticide contractor's license, which is proof that it has liability insurance.

- Memberships. Organizations like those listed above promote high standards of knowledge and customer service among their member companies. But some reputable land-scape companies are not "joiners."

This need not disqualify them from your search. If a company is unaffiliated, check it out through the Better Business Bureau and previous customers.

Demand a written contract. Verbal agreements invite misunderstandings. A good written contract is a must. Make sure it covers every detail of the job.

Finally, don't forget to take pictures of the areas you want fixed before anyone starts working. Then, later, photograph your finished project. If your landscape pro lives up to your expectations, you can show everyone what a great job he did.

4 Bs to a more beautiful yard

One of the biggest favors you can do for your lawn and garden is to invite bees, birds, butterflies — and, oh yes, bats — to congregate there. Each of these critters is both beautiful (in its own way) and beneficial. Bats and birds exterminate. Butterflies and bees pollinate. Birds and butterflies decorate.

Invite insect lovers. Some insects you want in your yard and some you just don't. So invite two guests that will be happy to help you get rid of the pesky ones — one by day, another by night.

Songbirds and hummingbirds consider insects a delicacy. Four surefire ways to make your yard an inviting place for them are:

- eliminate chemical pesticides
- provide them with refuge
- grow plants they can eat
- give them water and lodging

Don't be concerned that providing your winged guests with seed — either at feeders or with flowering plants — will make them any less eager to eat insects. They love variety. They also love fresh, preferably running, water. Just make sure your yard has some hedges or clusters of trees, shrubs, and flowers of varying heights for "refuge." That way it will be a welcome site for all your bird friends.

You may be surprised at the mention of bats, but a bat can eat 1,000 mosquitoes in a single night. No, they won't nest in your hair or attack when the moon is full. They just love to eat the flying insect pests that populate your neighborhood.

If they're not already living in your rafters, you can build or buy bat houses to mount beneath your eves. For more information about bat houses, visit the Organization for Bat Conservation at *www.batconservation.org*.

Seek out pollinators. You may not be enthusiastic enough about honeybees to provide hives where they can colonize. But they're a boon to any yard because they give your garden more bloom.

It's the same with butterflies, which have the added benefit of being especially beautiful. While bees go for anything that flowers, your goal with butterflies is to lure them with flowers they use for food — like butterfly bushes, morning glories, and phlox. Be sure to plant varieties that will provide blooms throughout the growing season.

Few pleasures are as simple and easy to enjoy as your yard and garden. Enhance your pleasure with songbirds, hummingbirds, bees, and butterflies by making yours a place they will love to visit.

Banish yard pests naturally

Wouldn't it be great to have a pest-free yard without worrying about how it affects the environment? Well, you can, says David Mitchell, founder and director of Natural Insect Control (NIC) in Ontario, Canada. The solution is natural control.

"We want birds and pets and other beneficial visitors in our yards and gardens," he says. "But when we use chemical poisons, its first effect is to kill the pests, but later it also poisons the beneficial and invited animals and people."

Mitchell recommends a three-pronged approach to eliminating yard pests naturally and safely.

Invite predators. When Mitchell speaks of "predators," he's referring to creatures you introduce or invite to your yard to eat your yard pests — like purple martins, lady bugs, toads, and praying mantises. Some predators will just show up if you make your yard inviting to them. Others you can purchase and release in your yard and garden.

"Take advantage of these natural 'predators' to help combat destructive mites, caterpillars, aphids, and other harmful plant bugs," says Mitchell.

Bring on parasites. Did you ever think you'd hear someone recommend parasites? Well, Mitchell does. He says they're an essential part of your pest-control team.

These recommended parasites are "beneficial nematodes" — natural microscopic worms that infest and kill more than 250 different pest larva. Mitchell says 90 percent of all insects spend at least part of their life cycle in the soil, so they're easy prey for parasites you spray on your yard.

"Mix them with water, and spray them on the area you want to treat," he says. "I recommend twice per season. The nematodes will infest and kill their prey within 24 to 48 hours, continuing to reproduce. The young will seek out new hosts to infest."

Beneficial nematodes are available from NIC or through other garden suppliers.

Plant traps. The third member of the pest control team is traps, including barriers. Many effective traps can catch flies, apple maggots, fruit flies, gypsy moths, elm bark beetles, fleas, Japanese beetles, earwigs, yellow jackets, and more.

One example is a slug and snail trap. You simply bury a container to its top in the soil, and fill it with something that will lure them — like beer — to their death. If you don't want to make one yourself, you can buy a trap at any garden center.

Mitchell also recommends barriers, like tree bands. "They stop caterpillars, cankerworms, gypsy moths, and other tussock moths from climbing your trees and laying their eggs. By creating a barrier, you break their breeding cycle."

Other barriers include ground red pepper or cloves sprinkled on the ground. These kill or ward off a wide range of crawling critters — like ants, cockroaches, spiders, and fleas. Either they will die trying to cross the barrier, or they'll turn back and go no further.

"In a sense," concludes Mitchell, "every predator, every parasite, and every trap you have in your yard is a natural barrier to the pests that threaten your yard. And they do their job without jeopardizing the environment."

Build your own wasp trap

If you're a hummingbird lover, you know your beloved birds can be chased away by wasps and yellow jackets swarming around their feeders. Here's a simple trap from the Hummer/Bird Study Group of Clay, Alabama, that should rid your yard of these pests once and for all.

Remove the label from an empty 2- or 3-liter soda bottle. Cut four penny-size holes spaced evenly around the bottle about a third of the way up from the bottom. Using a needle and thread, sew a string through two cotton balls. Leave yourself an extra 5 inches of thread so you can dangle the cotton balls down from the cap inside the bottle.

Once you've tied the thread around the bottle's neck, soak the cotton balls with wasp and hornet spray. Then use a stick to push them through the mouth of the bottle and down the neck so they're hanging about three inches from the top. Screwing the cap on the bottle over your knot will secure the thread.

Now fill the bottle with about two cups of hummingbird nectar — a one-to-four mixture of sugar and water. Drop a small piece of apple or pear and a small piece of raw meat into your solution.

Place your traps near your hummingbird feeders to keep wasps and yellow jackets from harassing you and your invited hummingbird guests.

Grow garlic for fun or profit

If you like to garden, garlic is a healthy and beneficial addition to your flowers and vegetables. Not only will it help keep aphids and deer away from your plants, if you're really ambitious, you can even make money growing this popular disease-attacking herb.

You can choose from several hundred varieties, but one of the best is elephant garlic. It may not be the prettiest, but it will be the largest. "One bulb can weigh a pound or more, and a single clove can weigh up to 4 ounces," says garlic grower Loyd Hubbard, president of the Gnos Garlic Company.

Follow these five steps to grow the smoothest-tasting garlic anywhere.

Prepare your soil. You can grow elephant garlic on any amount of land. A 10x10-foot plot will support about 120 bulbs. Ideally, you want an area with a minimum of six hours of sun and deep, fertile, well-drained soil. If the soil is primarily clay, use a raised bed. Fill it with a mix of good soil and rich manure.

Sow at the right time. Plant the seed cloves in September or October when the fall rains start. Place them in mounds, pointy ends up, 8 to 9 inches apart and 3 to 4 inches deep, with rows 11 to 12 inches apart.

Shower with water. "Elephant garlic needs a lot of moisture at first, whether it's irrigation or natural moisture," Hubbard says. "Drainage is also very important, so an elevated piece of land is ideal." Keep the weeds under control, and add 5 to 6 inches of straw mulch to help retain moisture during dry, cold periods. Cut off the flowering stems before they bloom to redirect the plant's energy into the cloves, giving you larger bulbs.

Harvest bulbs quickly. Don't let the plants get overly mature. Harvest them when most of the leaves turn yellow and fall over. Don't pull the bulb out — dig them up. Get the harvested garlic out of the sun quickly, cut off the tops, and dry them in an airy, shady location for at least a month. After your garlic is dry, keep it fresh by storing it in a well-ventilated room between 60 and 70 degrees Fahrenheit with less than 70 percent humidity.

Think about next year. Unlike other garlic, you'll need to keep part of your harvest as seed stock for next year's crop. Some elephant garlic growers use their entire first year's crop to grow an even larger crop the next year.

If you'd like to earn a little extra money, elephant garlic is the ideal crop. "You can sell your bulbs to gourmet restaurants or from a roadside stand and charge anywhere from $5 to $9 a pound," Hubbard says. "To make a good profit, though, you'll need to plant at least an acre. One acre can produce as much as 6,000 pounds of elephant garlic."

So whether your goal is to make a little money or simply add this healthy herb to your dinner table, take the plunge into the world of elephant garlic. As Hubbard says, "Suddenly, it's chic to reek!"

> All the information you'll ever need to grow or cook elephant garlic is in the *World's Largest Elephant Garlic Book* from Gnos Garlic Company. It features 101 recipes from some of the country's best chefs. Contact them at:
>
> Gnos Garlic Company
> P.O. Box 640
> North Plains, OR 97133
> 800-661-1799
> 503-244-0995 (fax)
> *www.elephantgarlic.com*

How to grow great tomatoes

Ever had a neighbor who supplied the whole neighborhood with homegrown tomatoes? Well, here's your chance to create your own bountiful harvest by following these simple tips.

Keep them cozy. Tomatoes love warm weather, so beware of frost. Warm spring days can be followed by cool nights. Even temperatures below 55 are a strain on tender, young plants.

Pick your favorites. You have lots of choices when it comes to tomatoes — color, size, shape, flavor. Ask other gardeners or your extension service which varieties do best in your locale.

Know when they'll grow. Choose varieties that will produce when you want them to — early, late, or mid-season. Also, learn whether the plants you're buying are "determinate" or "indeterminate."

Determinate plants grow to a certain height, then flower and yield their fruit within a short time. You'll like these if you're growing them for canning. Indeterminate varieties grow, flower, and produce throughout the growing season.

Plant smart. Buy plants with four to six leaves and straight, sturdy, pencil-thick stems. Smart gardeners pinch off all but the top two leaves and bury everything but the tip top of the plant. The entire buried stem will produce roots — vital for thirsty tomatoes.

Planting time is when you should stake or cage your plants. As they grow, suspend the stems to the stake or cage with quick-drying fabric such as pantyhose. Plant staked or caged tomatoes 2 to 3 feet apart. Mulch unstaked plants well to keep the fruit from touching the moist soil. This will prevent your tomatoes from rotting.

Give them some TLC. Once your young plants are established, employ some tricks of the tomato-growers' trade.

- If you stake or cage your plants, prune away all but the main stem and one sucker (branch) near the base. Pruned plants produce larger tomatoes. Also, pinch off the first flowers. This prevents the premature arrival of fruit and produces stronger, heartier plants.

- Tomatoes are especially fond of calcium, which helps prevent blossom-end rot. Try two novel ways of feeding it to your plants. Either lodge a piece of broken wallboard (gypsum board) in the soil near the roots, or mix powdered milk with your plant's water. By serving your plants these calcium-rich supplements, you're sure to have the sweetest, juiciest tomatoes ever.

- Here's a trick to discourage birds from feasting where they shouldn't. Decorate your tomato bushes with red Christmas tree ornaments before the plants start producing. Hungry birds will give them a try, find them unappetizing, and not return when the real thing arrives.

Enjoy the fruits of your labor. At harvest time, pick your tomatoes before they are fully ripe, and let them ripen indoors, sheltered from direct sunlight. This prevents them from splitting and keeps them looking as good as they taste.

Compute like a pro

Buy the perfect computer

If you thought using a computer was complicated, try shopping for one. The options can overwhelm you. Here are some important things to keep in mind during your search.

Know your needs. Why do you want a computer? Knowing the answer to this simple question can save you a lot of hassle — and money.

"Purpose is the most important thing to consider when buying a computer," says Derrick Lee, managing member of Lee's Computer Maintenance in Atlanta.

For example, if you're only going to use your computer for word processing, e-mail, and surfing the Internet, there's no need to spend $1,500 on a state-of-the-art system.

"Many people buy overpowered computers that could run a business and end up playing solitaire, while there are others who buy an underpowered computer and are confused by its inability to perform," Lee says.

"It's smart to buy the best machine your budget will allow while keeping the purposes for the machine at the forefront of your mind."

Do some research. Like a car or large appliance, a computer is a major purchase. Read reviews of products, ask computer-savvy friends and family members for recommendations, and comparison shop.

"Definitely shop around for the best bargain. Many times there are smaller stores that have better prices than the major computer chain stores," says Lee.

Some good magazines to look at include *Consumer Reports*, *PC World*, and *Computer Shopper*.

Tailor it to fit. Get what you really need without spending money for what you don't need. Some stores or manufacturers let you configure your own system. It's a good way to save money on some areas and improve your computer in others.

Give your old computer the reboot

Don't throw away your old computer. Recycle it. There are plenty of people who'd be happy to have it.

You can donate your old computer to schools, nonprofit organizations, and people with disabilities through Share the Technology. For more information, go to *www.sharetechnology.org*.

For an extensive list of recycling and reuse opportunities near you, check out the Consumer Education Initiative at *www.eiae.org*.

Other options include businesses like RE-PC (*www.repc.com*) or Back Thru the Future (*www.backthruthefuture.com*) which buy, sell, and refurbish used computers.

"You can have a computer custom built so it is specially made for your purposes," Lee says. "Often these systems deliver more bang for your buck."

Get more info. Besides a good price, you should also consider the following when shopping for a computer.

- Technical support. If you have problems — and you probably will at some point — you need to know how to get help. Can you get help 24 hours a day? Do the experts respond quickly to your questions? Is there an 800 number you can call? Get all the information in writing.

- Warranty. Aim for a three-year warranty, and never settle for less than a one-year warranty.

- Return policy. Make sure you can return the computer without any hassles or restocking fees. That means you don't pay the store to put the computer back on the shelf.

- Demonstrations. Ask the salesman to demonstrate anything he claims the computer can do. Sometimes salespeople might not know what they're talking about, make promises the computer can't keep, or lie just to clinch the sale.

Printer primer

Shopping for a printer? Don't just look at the price tag. You should also consider the following factors.

- Print quality. This is measured in dots per inch, or dpi. In general, the higher the dpi the better, or clearer, the image.

- Printer speed. If you're going to print a lot of documents, speed might be the most important factor. Just remember, sometimes you have to sacrifice quality for speed.

- Hidden costs. The cheapest printer is not always the best deal in the long run. You might spend much more on expensive ink cartridges or repairs later.

Maintenance made easy

A little preventive maintenance can make a big difference. For instance, a sensible diet and regular exercise keep you healthy. And regular oil changes and tune-ups keep your car running smoothly.

Your computer needs an occasional tune-up, just like your car. Find out what you need to do to keep your computer in tip-top condition.

---

5 easy computer upgrades

Before you buy a new computer, consider upgrading your current machine. Upgrading saves you money and extends the life of your computer.

Here are five ways to improve your computer's performance.

- Add more RAM, or memory, to speed things up.

- Add a second hard drive for more disk space.

- Add a CD-RW drive or DVD drive for more options.

- Replace your sound or video card with better ones.

- Replace your CPU, or processor, with a faster one.

Make sure any computer you buy has plenty of extra ports, drive bays, and expansion slots. It will be easy to upgrade later.

Piece it together. Think of the memory on your hard drive as a book. When your computer is new, your programs and files start on the first page and run in order. All the empty pages at the end of the book represent free memory. Pretty soon you start to add and save files, and your long continuous block of free memory fills up. Then you change and delete files, creating blank pages here and there — scattered chunks of free memory.

Eventually, a new file can't be stored all in one space because you don't have enough empty pages all together. So your computer automatically splits — or fragments — the file. Fragmentation slows down your computer because to access a file, it must go hunting for each piece.

To get your computer back up to speed, you need to defragment, or defrag, your hard drive.

"Defragging your hard drive on a regular basis keeps your programs running smoothly," says Derrick Lee, managing member of Lee's Computer Maintenance in Atlanta.

To do this, run Disk Defragmenter. This program looks at all your files and tries to reorganize them. First it moves files to create larger chunks of free memory, then it reconnects as many fragments as possible. This could take some time — up to a few hours — so plan to do something else while it runs. You'll be surprised how much faster your computer can operate.

Plan to scan. Scan-Disk acts like a computer watchdog. It checks both your files and your hardware to see if there are any glitches or problems. When it finds one, it solves the problem for you.

When the program finds errors, it will open a dialog box asking what you want to do about a particular file. You can ignore the problem, fix it, or delete the file.

Run ScanDisk about once a month. Plan to do it when you can step away from your computer for a while.

Clean it up. Useless files, like temporary Internet records and old updates, can clog up your computer. Disk Cleanup hunts down these files so you can delete them.

With a program called Maintenance Wizard, you can set up an automated schedule for regular cleanups. Pick a date and time when your computer will be on, but not in use.

Also, remember to back up your files and your hard drive just in case your computer crashes.

Speed up your system. Try these tactics if your computer seems sluggish.

- Close all programs you're not using.

- Empty the recycle bin.
- Find and delete unnecessary temporary files.
- Uninstall outdated programs as well as those you no longer use.
- Run Disk Defragmenter at least once a month.
- Add more RAM (Random Access Memory).

Stay on top of these simple maintenance tasks now, and you'll save yourself a hefty repair bill later.

Delete strains and pains

You might think you're perfectly safe sitting at a computer. Think again.

Problems associated with computer use include headaches, fatigue, eyestrain, neck and shoulder discomfort, lower back pain, elbow injuries, and wrist problems such as carpal tunnel syndrome.

That's why it's important to set up and use your computer ergonomically. This simply means your working conditions and your body are not at odds.

Professor Alan Hedge, Director of Cornell University's Human Factors and Ergonomics Laboratory, offers these guidelines for safe computer use.

Choose the right chair. You don't need a fancy, adjustable office chair if you're the only person who uses the computer. Just make sure it's comfortable for you.

"As you sit back in a chair, you need to support the lower back," Hedge says. "If you don't have a cushion, you can use a rolled-up towel if your chair isn't giving you good lower back support."

When sitting, plant your feet firmly on the floor or some other support surface for stability.

Take charge of the keyboard. Your keyboard should be at a comfortable level. If it's too high, you'll type in an awkward position and hunch over your keyboard while you work — two very dangerous postures.

Position your keyboard about 3 or 4 inches above your lap. It should be as level as possible so you can type with your hands in a flat and neutral position. To do this, you might need to use a keyboard tray, which fits beneath a high table, or a keyboard platform, a tray that tilts downward to take the slope out of the keyboard.

Other useful products include document holders and voice recognition software, which lets you dictate rather than type. But watch out for wrist rests.

"A lot of people go out and buy wrist rests and then they actually rest their wrists on them. And that is what you're not supposed to do," Hedge says. "Actually, the products are misnamed. They really should be called palm rests."

Resting your wrist on the wrist rest blocks circulation to your hand, puts pressure on the tendons, and compresses the median nerve. Instead, use the pads to rest your palms when you're not typing.

Move your mouse. Like your keyboard, your mouse should be in the proper position.

"Bring your mouse as close in to the body as you possibly can get it, and make sure it's at a comfortable height as well," Hedge says. "If you're doing a lot of mousing work, make sure you adjust your body to use the mouse, rather than reaching way out to the side or reaching way out in front of you to try and get to the mouse."

If you have trouble using a mouse, you can use a trackball instead. With this device, you roll a ball with the palm of your hand to maneuver around the computer screen.

Monitor your monitor. Once you've positioned your keyboard and mouse, line yourself up with your monitor.

"Ideally, the center of the screen should be in line with the center of the keyboard, which is the H key," Hedge says. "And you should be lined up with that so everything's in a nice straight line."

Sit back in your chair and hold your arm straight out in front of you. Your fingers should just about touch the center of your computer screen.

Ease eyestrain. Follow these tips to protect your eyes while using the computer.

- Use the Zoom features of software programs. They let you increase the size of the fonts so you don't have to lean forward to read your screen.

- Supplement normal room lighting with a good task light. "To see a computer screen effectively, you want to have fairly dim lighting in the room," says Hedge. "But if you're reading from any paper, you want to have pretty bright light on the paper."

- Buy a screen magnifier. Put it over the front of your screen so you can blow up the whole screen at once.

- Invest in a liquid crystal display (LCD) monitor. It's easier on the eyes than the standard cathode ray tube (CRT) because it doesn't flicker.

- Avoid sitting with a window facing you or at your back. The contrast between the window, walls, and computer screen can cause vision problems. You can also close drapes or blinds while computing.

• Work with screen fonts and colors that are easy for you to see. Many programs let you customize things such as the font size of folder headings or file names. "It's always a good idea to make use of those features because it just reduces the amount of work that your eyes have to do," Hedge says.

Take breaks. Work for 20 to 30 minutes, then get away from your computer. Stand up, move around, and look out the window. It will give your muscles a chance to recover and your eyes a chance to rest. You might even want to set an alarm to remind you to take a break.

"One thing that happens is you tend to lose track of time when you're sitting in front of the screen," Hedge says. "Before you know it, an hour or two hours have gone by."

Learn the ropes for less

You're finally ready to jump into the fascinating world of computers. You just need a little guidance.

Luckily, there are several low-cost computer classes available. You might even be able to find free computer classes for seniors. Many cities and computer stores offer free classes on how to use a computer. Here's how to find out about classes in your area.

Study at the library. Many libraries provide free use of online computers. They may even offer free computer training. Give your local branch a call and see what's available.

Stop at the store. Some computer stores, like Gateway, offer classes. So if you are looking to buy a new computer, ask if you can get free training as part of the package. If you already have a computer, you can probably enroll by paying a fee.

Stay in school. Most colleges and universities have continuing education departments that offer low-cost classes. Once you learn more about computers, you might want to graduate to classes in the regular curriculum. Many schools let senior citizens enroll in academic classes at reduced rates or even for free.

Sample a learning center. The not-for-profit organization SeniorNet provides folks over 50 with low-cost computer training in more than 200 learning centers in the United States, Europe, and Japan.

"The only kind of classes that really make any sense are the ones that are hands-on," says Judy Sobel, SeniorNet Program Coordinator for the Marcus Jewish Community Center of Atlanta.

Classes accommodate all types of learners — those who learn best by listening, those who learn best by seeing, and those who learn best by doing.

Other features of the program include:

- Small classes. Classes are limited to 12 students. Each student has his or her own computer.

- Personalized instruction. Each class has an instructor and a few coaches to help. "Our instructors are seniors, they're volunteers, they're extremely knowledgeable, they love teaching, and they love sharing their information," Sobel says.

- Wide selection. Courses are offered in beginning, intermediate, and advanced levels. Classes range from the very basics to in-depth courses on Microsoft Word and Windows XP to specialized classes on digital photography, online genealogy, and eBay.

- Low cost. Everyone must first pay a $40 fee to join SeniorNet. A seven-week course, like the beginning class, costs only $60. The fee includes a textbook with step-by-step instructions so you can review and practice at home.

• Fun. In the beginning class, instructors use games to teach mouse control. "We want to make it fun. We want to take the technological mystique away from it," Sobel says.

Best of all, the program takes seniors' needs into account. "We recognize that for seniors who have never used computers, it's like learning a new language. It's like learning Greek. After two hours, you wouldn't expect to be able to go to Greece and converse with anyone. It's the same thing with computers," Sobel says.

"You have to repeat something at least seven times — at least — before it sticks. We don't repeat the same thing seven times, but we may present it seven different ways so it makes an impact on the person taking the course."

To find a SeniorNet learning center near you, go to *www.seniornet.org* or call 415-495-4990.

Check out other senior centers, recreation departments, and YMCA or YWCA programs, as well. The odds are good they also offer computer lessons that are discounted or even free to seniors.

Besides taking classes, you can learn more about computers using these strategies.

Try a tutor. If you want one-on-one instruction, hiring a personal tutor might be your best bet. Options include local college students, computer-savvy friends or neighbors, or even your own grandchildren. It could be a great chance to bond while you're learning.

Log on and learn. Some Web sites, including *www.seniornet.org* and *www.thirdage.com*, offer free online tutorials. You can expand your computer knowledge from the comfort of your own home.

Keep looking. Pick up a self-help computer book — like FC&A's *Easy Computing for Seniors* — or read computer magazines to find more tips. Once you get up to speed on the Internet, you'll probably find even more tricks and traps online. Remember, when it comes to computers, you can always learn more.

Select super Internet service

The Internet can enrich and improve your life — but first you have to get to it. Here's how to find the service that's best for you.

Phone it in. Dial-up service, the traditional way to connect to the Internet, uses a modem and your phone line. For about $20 a month, you'll get access to the Internet. It's a good deal, especially for beginners. But if you download photographs or music or do a lot of Web surfing, dial-up might be too slow.

Full speed ahead. If dial-up seems too slow, you can opt for faster, more expensive options. Digital Subscriber Line (DSL) and cable — collectively known as "broadband" — cost about $50 a month, but that might be worth it for the added speed. Your Internet connection stays on continuously, and you can still use your telephone while you're online.

One problem with a continuous connection is that you leave your computer open to anyone on the Internet who wants to get into your system and cause mischief. Block them out with a piece of software aptly called a firewall. It will protect your files from tampering.

Pick your poison. Whether you opt for dial-up or broadband, you still need to choose an Internet service provider (ISP). Below are the three types of ISPs. As you'll see, each has its pros and cons.

- Commercial providers like AOL, Microsoft, and Earthlink. These popular sites essentially give you a guided tour of the Internet. But sometimes connection and customer service can be spotty.

- National telecommunication services like AT&T, Bell, or cable. You'll get fast, reliable service, but you might have trouble accessing customer service when you need technical support.

- Local providers. These small outfits boast the best customer service, but they are prone to going out of business. You could lose money if you prepay for service.

Do your homework. Having trouble choosing a provider? Try these tactics.

- Take advantage of free trial offers you get in the mail. Just make sure to disconnect before they start charging you for service.

- Ask around. Your friends and neighbors might have recommendations.

- Read ISP ratings in consumer and computer magazines.

- Check the Yellow Pages or ask your phone company if it offers online service.

- Use your local library to research online. You can usually get free access to the Internet. Log on to these Web sites to research and order your ISP software.

The List of ISPs	www.thelist.com
All Free ISP	www.all-free-isp.com
Find an ISP	www.findanisp.com

Consider these questions. When researching an ISP, you should keep the following questions in mind.

- Is my access limited or unlimited? If you don't use the Internet much, a cheaper service with limited access might make sense. Otherwise, opt for unlimited access.

- How much will it cost, including setup?

- Do you have local access numbers? You don't want to pay long-distance charges every time you log on.

- Do you have a free 24-hour customer support line? What's the phone number? Make sure you can get through outside regular business hours.

- Do you have a trial period? Try the service for a few months before signing a year-long contract.

Protect your privacy online

You have a whole world of information at your fingertips with the Internet. Unfortunately, the whole world can just as easily get information about you.

That makes going online a little scarier — but there is good news. You can "surf the Net," keep in touch with friends, and still protect your personal information from being broadcast all over the Internet. Here's how.

Play it smart with passwords. You need plenty of passwords while computing. Make it harder for computer criminals to guess yours and access your information. Pick passwords at least six characters long. Use a combination of letters and numbers, and mix uppercase and lowercase letters. Don't use any part of your name or any significant numbers, like your birthday or telephone number. Don't use the same password for everything.

Snatch a patch. Check for the latest security patches. They're usually free from the software maker's Web site. They prevent hackers from taking advantage of new security holes in browsers and other software.

Stymie spyware. Spyware, also called stealthware or adware, gathers information about all your computer activities, then sends it back to its home company. The company uses this information to match advertisements to your interests. Spyware hides within a software program. When you download the program, the spyware runs, too.

Read license agreements carefully to see if you will be monitored. Don't install the software if you suspect it includes spyware. You can also get a firewall to block spyware from sending information out of your computer.

Crumble cookies. Cookies are tiny text files that Web sites place on your hard drive to send information back to them. They help personalize your Web pages or match ads to things you like. They can also track where you surf and shop. Set your browser to prompt you every time a site tries to set a cookie. Or just set the browser to reject all cookies.

Erase your browser profile. Your browser probably stores your name and contact information so you can give it out to Web sites easily. Block this information by cleverly altering your profile. Type in a fake name and make all other fields blank.

Be anonymous. Don't register with online people directories, such as Switchboard or Bigfoot. If you're already registered, remove yourself from the list.

Shop safely. It's hard to beat the convenience of online shopping. Just remember to follow these guidelines.

- Stick to familiar companies. Avoid companies that don't have a phone number, street address, or other contact information readily available.

- Check with the Better Business Bureau before ordering if you're not sure about a company.

- Look for a secure server. You can tell if a Web site is secure by the unbroken padlock or key symbol in the browser corner. You might get a Security Notice dialog box that says you are entering a secure page. Or you may see "https" in the address line. Make sure the site uses encryption, or a secret code, to store your information.

- Read the site's privacy policy. Only do business with sites that won't share your personal information with other businesses.

- Don't register with the site if you don't have to. If you choose to register, fill out only "required" fields on the registration form. Never give out your Social Security number. No shopping site should need it.

- Pay with a credit card. This limits your losses to $50 in case of fraud. Get a record of the transaction.

Communicate cautiously. Take the following precautions to help your private e-mails stay private.

- Don't share the password to your e-mail account with anyone. Always sign out when you close your e-mail connection.

- Read and compose messages offline, then go online to send them. Less time online means less danger.

- Save copies of personal e-mails on a floppy disk or CD and store them in a private place. If you leave them on your computer, a hacker may find them.

- Check out your mail program's encryption option. It scrambles messages between your computer and that of the recipient so no one else can read them.

- Never e-mail your Social Security number or credit card number to anyone. In fact, think twice before you send anything in an e-mail that you wouldn't post on a bulletin board.

Zip your lip. Chat rooms are a great way to meet people and make new friends who share similar interests. But don't be too chatty.

Never give your real name, address, or other personal information in a chat room. Even if you don't intentionally reveal yourself, you'd be surprised at the clues you can innocently drop into a conversation — where you live, if you live alone, when you plan to be away from home, even your financial status.

The problem is, people can pretend to be anyone they choose online. That friendly grandmother you share family stories with could really be a 30-year-old male con artist. But that shouldn't keep you from enjoying online connections. Just don't be too trusting.

Vaccinate against viruses

Every year, you get a flu shot to protect yourself from a nasty virus. But what can you do for your computer? A virus can also make your computer sick. Find out how to protect your information and your investment.

Spot the symptoms. Just like a sore throat, achiness, and stuffy nose can signal the flu, certain symptoms can signal a computer virus.

Yet, symptoms can vary. A relatively harmless virus might just display words or images on your screen. But viruses can also change, delete, or damage your files. Some viruses can even keep your computer from working at all.

Be on the lookout for jumbled words, disappearing files, a slow or unresponsive system, and changes in memory.

Take care not to catch it. If you shake hands with someone who has the flu, you could get it next. Here are some ways your computer can catch a virus. You could:

- receive an infected e-mail attachment. "Be aware of who is sending you e-mails with attachments," says Derrick Lee, managing member of Lee's Computer Maintenance in Atlanta. "If you don't know who sent it, do not open it!"

- download a file with a virus from the Internet.

- get an infected disk or CD.

- use a software program with an infected macro. A macro is a small file that automatically runs several commands back-to-back.

Fight back. A healthy immune system can help ward off sickness. Take these steps to prevent a virus.

- Install anti-virus software, such as Norton Antivirus or McAfee's VirusScan.

- Keep your anti-virus software enabled and running.

- Make an emergency disk if your anti-virus installation instructions encourage you to do so.

- Schedule and run automatic or manual scans every week.

- Get virus updates several times each month. New viruses break out constantly, so don't assume your computer is protected.

  "To prevent viruses from infecting your computer, you must always keep your anti-virus software up to date," Lee says.

- Set your anti-virus program to check all incoming files, downloaded files, and e-mail attachments.

- Download only from reputable Web sites.

- Scan any floppy disks or zip disks.

- Scan compressed files before and after unzipping.

- Back up data files. If a virus does damage your computer, you won't lose your valuable data.

"If you happen to get a virus on your computer, then you must make sure your anti-virus software definitions are up to date and run a scan of your entire system," Lee says. "When the scan finds the virus, then follow the prompts from the software's author and clean the infection. If this doesn't work, then you will need to call a professional."

For more information on current virus threats and what to do about them, check out these Web sites.

Symantec	www.symantec.com/avcenter
The WildList Organization	www.wildlist.org
McAfee Security	www.mcafee.com

Slam the door on spam

Junk mail has gone high-tech. Now, instead of just arriving in your mailbox, it also appears in your e-mail inbox.

Called "spam," unsolicited junk e-mail can be quite a nuisance. Spam includes shady work-at-home offers, advertisements for miracle products, and lurid plugs for pornography. Whatever form spam takes, you don't want it — but you might receive hundreds of these messages a day.

Laura Atkins, President of SpamCon

⚠ Stop pop-ups

Spam isn't the only nuisance you have to put up with as a computer user. Windows messenger pop-up ads can interrupt you whether you're surfing the Internet, e-mailing, or even word processing.

These ads affect all computers running the Windows 2000 or Windows XP operating systems. While terribly annoying and distracting, they are not a danger.

You can thwart these pop-up ads by disabling Windows messenger service and enabling your Internet connection firewall. Both tasks can be done through your control panel.

Foundation, an anti-spam organization, offers these tips to avoid or limit spam.

Keep it secret. Guard your e-mail address closely. "The single most important thing to do to minimize the amount of spam is don't give out your e-mail address," says Atkins. Do not publish your e-mail address on a Web page. Spammers will find it.

Set up a new account. Atkins recommends using a disposable e-mail address (DEA) if you want to make an online purchase or sign up for a list. You can get free DEAs at the following Web sites.

SpamCon Foundation	spamcon.org/services/dea
spamgourmet	spamgourmet.com
Yahoo! Mail	mail.yahoo.com

Just say no. As tempting as a spam offer might sound, do not respond to it. You'll only end up with more spam. "Never buy anything advertised by spam," Atkins says.

Filter it out. You can buy filters and other software programs to combat spam, but Atkins doesn't recommend them. Instead, she says to rely on your Internet service provider, or ISP.

"Most of the anti-spam filters that run on your own machine are pretty bad," Atkins says. "ISPs are much more effective against spam, so look for a provider that does filtering for you. All of the big ISPs do a lot of work on filtering, but often the small, local ISP is more responsive to customers."

Make a complaint. An e-mail header — the details of the path the e-mail took from the originator's computer to yours — can provide useful information.

Atkins recommends learning how to read headers and sending complaints about spam to the appropriate ISPs. "As spammers get better and better about hiding their sources, this becomes a bigger challenge," Atkins says.

You can learn how to decipher headers at *www.stopspam.org/email/headers.html.*

Avoid attachments. An e-mail attachment could make you an unwitting accomplice to spammers. "Never click on an attachment as they are spreading viruses like mad these days," says Atkins. "Those viruses are allowing spammers to hijack home computers and use them to send spam."

And another thing — make sure to use and regularly update anti-virus software.

Do your best. It might seem like no matter what you do, spammers are out to get you. Just make it harder for them to find you.

"Spammers don't 'target' anyone. They will send mail to any e-mail address they can find or create," Atkins says. "Keeping your address hidden can help. Not signing up for contests, Web sites, or sweepstakes will also help."

Put your computer to work

Your computer is a tool — use it. Whether it's a personally rewarding project, like researching your ancestors, or a financially rewarding one, like starting a home business, your computer can handle it.

Bark up your family tree. You've always been interested in your family's history. Now, thanks to your computer and the Internet, it's easier than ever to trace your family tree back to its roots ... even if your tree was planted in another country.

- Start slowly. Genealogy can be overwhelming. These general sites are good places to start.

About Genealogy	www.genealogy.about.com
FamilyTree	www.familytree.com
Genealogy Today	www.genealogytoday.com
Family Search	www.familysearch.org
RootsWeb.com	www.rootsweb.com

- Get more specific. Find historical records like birth, baptism, marriage, and death certificates at *www.vitalrec.com* or military service records at *www.vetfriends.com*. The National Archives at *www.nara.gov* can also be helpful.

- Go international. Learn how to find your immigrant ancestors at *www.genealogy.com/uni-immi.html*. You can also trace your family's journey to America at *www.ellisisland.org*.

- Get organized. Download helpful free software from Family Tree House at *www.usaafter.com* or Ancestry Family Tree at *http://aft.ancestry.com*.

- Learn more. At *www.genealogy.com*, you can sign up for an online genealogy class. With their self-paced tutorials, you'll explore various topics one lesson at a time.

Earn money. There are many jobs that can be done in the comfort of your home, and all it takes to get started is your computer and the information that follows.

- Telecommute. If you currently have a job, ask your boss about telecommuting, or teleworking. You might be able to do your job from home.

- Make extra money using the skills you've acquired. Edit term papers, sell crafts, or provide accounting or secretarial services to small, local businesses. Proofread, transcribe medical records, or work in sales or customer service.

- Build a Web page and get paid for displaying advertising banners. Learn how to set up a Web page at *www.htmlgoodies.com*.

- Watch out for scams. Check out any work-at-home opportunities with the Federal Trade Commission at *www.ftc.gov/bcp/conline/pubs/invest/homewrk.htm* or Better Business Bureau at *www.bbbonline.org*. These sites list scams, let you know how to avoid fraud, give common signs of an unscrupulous scheme, and tell you what to do if you are a victim of a work-at-home scam.

- Check out these Internet sites dedicated to helping you find work at home.

Independent Homeworkers Alliance	www.homeworkers.org
2Work at Home.com	www.2work-at-home.com
HomeBasedWork.com	www.homebasedwork.com
Work At Home Dot Com	www.work-at-home-dot.com
Work at Home Index	www.work-at-home-index.net

Upgrade your memory

As usual, you find yourself scrambling for a last-minute birthday present. Never forget again. Create a calendar that will remind you of important birthdays and anniversaries, doctor appointments, or any other information you want to keep track of. It's easy with your computer.

Some software programs, like Entourage, come with a calendar function. You can record your entire schedule — and even set it to make a notification sound at the proper time. A box will pop up on your computer screen with the text of your reminder. No more belated birthday cards for you.

Keep in touch and save much

You might think of computers as cold and impersonal — but a computer is one of the best tools for communicating with other human beings.

When you have a computer, it's like having free phone calls and postage! You can talk to the grandkids in Tampa, send birthday greetings to your sister in Des Moines, and keep in touch with old friends all over the world, with a click of a button.

Dial for no dollars. With the right software, you can make free calls from your personal computer to someone else's. Of course, the other person must have the same software and be online at the same time in order to talk.

You can download the program for free through PC-Telephone at *www.pc-telephone.com*. With this service, all PC-to-PC calls are free, while PC-to-telephone calls are extremely cheap. For example, calls within the United States, except Alaska and Hawaii, are only 3.5 cents a minute.

Other companies provide amazingly low rates on PC-to-telephone calls. Here are a few worth checking out.

Dialpad	www.dialpad.com
Net2Phone	www.net2phone.com
iConnectHere	www.iconnecthere.com

Enjoy e-mail. If you don't need the extra pizazz of an electronic greeting card, you can always just send a plain old e-mail. It's an easy and inexpensive way to keep in touch with friends, whether they live down the block or halfway around the world. You can even send or receive digital photos. That way, you can enjoy the memories of a special event even if you couldn't make it there in person.

Send greeting cards. Maybe you forgot a special occasion and need a last-minute card. Or perhaps you just don't want to shell out the money for a fancy greeting card. Then electronic greeting cards are for you.

The following Web sites offer a wide variety of free electronic greeting cards for any occasion — or no special occasion at all. They can be funny, sentimental, or even musical. Just pick one out, add a personal message, and send it to that special someone's e-mail address. Some sites might want you to join for a small yearly fee, but you can usually sample their cards during a free trial period.

AmericanGreetings	www.americangreetings.com
Blue Mountain	www.bluemountain.com
Egreetings.com	www.egreetings.com
Cardmaster	www.cardmaster.com
Greeting-cards.com	www.greeting-cards.com
Hallmark	www.hallmark.com
MyPostCards	www.mypostcards.com

Post your pictures. Another good way to share photos with friends and family is through an online photo album. Some Web sites allow you to store digital photos online. Your family or friends can access them with a secret password. It's almost like thumbing through old family photo albums on the living room couch — only not as crowded. Here are just a few photo-sharing sites.

Club Photo	www.clubphoto.com
dotPhoto	www.dotphoto.com
ImageStation	www.imagestation.com
Ofoto	www.ofto.com
PhotoWorks	www.photoworks.com
PictureTrail	www.picturetrail.com
Snapfish	www.snapfish.com

Put a halt to hoaxes

You might not fall for a hoax or believe a rumor when you hear it from your crazy cousin Larry. But when it arrives in your e-mail inbox, it seems much more official. You might even forward it to all your friends and family.

Hoaxes can be a harmless waste of time — or they can cause you to lose money or try something dangerous. Avoid becoming a victim with these tips.

Learn to spot a hoax. Most hoaxes contain the following three parts:

- the bait, often something shocking, to make you read it
- a threat that something bad will happen if you don't pay attention
- an urgent request to spread the word to others

Let these be red flags that warn you to investigate before you send it to others or take any other action.

Beware of deceptions. Here are some of the most popular types of hoaxes. How many have you fallen for?

- Computer viruses. These alerts warn you that opening certain e-mails will erase your hard drive. There are enough real virus threats around without spreading false rumors of more.

- Sympathy hoaxes. It's hard to resist a message from a little girl with cancer — especially when the American Cancer Society will donate 3 cents toward her treatment every time the e-mail is forwarded. Unfortunately, it's not true.

- Financial scams. A mysterious Nigerian official contacts you with a tempting offer — let him use your bank account to transfer millions of dollars out of his country, and you'll get to keep some of it. Sounds great — if you want to lose money. Beware of this and other scams, like work-at-home deals, credit repair offers, and chain letters.

- False medical information. Watch out for kidney thieves or people who prick you with HIV-infected needles at the movies. Better yet, watch out for these types of preposterous warnings.

- Phony legislation. Don't get hot under the collar over the warning that e-mail will now require postage. No such law has been passed, nor is a bill like that under consideration by Congress.

- E-mail tracker cons. Neither Bill Gates nor the Gap will give you money or merchandise for forwarding e-mails. Even if they wanted to, there's no way to track the number of times an e-mail is forwarded.

- Urban legends. Maybe you've heard of the lady who was charged $250 for the Neiman Marcus cookie recipe and is now forwarding it to everyone for revenge. It makes a good story, but it's not true. Feel free to try the cookie recipe, though.

If you come across a sensational story or warning, check it out on one or more of these Web sites.

Centers for Disease Control	www.cdc.gov/hoax_rumors.htm
Hoaxbusters	http://hoaxbusters.ciac.org
McAfee	http://vil.nai.com/VIL/hoaxes.asp
Scambusters	www.scambusters.org/legends.html
Snopes	www.snopes.com
Symantec	www.symantec.com/avcenter/hoax.html
VMyths	www.vmyths.com

Trouble-free gadgets

Winning ways to shop high-tech

No question about it — high-tech appliances and electronics are a boon to today's consumer. Not only has technology simplified people's lives, but high-tech products seem to defy the laws of inflation. As technology advances, prices retreat. Smart shoppers are seizing the opportunity to buy cutting-edge products at bargain prices.

If you hesitate to plunge into the world of technology, Donald Norman, co-founder of the Nielsen Norman group and author of *The Design of Everyday Things* and *Emotional Design,* offers sound advice.

"First, I think being frightened of technology is a perfectly sensible reaction. We are afraid to experiment for a very simple reason — we're afraid we will break it. It's because we've been burned so many times in the past, we don't want to be again." But if you really want to learn something, Norman says, you have to just keep trying.

Of course, you shouldn't buy a product unless you really want and need it, Norman says. "You really have to imagine using it in your home," he points out. "Imagine where you are going to put it, and imagine yourself trying to go over and use it and do it."

Once you decide to buy, take the time to try out the product in the store. And don't let the salesman interfere and try to show you how to use it, Norman warns. After all, he's spent hours practicing with it so he can give a quick and easy demonstration. You need to feel comfortable operating it yourself.

"There is a wonderful phrase salespeople use when you have problems, they say, 'Oh, don't worry, you'll get used to it.' When someone says that to you, say 'OK, that's one product I don't want.' You don't want a product that you have to get used to."

Norman's final advice is to resist the temptation to invest in high-priced features. "Every company makes three versions of every product — the cheap version, the middle version, and the expensive version," he says, adding that the cheap version is usually the easiest to use. "Never buy the most expensive version. The more expensive, the more stuff they've thrown in, and the more complicated it is."

Norman speaks from personal experience. "I have a home theater — spent a lot of money on it. It's really wonderful. It has fantastic sound and picture. But I have something like 12 remote controls, and it's a disaster to try to set up and use."

Norman recommends making user-friendliness your benchmark for judging each product. That should be easier to do as more and more manufacturers give in to the public's demand for user-friendly goods.

Norman's most recent book, *Emotional Design,* addresses one common complaint about user-friendliness — that products designed to be useable are doomed to be ugly.

"I've always been upset by that comment," admits Norman. "But I've finally figured out how these things fit together, and that's emotional design. The best product will be both useable and beautiful."

Preserve your digital pictures

Like many people, you've probably spent years taking pictures and arranging them in photo albums. But now the digital camera has come on the scene, and suddenly you can take a hundred pictures on a single reusable card, edit them yourself, send them worldwide in an instant, and store an album's worth on a single CD. Welcome to the digital revolution!

Such high-tech wizardry may be intimidating, but you don't need to feel left out. As David Pogue says in a recent *New York Times* article, "There's a terrific camera for just about every sort of shutterbug, including the technophobe, the style maven, the outdoorsy types, the quality diva, and the bargain hunter."

Any reputable camera shop can provide you with help in choosing the right camera. The challenge in the digital era is knowing how to preserve the memories you gather on your new technological toy.

Here are some suggestions from the Image Permanence Institute (IPI) and Creative Memories (CM). These groups have teamed up to offer guidelines for preserving your photographs — and your digital images — so they'll be available for the enjoyment of your great-grandchildren.

Make lasting prints. You can store lots of images on a CD or your hard drive, but who knows if you'll be able to access them 20 years from now? If you store photos or anything else on a computer, it's important to update your record-keeping software regularly.

But if you really want to make sure you don't lose photos, you need to make color prints from your digital files. And not just with your computer printer, but at a professional photo lab. IPI and CM say this is the best way to preserve digital images for future generations.

Use the best supplies. Use "stable" photo-finishing materials, and you'll enjoy long-lasting, eye-pleasing color prints, say the experts. Inferior paper and ink will reduce clarity, lead to rapid fading, and result in premature aging. This probably won't be a problem if you have your digital images "developed" professionally, but they will if you print your images with an ink jet or laser printer.

Protect them from damage. Once you have your prints, take care of them. They can still be ruined by light, moisture, air pollution, and improper handling. If you place them in cheap photo albums, stack them carelessly in shoe boxes, or mount them on your refrigerator door, you're asking for trouble.

Make the extra effort to properly frame photos, and pay the few extra dollars for high-quality photo albums. You'll be rewarded with images that will outlive even your own memories.

7 tips for super-safe dryers

A clothes dryer is one of the most helpful appliances you can own. But it's also one of the most deadly. Just look at these statistics reported by the National Fire Prevention Association (NFPA) of Quincy, Mass.

Each year in the U.S., clothes dryers are involved in an average of:

- 14,800 house fires
- 16 deaths
- 309 injuries
- $75.8 million in property damage

And most of the time, it's simply because of a lack of routine maintenance. That's enough to make you want to resurrect your clothesline.

But the NFPA recommends some house rules for keeping your dryer a blessing rather than a curse.

Clean the lint filter before and after each use. That dust and lint is like kindling for a house fire. And don't forget to remove lint from around the drum. It builds up there, too.

Don't operate your dryer without the lint filter. That's like supplying the dryer element with fuel for a house fire.

Make sure the exhaust vent pipe isn't restricted. A kink or congestion in that pipe makes the temperature inside the dryer rise above safe limits.

Check the outdoor vent. The flap on the outdoor vent has to open and shut freely when the dryer is running. And the vent needs to be outdoors, not in the basement or crawl-space.

Don't leave the dryer running when you leave home. The possibility of it causing a house fire skyrockets once you leave.

Recycle your large appliances

Buying a new refrigerator, washer, dryer, range, or other appliance is a simple task. Delivery and installation is a cinch for your suppliers. But knowing what to do with your old "white goods" may not be so easy if your supplier won't haul them away for you.

Help is a phone call away. The Appliance Recycling Information Center has a toll-free number for you to contact recyclers in your area. By calling 1-800-YES-1-CAN (937-1226), you reach a national listing of recyclers for appliances and other products. Take advantage of their assistance, and you'll help your environment as well as yourself.

Keep the area around your dryer free of combustibles. Remove items like cardboard boxes and baskets full of clothes.

Have your dryer installed and serviced by a professional. He can make sure it's kept in good working order to avoid problems that arise from lack of maintenance and parts failures. And gas dryers need to be inspected regularly for leaks.

The care you take to make certain your dryer is kept in good, safe running order will be worth the effort — and keep your house from becoming one more sad statistic.

Simplify vacuum cleaner buying

Choosing a new vacuum cleaner is a tough job. More than a dozen makes and hundreds of models to choose from can leave you bewildered. But take the time to sort through some basic questions, says vacuum cleaner expert Nathan Howell with AllBrands.com, and you'll end up with just the right vac.

Upright or canister? These are the two basic types of portable, household vacuum cleaners. Figuring out which one will serve you better is how you should begin your search.

Uprights. If you mostly clean large, carpeted areas, this is probably your best bet. It has a rotating brush that sweeps down into the carpet. "Some models even allow you to turn the rotating brush off for use on bare floors," says Howell.

Its bag or capture chamber is usually larger than those available in canisters. Many models come with a hose and attachments for above-the-floor cleaning. They're also easy to store.

Canisters. If you have lots of stairs, more hardwood floors than carpet, and many hard-to-reach areas, the canister is your best choice. "Canisters are best for multi-surface cleaning," Howell says.

And that's not all. Canisters are powerful, yet lightweight, and have a retractable cord. They're easy to use on stairs and under beds and furniture and more efficient at filtering dust and dirt.

Gimmicks and extras. As with many products, you'll find yourself enticed with gimmicks and extras. These expensive accessories allow your vac to perform some extraordinary — but rarely necessary — tasks. Don't fall for them. According to several consumer organizations, most no-frills, inexpensive vacuum cleaners do what you want done just fine.

That's not to suggest certain options aren't worthwhile. The optional HEPA (High Efficiency Particle Arresting) filter, for example, helps the vac do its job by filtering exhaust air — important if you suffer from allergies. "But," cautions Howell, "you can't just let a vacuum cleaner run and expect it to filter the air in your room." If you want cleaner air, rely on your heating and air conditioning system, not your vacuum cleaner.

Variables. Know your limits. The weight of a vac is an important factor if you do lots of vacuuming or lugging it up and down stairs. If you clean your carpet with a canister vacuum, be sure it's equipped with a rotating brush. Before you buy, make sure the vac's roar will be tolerable to you and your family.

Bagless vacuum cleaners have become very popular in recent years. They capture dirt in a clear plastic chamber. You can see when it's full, so you won't have to change or empty a bag with these models. But the savings on bags will likely be offset by the cost of replacement air filters.

Special jobs. Vacuum cleaners can be great helpers. Certain models are great for special tasks. "Hand vacs are great for quick spills on counter tops or floors. You can also use them to get in tight spots, or in the car, where a larger machine won't fit," says Howell.

Wet/dry models are the only vacs that can clean up after construction projects or when water and food spills are a problem.

"Don't use any household vac to pick up Sheetrock dust, sawdust, chimney ash, or water," warns Howell. "It'll do serious damage to your vacuum if you do."

It isn't necessary to find a single vacuum that can do all your jobs. Figure out which one will be best for the jobs you do the most. Then, when the need arises, buy a specialty model to add to your cleaning arsenal.

Cell phone strategy for hearing impaired

Buying the right cell phone can be a challenge, especially if you're hearing impaired. But the National Information and Training Center for Hearing Assistive Technology has some helpful phone-shopping tips to make the job easier.

Go to the store. Try out several activated cell phones at Verizon Wireless, Sprint PCS, or Nextel stores. These service providers offer technologies to reduce hearing aid interference. First, try out several varieties of phones at the store. Then go home and do your research by logging on to the service provider's or phone manufacturer's Web site.

Shop for features. You'll probably be interested in Web access, text and instant messaging, and TTY (teletypewriting) and VCO (voice carry over) compatibility. Keep an eye out for new technologies and products.

Beware of interference. Does the phone interfere with your hearing aid? Place a call. If you hear continuous interference, see if turning off the backlight solves the problem. Also, slowly move the phone around your hearing aid to see if there's a place you can hold it to get rid of the interference.

Test every feature. How is the sound quality? Call a recorded message, like Time and Temperature, using several different phones, but the same service provider. Compare volume and clarity.

Vibrating alerts — can you feel them? Ringers — can you hear them? Does the phone display a visual alert when it rings?

Consider travel needs. Consider a phone that works on both analog and digital networks. Then you'll have a phone that works in remote areas where digital wireless signals can't reach you.

Look for comments and reviews. Try *www.cnet.com* (Product reviews), *www.zdnet.com* (Reviews & Prices), *www.epinions.com* (Electronics), or contact a local chapter of an organization like Self Help for Hard of Hearing People (SHHH) *www.hearingloss.org*.

Make good use of trial period. When you buy a phone, ask about the trial period. During that time, test everything. Make sure you can sense the phone's alerts — low battery, call waiting. Be sure you're satisfied with its reception and sound quality — at home, work, or other places you frequent. Check the user-friendliness of its features — three-way calling, address book, messaging, Web access, appointment reminders, alarm clock.

If you're not satisfied with the phone, return it to the phone store and cancel your service with the service provider. If you let the service provider know you have a hearing loss and the phone didn't work for you because of it, they may waive the service fee.

Choosing a cell phone isn't easy. But shopping with a strategy will pay off — you'll find a phone that will meet your needs and serve you well.

Car smarts

Negotiate a successful deal

Everyone likes a new car. Trouble is, in order to buy one, you have to face a salesperson. If you're lucky, he'll be friendly, helpful, and honest. If not, you may be in for an unpleasant experience.

To successfully negotiate with even the most aggressive salesperson, you need to be prepared. Jeff Ostroff, CEO of CarBuyingTips.com, recommends you arm yourself with a folder containing the MSRP (manufacturer's suggested retail price) and invoice price of the car you want, plus your credit report and score.

Arrive at the showroom with "the folder," and you'll drive away in a great car at a great price.

Know the invoice price. The MSRP is the window sticker price — for example $36,499. The invoice price is what the dealer pays — say $33,700. The dealer would like to sell you the car for the MSRP for a profit of $2,799. You want to pay the invoice price — or less — and save thousands.

"Know how much you should be paying for that car before you even set foot on the parking lot," says Ostroff. "Don't wait until you get there to chisel them down and decide what you're going to pay. You should know that ahead of time."

Obtain your credit score. Your credit report is the other key document in your folder. "Have all your credit information, and make sure it's clean before you go to buy a car," Ostroff advises. "We suggest you shoot for a score of 680 or higher."

Ostroff warns that unscrupulous salespeople see people who don't know their credit score as suckers.

"They will lie to you about your credit score and tell you it is a lot less than it really is in order to jack up the interest rate. People who have bad credit or don't know what their current score is stand to lose the most money," says Ostroff.

Beware also of the "0% financing" lure, he warns. "A lot of people, especially ones with bad credit, think they are going to go in there and get 0% financing. But that is usually reserved for people with the very best of credit."

Your chances of securing a good interest rate improve if you get yourself fiscally fit and raise your score before you apply for a loan.

Get pre-approved financing. You can avoid a financial power struggle altogether simply by arranging your financing before you arrive at the dealership.

"It's just like buying a house," Ostroff says. "When you go to buy a house, real estate agents will run your credit and make sure you have approval from a bank before they even work with you."

Prepare for buying a car the same way. Don't finance your car on the dealer's terms. It's too expensive.

Bring on the competition. Ostroff believes the real key to saving money is competition. "We tell people to get quotes from several different online sites, because you never know who is going to have the lowest price. Once the salesman knows he's in competition with other dealers, that usually helps keep him in line."

Don't be hoodwinked by car dealers

Learn the games new-car dealers play. Their tactics may vary, says Jeff Ostroff, CEO of CarBuyingTips.com, but you can protect yourself by knowing the scams they're likely to try.

VIN window etching. Don't believe them if they say you won't get the loan without it. That lie could cost you $300 to $900. The bank does not need it, and you can have the VIN etched yourself for around $30.

Denied financing. You signed for a low interest rate and thought your worries were over. Now, two weeks later, they're saying you didn't qualify, and they'll be raising your rate and your monthly payments. Next time read the fine print that says "subject to financing."

False credit score. "Your credit score is 580," they say, "so we can only give you 10.9 percent APR." Good thing you have proof your score is 780, which qualifies you for the best rates. Not knowing your score may cost you the difference between a low rate and a much higher rate over the life of your loan.

Forced warranty. The bank does not require an extended warranty. That could cost at least $2,000.

Dealer prep. They might say, "Our dealer prep fee covers the cost of getting your car ready to drive off the lot." This fee is $500 for a job that only takes the dealer two hours. That's $250 per hour! Why are you charged when the factory already pays the dealer to do this?

Additional dealer markup (ADM). This is padding, pure and simple. It doesn't even pretend to be the cost of a service or benefit. The ADM "hides" on a little orange sticker next to the MSRP sticker. Cost — $2,000.

Loan pay-off. They may offer to pay off your loan, but the amount you owed, plus the penalties for breaking your loan contract, is folded into your monthly payments. The dealer doesn't pay it. You do. This huge added fee lies hidden in your monthly payments, spread out over 60 or 72 months.

Bounced bank checks. You arrive at the dealership with a draft from your bank, credit union, or lender. The dealer says, "We don't take their checks. They always bounce." The dealer then offers you its own financing package, but at a higher APR. Cost — higher payments over the life of your loan.

Forced credit application. You come prepared to pay cash, but they insist you complete a credit application. Contrary to what the salesperson says, there is no state law requiring you to fill out a credit application. If he claims it is company policy, then, according to Ostroff, maybe you need to find another company to deal with.

Remember, you are in control of the deal, not them. Any time you encounter one of these scams, or feel uncomfortable in any way, simply get up and take your business elsewhere.

Look out for blind spots

Whether your dream car is a luxury sedan, sports coupe, or SUV, make safety priority one when you decide to make your purchase. You might be surprised to know that even "safe" new cars can have built-in road hazards.

Your car's distinctive style — or even some of its safety features — may make it difficult for you to see while you're driving. For example, a sleek sports car may be a thing of rare beauty, but its small back window or high rear deck may make it nearly impossible to see what's behind you. Even practical necessities like headrests and roof pillars on ordinary sedans can create blind spots — and that's dangerous.

Recent government statistics show that about 9 percent of all reported automobile crashes involve lane changes, a classic example of a blind spot situation. When you back up and merge you're also likely to have limited visibility.

Here are things the National Highway Traffic Safety Administration says you can do to improve the view in your existing car.

- Adjust your seat height so you can see at least 10 feet of road in front of your car. Use a cushion if necessary.

- Get your doctor's approval for neck stretching exercises. These will increase your flexibility and help you look over your shoulder and to your right and left.

- Adjust your outside mirrors to eliminate blind spots. Lean your head against the window and move the driver's side mirror outward so you can barely see the side of your car.

- Use a passenger as your second pair of eyes.

If you're in the market for a new car, follow these guidelines to stay safe on the road.

Test before you buy. Slide into the driver's seat of that showroom demonstrator. What can you see when you peer into the mirror? Ask a friend to walk around behind the car. Does he ever just vanish? If you're looking at SUVs or pickups, see how far beyond the tailgate things disappear from view. Headrests and roof support pillars are important and necessary, but you don't want them in your way when you turn your head. Make sure you can see all around you from the cockpit.

Choose top-rated vehicles. Government safety and consumer advocacy groups have found that full-size sedans are among the best for rear and side visibility. Drivers believe they have the worst view in convertibles and big vans. Check out magazines and Web sites that focus on auto safety issues, or check with your car insurance company about safety ratings.

Get help from new features. Consider these options that may help you overcome the "blind-spot syndrome."

- A rearview camera is a neat option already available on a few cars, although aftermarket systems are available, too. These are pricey, however, and you'll need an on-board navigation system with a monitor to make it work for you.

- Sensors that "see" things behind you as you back up will beep a warning if you get close to an obstacle. While this system starts at around $500, some drivers actually end up ignoring the constant beeping.

- Lenses and mirrors are two inexpensive alternatives to cameras and sensors. Plastic fisheye lenses attach to the rear window of your van or SUV, and convex mirrors stick to your side-view mirrors. Both are easy to install and help you see objects, pets, and people you might otherwise miss. Convex mirrors make lane changing much safer and do a great job of displaying cars coming up quickly from behind.

When you go car shopping, be assertive. Let sales associates know you're serious about a safe car. Do your homework. Then don't forget to look behind you.

Land the best car lease

Financial experts will tell you that buying a new car is usually smarter than leasing. But a lease can be a practical choice under certain conditions. You're a good candidate for a car lease if:

- a new car is more important to you than ownership.

- you trade every two or three years.

- you drive fewer than 15,000 miles a year.

If that describes you, here are some pointers that will help you secure a winning lease.

Know your total costs. It's harder to compare prices on a lease than it is when buying, so be sure to find out your total amount for payments and fees. Be suspicious if the numbers appear too good to be true.

Negotiate carefully. Haggle with the dealer over price and payments just as if you were buying the car. Or, if you prefer, use a service like LeaseWise (800-475-7283 or *www.checkbook.org*) to negotiate for you. For a fee, LeaseWise will help you land the best deal by making dealers bid for your business.

Be aware of penalties. The penalties are high if you back out of your lease before it ends. Also, you'll be charged a pricey mileage fee if you drive more than your annual limit — usually 12,000 to 15,000 miles. Make sure you know exactly what you're getting into.

Steer clear of maintenance agreements. When you lease, you get a new car with a factory warranty. Major maintenance is not your financial responsibility.

Snoop around for a good used car

You're in the market for a good used car but don't want to buy a lemon. The key is to shop wisely. When you find a car that's a candidate for occupying your garage, here's a checklist for snooping out any problems.

Eyeball the body. How does the paint look? Does it match on each body panel? If not, the car may have been wrecked. If it was, it's not necessarily disqualified from the race. But if it's been poorly repaired, or if the frame has been bent, you can count on costly problems down the road. Also, look for signs of rust. Bring a friend along who can help you check it out and be an objective critic.

Explore the interior. Have your companion tell you if the lights all work as you toggle the switches from the driver's seat. Don't forget brake, interior, dash panel lights, and turn signals. Check out every knob, switch, and gizmo you can find — hood, trunk, and gas tank releases. Can you easily adjust the side view mirrors? Look for worn and torn upholstery and carpeting. Do the doors close easily?

Beware of fragrances. Air fresheners are sometimes used to mask the smell of moisture. Are there leaks? Is this car a flood survivor? If it is, more than the car's interior has suffered.

Raise the hood. Beneath the hood lies a treasure trove of information about the car you're thinking of buying. Be sure the motor is cold, then check the fluids. When any fluid is so low you can't get a reading on the dipstick or see it in the reservoir, it's a bad sign. Another bad omen is dirty fluid that is discolored or no longer translucent. That tells you it hasn't been changed often enough.

> ⚠️ **Know your rights**
>
> When shopping at a used-car lot, insist on a Buyers Guide sticker, and read it carefully. "It basically tells you your rights — if there is a warranty or if you're buying 'as is,'" says Jeff Ostroff, CEO of CarBuyingTips.com. Never buy a used car from a dealer "as is," he warns. Signing the deal means you assume all risks. Even if the dealer lied, you have no rights.

These are telltale signs that the internal parts of the engine and transmission are worn, since dirty fluids speed up wear. Also, look for radiator hoses that are cracked or bulging or pulley belts that are loose, worn, or frayed.

Examine the tires. Check for irregular wear patterns on all the tires, including the spare. That wear may point to an easy remedy like balancing the tires. But it could also be a symptom of suspension problems, which involve costly repairs.

Hit the road. The test drive is one of the most crucial parts of the car-shopping process. Once again, your friend can help. When you crank up the car, does the exhaust pipe belch a plume of smoke? When you drive away, are there fluid spots on the pavement?

Listen carefully for bad sounds when you accelerate or brake. Does the car drift off course when you're cruising or pull to the side when you brake? Does the transmission shift smoothly and effortlessly?

Search the history. If you suspect the car has a hidden past, use the Vehicle Identification Number (VIN) to investigate its history. Carfax.com (*www.carfax.com*) and Autocheck.com (*www.autocheck.com*) are two companies that will search a car's history for a fee. The Center for Auto Safety (*www.autosafety.org*) provides information on safety defects, recalls, and lemons, as well as service bulletins.

Call in the experts. If you're still not sure after all your "snooping," turn the car over to an expert. It's always smart to get a trusted mechanic or auto diagnostician to check a car before you buy. For a fee, he'll give that car a thorough going over and save you the stress and expense of untimely repairs.

Find the right fix-it shop

Make car repair a pleasure rather than a pain by heeding the advice of veteran mechanic Ken Smith, owner of Smith's Auto and Truck Service, a NAPA Car Care Center in Fayetteville, Georgia.

The best way to find a good repair shop, he says, is to shop around. "Go by word-of-mouth recommendations," he suggests. "Look for some certification — ASE in particular — and their time in business. Check their affiliation with a reputable parts distribution and repair network." A network — such as NAPA — will assure you the service center has:

- the parts you need.

- the latest repair information for every vehicle.

- good warranties on parts and service.

- access to technical hotlines for hard-to-solve problems.

No one likes "misunderstandings" when he's having his car repaired. Smith, who has been in the auto repair business since 1962, has several suggestions to improve communication and prevent unpleasant surprises.

Describe the problem. Don't leave it up to the shop to discover the symptoms. "An accurate description of the problem or service needed is good at the onset," says Smith. Describe that noise or vibration, and they'll quickly pinpoint the cause.

Expect honesty. One clue that you've found a good shop is their willingness to point you to a specialty shop or dealer. "A reputable, honest repair facility would refer you to a dealer if it's necessary," says Smith, "especially if the repair involves warranty work." If he can't or shouldn't make the repair himself, he'll refer you to someone who can or suggest a choice of service providers.

Schedule an appointment. Avoid a long wait or unnecessary delay. "Scheduling allows proper time for the service or repair to be performed," Smith says.

Be reachable. Give the shop a way to contact you. Leave phone numbers in case a problem arises during the repair. A reputable shop will hold off making further repairs if they discover a new problem beyond the scope of your work order and can't reach you.

Be reasonable. Allow adequate time for your repair, and understand that in the auto repair industry there are few "quick fixes." "If you've got to have your car back today, and you've got a repair that's going to take two days, naturally, that's not going to happen," Smith says.

Don't procrastinate. Some drivers delay having their cars serviced or repaired because they're worried about the cost. "There needs to be some communication and some understanding," Smith advises. "If you're limited with how much you can spend, let the repair facility know that to start with." Then they will know what you can afford and take whatever steps are necessary to make your car roadworthy — within your budget.

Lots of problems can arise in the world of car repair. "If you have repairs that exceed the car's value, we certainly don't want the customer unhappy." Smith believes that a good shop will assume the responsibility of explaining what your options are.

Stay in the driver's seat. You can expect a good repair shop to:

- diagnose your car's problem.

- estimate how long a repair will take and its cost.

- give you expert advice.

- repair your car so it's safe to drive.

But it's your car and your responsibility to make sure things are done right. So be sure to communicate with the shop, and stay informed about what your mechanic is doing each step of the way. You'll drive away a happy, satisfied customer.

7 ways to pump up your mileage

The U.S. Department of Energy recommends these good habits to improve your mileage and make your car run better. Follow them faithfully, and you can save over $200 a year at the gas station.

- Keep your engine tuned, and your mileage will be from 4 to 40 percent better than its un-tuned twin's. Replacing a faulty oxygen sensor alone can improve your mileage by 40 percent.

- Regularly replace your air filter for an extra 10 percent savings. That's an extra 5 to 10 miles per gallon.

- Use the recommended grade of motor oil and improve your mileage by 1 to 2 percent.

- Maintain the recommended tire pressure, and you'll save an additional 3 percent.

- Drive conservatively. No jackrabbit starts. Aggressive driving diminishes your mileage by 5 to 33 percent.

- Observe the fuel-savings speed limit. Every 5 mph over 60 is like paying an extra 10 cents per gallon. Keep it at 60, and save 7 to 23 percent.

- Travel light and aerodynamically. A loaded roof rack's drag reduces mileage by 5 percent, and every extra 100 pounds knocks it down another 1 to 2 percent.

Target tire pressure to inflate safety

Most drivers make monthly car washing a priority, but only 14 percent check tire pressure that often. One thing's for sure, once you learn how important this one detail of car maintenance is to your safety and your pocketbook, you'll get the habit.

Driving on underinflated tires:

- is a major cause of tire failure.

- wastes gas — over a billion gallons per year in the U.S. alone.

- decreases handling and life-saving traction.

Spare the gauge, spoil the tire. To make sure your tires live long, behave well, and remain well-treaded, follow these simple guidelines from the National Highway Traffic Safety Administration (NHTSA).

- Own a good gauge. It will cost less than the gas you'll waste by driving on underinflated tires.

- Check tire pressure often — at least once a month, before going on trips, and when there are big temperature swings. And don't forget your spare.

- Measure pressure when your tires are cold. Driving warms the tires up and the pressure reading won't be accurate. Look for the correct "Cold Tire Pressure" for your car in your glove box, on the door, or in your owner's manual. Don't use the figure embossed on the sidewall of your tires. It will be too high.

- Make sure your tire valves have caps.

- Don't overload your vehicle.

In addition, the Rubber Manufacturers Association (RMA) says 45 percent of drivers believe, incorrectly, they should deflate tires a little when preparing for a trip.

Scan the tire-tech horizon. Tire makers are working hard to perfect on-the-go tire pressure monitoring — tires with their own built-in pressure sensors that warn of low tire pressure while you're driving. This is already available on some models, but the NHTSA may soon require it on all new cars. Experts caution that even if your car has such a system, you should continue to check your tires with a gauge.

"Run-flat" tires are made to do just that — run in the event of a puncture, without causing damage to the tire or wheel. Because you can't feel when run-flats are flat, they require on-the-go pressure monitoring.

There's a day coming when your car will keep its own tires correctly inflated. But until then, take responsibility for checking them. Keep your tire pressure gauge handy, and enjoy the benefits of saving money and staying safe on the road.

4 smart ways to thwart thieves

Every once in a while you'll hear someone reminisce, "I remember the good ole days when I could leave my doors unlocked and the keys in the car." But it's a new day, and it takes some effort to be safe and secure.

"The nation's number one property crime is auto theft — occurring every 26 seconds in America," says Teri Vlasak, Director of Corporate Communications at the National Insurance Crime Bureau (NICB). That's unsettling news, but the NICB has some great advice to help car owners like you achieve peace of mind.

Begin with basics. "It may seem very basic," says Vlasak, "but your car is most vulnerable to thieves when it is left running with the doors unlocked. When the weather is cold or rainy, or you're just running a quick errand in the convenience store — never leave the car running or unlocked. Your car is safest when it is out of sight, out of mind — locked in a locked garage."

"When parking your car," she adds, "turn the wheels to the curb, click the steering wheel into the lock position, close your windows, and lock up. If your car has been broken into or is stolen, call 911, and report the theft immediately to the police."

Use layered protection. You protect yourself in cold weather by piling on layers of clothing. Layered protection for your car is the same thing using safety devices, Vlasac says. NICB recommends four layers — common sense, visible or audible devices, car immobilizers, and a vehicle tracking system.

- Common sense is as simple as locking your doors, removing the keys from the ignition when you leave the car, closing your windows, and parking in well-lit areas. "Common sense is your strongest deterrent against theft, and it doesn't cost you a thing," says Vlasak.

- Visible or audible devices can include alarm systems, steering wheel locks, steering column collars, deterrent decals, and window etching.

- Car immobilizers make it more difficult for thieves to bypass your ignition system. "Smart keys with computer chips, fuse cut-offs, kill switches, and starter, ignition, and fuel disablers are some of the immobilization systems currently available," Vlasac says.

- Tracking systems emit a signal to the police or a monitor service when your car is reported stolen.

The coat of common sense won't cost you a penny, so put it on today. Install a visible device. Potential thieves will see it and know you mean business about protecting your automobile. Keep your car safe, and enjoy it as long as you own it.

Senior drivers: Know when to quit

The privilege of driving is a necessity few can live without. But there comes a time when you or someone you love may have to scale back or retire.

"We all hope when we reach that magic age where we just can't handle it out there anymore, we'll limit our driving, and then back off from there," says Senior Sgt. Terrance D. Martin, retired veteran of the Vermont State Police.

Unfortunately, many older adults are reluctant to give up their car keys. But doing so could be critical to their health — and their lives. A recent study showed that drivers over age 65 are almost twice as likely as middle-aged drivers to die in car crashes. And the Insurance Institute of America predicts that by 2030 older drivers will be involved in 25 percent of all fatal accidents.

Know thyself. If you're unsure about your driving abilities, look for red flags, Martin says.

- Do you have difficulty seeing at night or at a distance?
- Are you suffering from cataracts or other eye problems?
- Do you react to surprises more slowly than you used to?
- Do you take medications that could affect your alertness?

If you've answered "yes" to any of these questions, you're probably not as safe behind the wheel as you once were.

If that's the case, think about setting limits on your driving. Drive only in daylight, and keep your trips short. Let someone else drive at night. Don't drive in bad weather. Make use of shuttles and public transportation. And enjoy the scenery from a plane, train, or bus on longer trips.

Come to the rescue. If it's a loved one rather than yourself who is an accident waiting to happen, what should you do? You'd never forgive yourself if he had a wreck and you could have prevented it.

Martin has known a lot of situations like that. "Contact your local department of motor vehicles," he advises. "Most of them have an instrument within the law that allows them to retest that person."

This is especially important if your state does not require mandatory retesting at a certain age. But be aware that you have to present reasonable grounds — like a minor accident. You can't request a retest just because they are senior citizens.

"It's a hard thing to do, but sometimes you have to for grandma or grandpa or that neighbor you've seen make so many close calls," Martin says.

Recognize the problem. Many people claim road conditions or mechanical failure cause their driving mishaps. But if you combine mechanical and environmental factors, they cause only 5 to 10 percent of all collisions, Martin says. It's usually the "human factor" that is responsible. "Most of the time, it's the person who chooses to 'overdrive' the conditions," he says.

So if you find yourself faltering on the road, take an honest look at the situation. The Automobile Association of America (AAA) has an online quiz at *aaafoundation.org/quizzes* to help analyze your driving skills. Or you can call 202-638-5944 to request the quiz be sent to you. The user-friendly Web site *www.seniordrivers.org* also offers a wealth of driving information and resources.

Giving up your car keys does not mean surrendering your independence. If you approach this phase of your golden years with acceptance and a positive attitude, you can make it an enjoyable — and safe — time of your life.

Fun for less

Free tickets — that's entertainment!

With age comes wisdom. And an amazing number of entertainment discounts. Sometimes you have to use that wisdom to find the senior discounts — but you should rarely have to pay full price for your entertainment.

Snare senior discounts. David Smidt, President and CEO of SeniorDiscounts.com, knows a thing or two about discounts for older adults. Here are some of his suggestions for common entertainment deals.

- Movie theaters. "Almost every movie theater gives a senior discount. Those tend to be in the 40 percent range," Smidt says.

- Museums. "Almost all museums give free admission to seniors or a senior discount at least."

- Amusement parks, such as SeaWorld or Disneyland. "Most of them will give some sort of senior discount, and you definitely should ask."

- National parks. Residents of the U.S. who are 62 or older can get a Golden Age passport for $10. This serves as a lifetime pass to all national parks, monuments, and historic sites.

- Ski areas. "A lot of them," says Smidt, "when you're over 70, you ski free, or if you're over 60 you get a discount."

- Smidt also suggests you ask about senior discounts when you go to the opera, theater, or even bowling alleys.

You can search for local senior discounts at *www.seniordiscounts.com.* You can also submit discounts that aren't currently listed. That's how the company builds its database, which currently contains about 125,000 deals for seniors. In addition to entertainment deals, you'll find discounts for local restaurants, dry cleaners, moving companies — even car dealerships.

"It really goes across every service and product industry out there," says Smidt.

Ask for it. Even if the place doesn't advertise a senior discount, ask for one. It can't hurt. "A lot of times, even if they don't offer one, we have found seniors can create the discount just by asking," says Smidt.

Remember, different venues have different age requirements. You may qualify for a senior discount and not even realize it.

"At 50 is the time you want to just be on the lookout for discounts — if you're willing to admit you're a senior at that point," says Smidt.

Try these tactics. You don't have to be a senior to take advantage of free or discount tickets. Here are some other strategies for low-cost entertainment.

- Volunteer to usher at a local theater or concert venue.

- Take in a matinee, or wait for your movie to come to a dollar theater.

- Be quick and call when your radio station offers ticket giveaways.

- Write to the Guest Relations departments of television networks to get free tickets to live tapings of TV shows.

- Buy coupon books with entertainment vouchers.

- Join art organization mailing lists to find out about last-minute discounts.

- Check your membership benefits through AAA or any other clubs you might belong to.
- Subscribe early to the theater or symphony for deep discounts.
- Keep your eye open for free public events or festivals.

Read up on book and magazine deals

There's nothing quite like curling up with a good book — especially when you get that book for a good price.

Here are some ways to enjoy your favorite books and magazines without spending top dollar for them.

Borrow a book. For free books, you can't beat your local library. It has more books than you can read in a lifetime and provides a nice, quiet place to read them. Or take some home and return them when you're done. You don't pay a dime — except for late fees — and you don't clutter up your home.

Become a member. Join a book club, like the Book-of-the-Month Club. You can expand your personal library without leaving your house.

Look closely into any book clubs before joining. Make sure you can afford their prices. Check things like shipping and handling charges and how easy it is to return a book you don't want.

Seek out sales. Keep your eyes peeled for community book sales. The American Association of University Women (AAUW) and your local library usually have one every year. You'll find great books at amazing discounts. In the final days of the sale, you might spend $5 for a paper bag full of paperbacks.

Shop around. Used book stores and garage sales can yield some remarkable savings. It might take some looking, but you'll find a deal.

While you're at it, don't forget to check the bargain book tables in large bookstore chains. You might not find the latest bestseller, but chances are you'll find something neat.

Browse the Internet. Think of the Internet as a giant library or discount bookstore. Take advantage of this exciting technology.

- Read books online at Web sites like Bartleby.com at *www.bartleby.com*, Project Gutenberg at *www.promo.net/pg*, or The Online Books Page at *www.digital.library. upenn.edu/books*.

- Order books from online retailers. You can find discounts at the following Web sites.

All Books 4 Less.com	www.allbooks4less.com
Amazon	www.amazon.com
Barnes & Noble	www.bn.com
Book Closeouts	www.bookcloseouts.com
Books-A-Million	www.booksamillion.com

- Swap books. Check out *www.thebookcart.com*, a Web site that lets you borrow and lend paperbacks through the mail for just the cost of postage.

Maximize magazine savings. If you enjoy thumbing through magazines, try these thumbs-up ideas.

- Resubscribe. Instead of renewing your subscription at the regular price after the low introductory rate expires, simply resubscribe at the introductory rate.

- Ask for old magazines at your local recycling center, beauty salon, or library.

- Read your favorite magazines at the library.

- Take advantage of free trial offers.

- Go online. Some magazines let you read articles online for free. You can also save on magazine subscriptions at sites like *www.magazines.com*, *www.magsdirect.com*, *www.magazineoutlet.com*, or *www.absolutemagazines.com*.

Get in tune with music deals

Music used to soothe the savage beast — now it sounds like it's being played by one. What happened to the good old days when you could understand the well-crafted lyrics or enjoy a smooth melody?

Relive them with records and compact discs. Here's how to find great deals on the music you love.

Unearth used gems. Shop at used record or CD stores. Often, you can find great deals on CDs that are as good as new. Make sure to check for scratches — and make sure the CD inside the case is the one you want.

Garage sales and thrift shops can also provide a treasure trove of old albums. One Gospel music lover found an extremely rare record, with an estimated value of $4,500, in a 25-cent rack at a Salvation Army thrift store.

Keep an eye out for CD and record conventions. Dealers from all over bring their wares and set up shop in a local hotel ballroom. For a small entry fee, you get to rummage for deals all day.

Join the club. Music clubs like BMG and Columbia House have wide selections of compact discs. It's an easy way to shop without leaving your home.

But there are pros and cons to these types of clubs. As an incentive to join, you get several free CDs right away. The bad news is you must buy a certain amount of regularly priced CDs over the next few years. Luckily, the clubs often feature special sales, like buy-one-get-two-free deals.

Log on and listen. You and the Internet can make — or at least find — beautiful music together.

- Tune in. If you don't need to own the music, but just want to enjoy it, tune in to an Internet radio station. You can get stations from all over the world specializing in just about every style of music. Go to *www.live-radio.net*, *www.radio-locator.com*, *www.radiotower.com*, or *www.virtualtuner.com* to find one that interests you.

- Download songs. You may have heard all the fuss about kids illegally downloading music from the Internet. Well, you can download songs legally, too, from sites like *www.emusic.com*. For just pennies, you can get a copy of a song you like. It beats buying a whole album just to hear it.

- Shop online. Many music stores you're familiar with have Web sites. Other companies sell exclusively through the Internet. Browse extensive catalogs, find deals, and order online at these sites.

Amazon	www.amazon.com
Barnes & Noble	www.bn.com
CD Universe	www.cduniverse.com
FYE	www.fye.com
Tower Records	www.towerrecords.com

- Bid on it. You might be able to find what you're looking for on e-Bay. Some people actually make a living selling records and CDs through this popular auction site.

Liven things up. Recorded music is great, but sometimes you want to see a performer in person. Check your local newspaper for live music in your area. Some cities have weekly papers devoted to local entertainment.

Another good way to find out which musicians are appearing where is to visit *www.pollstar.com*. You can search by city, venue, or artist. You'll be surprised who's still alive — and still performing.

'Priceless' tips for budget-minded collectors

Stamps, coins, comic books, baseball cards, toys, records, furniture — there's no limit to what you can collect. But there is a limit to your budget. Fortunately, you can still afford to enter the exciting world of collecting.

Harry Rinker, noted antiques and collectibles expert and host of HGTV's *Collector Inspector,* offers these priceless collecting tips.

Collect what you like. A collection won't be any fun if you don't actually enjoy the items you're collecting. And don't limit yourself — anything can become a collectible.

"You can collect everything from hotel soap to toilet paper," Rinker says. "What you really want to do is instead of asking, 'Why?' just ask, 'Why not?' It's a lot easier and you have a lot more fun with it."

Just make sure you can afford it. Rinker points out that you can find plenty of affordable collectibles. "Look around and find something you like but that's within your price range," Rinker says. "There's no sense trying to collect stuff that's outside your price range. It doesn't do you any good. It just drives you nuts."

Stay in control. Your new hobby may be exciting, but don't go overboard. Stay within your budget. "Collecting can be addictive," Rinker says. "One of the things that you don't want to do is wind up spending your food or rent money on the stuff. And there are people that can get caught up in it that badly that they do that."

Collect by condition. You may think you can save money by buying a damaged item and fixing it up. According to Rinker, this idea is silly.

"Don't buy anything that's damaged, chipped, broken, or whatever. It's better that you buy it in great shape," Rinker says. "Broken stuff isn't a bargain."

Comparison shop. Look on the Internet, check out garage sales and flea markets, attend antique shows or auctions. You'll find the best deals there. "Most everything you're going to collect is going to be mass produced. Therefore, it pays to shop around," Rinker says. "If you don't like the price, walk away. You'll find another one."

The price is most often best at garage sales, where you can discover super discounts and bargains that can save you up to 80 percent or more. In fact, Rinker says you should pay only 10 to 15 cents on the retail dollar at a garage sale. If you pay more than 25 cents, you're paying too much.

Switch things up. No one said you have to stick with your first choice. "If you get tired of your collection, switch collections. It's OK," Rinker says.

Be practical. Are your collectibles just collecting dust? Why not collect things you can use? Rinker does. He lists kitchen utensils, chairs, and furniture among his useful collectibles. As a bonus, antiques and collectibles are often cheaper than new items.

Beware of reproductions. Some bargains aren't bargains at all — they're fakes. Be especially wary at flea markets and antique malls. "If it looks new and it's supposed to be old, chances are it is new," Rinker says.

Stop speculating. Don't buy for investment or resale purposes. The antique business requires much more skill than you think. "People think they can just whip their wallet out, that they can buy cheap and sell dear," Rinker says. "It doesn't work that way."

Sell with sense. If you do decide to sell your collection, Rinker recommends trying an estate sale or garage sale first. An auction would be your next step — but if all the good stuff is picked over at a garage sale, you may not have anything left to interest an auctioneer.

Just don't expect to get rich selling your collection. Remember, unless you can find a buyer, your stuff has no value. "People always overestimate what their stuff is worth, and they always want more than the market will bear because it's personal to them," Rinker says.

"People have to understand that it's a trendy market out there. The value of things changes rapidly. It's totally dependent on the whims of the public."

Successful ways to locate a lost pet

Yikes! Your pet is missing. You're understandably worried, frightened, even terrified. Do not panic— but do act quickly.

"The sooner you start searching for your pet, probably the closer they will be," says Nancy Peterson, an Issues Specialist for the Humane Society of the United States. "Fast action is very important."

Peterson offers the following advice for finding a lost pet.

Search your house. This might sound like an obvious place to start, but it could save you a lot of trouble. Peterson says she's "lost" her cat in her house many times.

"I found her lurking somewhere sound asleep, just oblivious to the fact that I'm frantically looking for her," Peterson says. "Definitely check favorite hiding places in the house."

Take a walk. Walk through your neighborhood calling for your pet. If you've trained your pet to come when it hears the sound of jangling keys or a shaking can of dry kibble, try those tactics, too.

Alert the neighbors. Go door to door to let your neighbors know your pet is missing. Also alert any delivery people or mail carriers so they can be on the lookout. Show them a current photograph of your pet.

Call around. Call all animal shelters and veterinarians within a 50-mile radius. Some good Samaritan may have brought your pet there.

Advertise. Make posters with a picture of your pet and a description. You may want to leave out one telling characteristic so the finder can positively identify your pet to you. Include all your telephone numbers — home, business, cell phone — to make it easy for someone to contact you. Many newspapers will let you place lost pet ads for free.

Watch out for scams. A lost pet could make you an easy mark for a con artist. "There have been scams in the past involving lost pets so it is important to be careful," Peterson says. Make sure any caller can tell you the secret detail you left off your posters. Otherwise, he may not have your pet.

Beware of what Peterson calls the "Trucker's Scam." In this scam, the con artist will call and say, "I was traveling through your area, and I believe I found your dog." He'll say he's now in another state and needs some money to ship the dog back to you. Of course, he doesn't have your dog at all. But if you're not careful, he may end up with your money.

"If somebody has your pet and you're going to meet that person somewhere, make sure it's in a very public place," Peterson says. Also, insist you get your pet back before handing over any reward.

Take precautions. Do your best to prevent your pet from getting lost in the first place. Make sure screens are secure, train everyone in your house to be careful around doors, check your backyard for escape routes, and keep your pet inside when you're not home.

Most important, make sure your pet has some form of ID. "Even strictly indoor pets should always wear some visible form of identification," Peterson says. "That identification is going to be their ticket home."

A good backup to a collar is a microchip. Vets inject this tiny chip, about the size of a grain of rice, into your pet's back. When scanned, the chip provides your contact information. Make sure to keep this information updated.

A lost pet can be devastating. But, no matter what, do not give up hope.

"Sometimes you'll see stories about pets that are reunited with their owners after months or even years, which is pretty amazing," Peterson says. "Stranger things have happened."

Savvy traveling

Dodging the high cost of lodging

Your vacation would be much more fun if you still had your arm and your leg. Too bad that's what your hotel charged you for a night's stay.

Sure, you could have found cheaper accommodations — you'd just have to share them with the fleas and the cockroaches.

Here's how to find low-cost lodging without settling for the Hotel Fleabag.

Pick up the phone. Call ahead and ask for the best rate. If you just show up looking tired and desperate, the hotel has you right where it wants you.

Dial both numbers. Don't just call the hotel's 800 number. Try the local number, too. That gives you two chances to find a good deal.

Join the club. Just being a member of certain clubs like AAA, or participating in a frequent flier program, may make you eligible for a discount. Be sure to check.

Act your age. Ask for the AARP or senior discount. It can save you anywhere from 10 percent to 50 percent, according to David Smidt, President and CEO of SeniorDiscounts.com.

"Most hotels that we've found will offer an AARP discount but don't require you to have the card to get the discount," Smidt says. "Ask for the senior discount even if you're not an AARP member."

For hotels, the senior discount almost always begins at age 50.

Think fast. Plan ahead and make reservations early for the best rates.

Look online. Take advantage of the Internet to compare rates and find great bargains. "Check out Priceline and Hotwire and those bid-type sites, and see what you can come up with because there are some really good deals," Smidt says.

Go when it's slow. Book during off-season or off-peak times for big savings. For example, make midweek reservations at resort areas and weekend reservations at destinations that cater to business travelers.

Be flexible. You may be able to save money just by slightly changing the dates of your trip. Keep your travel plans flexible.

Haggle. Don't be afraid to bargain with hotels. Their prices aren't set in stone. If their prices are too high, make them a counteroffer. If they have extra rooms, they may be glad to get something rather than nothing.

Study, swap, and save on travel

Does your pocketbook need a vacation after your vacation? Next time, try one of these interesting low-cost alternatives.

Live and learn. Instead of being a run-of-the-mill tourist, be a student of the world. Elderhostel gives older adults the chance to explore new subjects and places at a reasonable price.

You can study art in Paris, jazz in New Orleans, or wine in Italy. With more than 10,000 programs in more than 90 countries, Elderhostel is bound to offer something that appeals to you.

"All of our programs include an educational component, and lectures are led by university faculty, local experts, and professionals, rather than tour guides," says Elderhostel spokeswoman Despina Gakopoulos. "Also, as a not-for-profit, Elderhostel is committed to keeping program tuition as low as possible."

That means an average of $115 per day for domestic programs and $220 for international ones. Keep in mind this price includes all accommodations, meals, lectures, activities, and gratuities. It even includes roundtrip airfare for most international programs. Programs vary in length from three days to more than two weeks.

Elderhostel also offers intergenerational programs that let you bring your grandchildren along for the fun, and active outdoor programs that combine learning with activities like birding, bicycling, sailing, hiking, or golf.

For more information, call Elderhostel toll-free at 877-426-8056, or visit its Web site at *www.elderhostel.org.*

Swap homes. Spend $0 on lodging or car rentals on your next vacation. Just participate in a home exchange program. While you and your family enjoy the comforts of another family's home, that family enjoys the comforts of yours. You'll have your own kitchen, TV, plenty of space, and even use of the family car.

Join one of several homeswapping services to browse the list of available homes and add yours to the list. Find a match, and work out the details with the other homeowner. Make sure to check references before entrusting your home to a stranger. Not only will you have a wonderful, cheap vacation — you might make a new friend for life.

Check out these home exchange services on the Internet.

Home Exchange	www.homeexchange.com
HomeLink International	www.homelink.org
Intervac	www.intervac.com
Digsville Home Exchange	www.digsville.com
Seniors Home Exchange	www.seniorshomeexchange.com

Be my guest. The Affordable Travel Club is similar to home-swapping except you host travelers — or stay with hosts — during your travels.

When you pay the small yearly fee to join this over-40 club, you get access to a directory of members in 47 states and 30 countries. Contact one in the area you're interested in visiting, and see if they're able to host you. For $20 per night, you'll have a place to stay and breakfast the next morning. Your host should also take some time to tell you about the local attractions and restaurants. Of course, you'll have the same responsibilities if you decide to host anyone.

To learn more about it, go to *www.affordabletravelclub.net.*

Here's an added bonus to these low-cost travel options — with all the money you save on your trip, you can buy more souvenirs.

Soar with senior flight deals

If it seems like senior discounts on airfare just flew into the Bermuda triangle, don't despair. You can still find a senior discount — you just have to look harder. And you may not even need one.

David Smidt, President and CEO of SeniorDiscounts.com, a company devoted to finding deals for seniors, explains how to land the best bargain.

Check online. This convenient option should be your first step. Most of the time, you can save more by booking through a Web site like Orbitz or Priceline than you would with a senior discount.

"But at peak traveling times, or on really off times when they're not doing deals, senior discounts are going to be the cheapest way to go still," Smidt says.

Here are some good places to check for low fares.

Best Fares	www.bestfares.com
Expedia	www.expedia.com
Cheap Tickets	www.cheaptickets.com
Hotwire	www.hotwire.com
Orbitz	www.orbitz.com
Priceline	www.priceline.com
Travelocity	www.travelocity.com

Call and ask. If you can't find a good deal online, take the next step. Call the airline and see how much you can save with a senior discount. Keep in mind that the age requirements differ from airline to airline. With some, you must be 65. Others kick in at 62, 60 — or even, rarely, 55.

"Basically, most companies don't advertise senior discounts. You really have to ask for them and look for them," Smidt says. "You'll be surprised at how many people will actually offer a senior discount if you just ask. That includes not just airlines, but everyone."

Know when to use it. Remember, a senior discount is not always the best deal. By planning ahead and booking your flight far in advance, you can probably take advantage of cheaper fares.

But if you want to fly next week, the senior discount might be your best bet. For example, if you're 65 or older, the most you'll pay for a one-way ticket on Southwest Airlines is $129.

Be aware of bonuses. Senior discounts aren't always limited to seniors. Some, like America West's Senior Saver Pack coupon program, can be transferred to your grandkids if they're between the ages of 2 and 11. And most airlines will give your spouse or traveling companion the same senior rate even if they don't meet the age requirement.

So how much can you expect to save with a senior discount? Because of the up-and-down nature of airline prices, it's hard to say.

"Depending on what the prices are at the time, it can be 10 percent or 50 percent. There really is no set percentage on airline tickets," Smidt says. "You can save $20 or a couple of hundred dollars on airline tickets, depending on when you fly and what airline."

Dream vacation could be a nightmare

Who wouldn't want to go on a free or deeply discounted luxury vacation? But before you jump at that tempting offer, take a deep breath. There's usually more to these trips than meets the eye.

Beware of the "trip trap." Free vacations that sound too good to be true usually are. Find out what to watch for with this advice from the Federal Trade Commission.

Do some research. Check out the company before you buy. Get its complete name, address, and local telephone number. Contact the Attorney General and Better Business Bureau in your state and where the company is located to see if any complaints have been lodged against it. Keep in mind shady companies often change names.

Try to deal with businesses that belong to professional associations, such as the American Society of Travel Agents, the National Tour Association, or the United States Tour Operators Association.

Take your time. Scam operators often pressure you to act quickly or say the offer won't be around much longer. Legitimate businesses don't force you to make hasty decisions.

Read all about it. Get all information in writing before you buy — and read it over carefully to make sure it matches what you've been told. Look out for additional conditions or costs. Request copies of the cancellation and refund policies.

Insist on getting the names, addresses, and phone numbers for the lodgings, airlines, or cruise lines you'll be using. Don't settle for vague terms like "major hotels" or "luxury cruise ships." Call to confirm your reservations.

Withhold information. Never give your credit card number or bank information over the phone unless you know the company. Con artists might say they need the number for verification purposes only — then use it to charge your account.

Curtail couriers. Refuse to send money by courier or overnight delivery. The business may be trying to avoid charges of mail fraud. Plus, paying with cash or check is riskier than using a credit card because you can't dispute the charges.

KO offers for ID. Watch out for "instant travel agent" offers. Companies may offer to sell you identification that will "guarantee" you discounted rates from cruise lines, hotels, or airlines. There is no guarantee — except you will lose money.

Pass on the presentation. Often, ads for great deals don't tell you that you'll have to sit through a sales presentation to qualify. Decline these offers.

If you're considering investing in a timeshare, think ahead. Will you be healthy and financially stable enough to enjoy it five years from now? Will the company still be in business? Be aware annual membership and maintenance fees may rise, and resale is very difficult. It is not an investment.

Just say no. If you have any doubts about the offer, turn it down. Trust your instincts.

If you think you've been victimized by a travel scam or just want more information, contact the FTC's Consumer Response Center.

```
Contact   Federal Trade Commission
          CRC-240
          Washington, D.C. 20580
          877-382-4357 (877-FTC-
          HELP)
          www.ftc.gov
```

Smart strategies for safe travel

The world is dangerous. But it's still a world worth seeing. You just have to take precautions to protect yourself and your valuables.

Mark Monday, member of the Strategic Security Systems team for Titan Corporation and co-author of the book *What Your Travel Agent Won't Tell You!*, provides these tips for safe travel.

Watch the roads. You might think terrorism is the biggest threat when traveling overseas — but you're far more likely to encounter danger on foreign roads.

"Driving conditions are generally quite hazardous," Monday says. "The roads are in terrible condition, too. You don't want to break down in the middle of nowhere."

Roadways might not be marked and might not have street lights, shoulders, or working traffic lights. Drivers might not use their headlights or obey traffic lights even if they are working. Remember, in some countries, people drive on the left side of the road. Make sure you look the right way when crossing the street.

If you rent a car, don't choose one that will brand you as an American or a Westerner. Blend in with a vehicle that's not flashy. Look out for carjackings, especially in rural areas.

Don't get into a taxi cab that you hail off the street. It could be a scheme to kidnap you. Have your hotel concierge call a cab for you instead.

Guard your health. Check with the World Health Organization and Centers for Disease Control to find out what health issues you might be facing where you're going.

Make sure you have all the proper innoculations, and ask your insurance company if your policy applies overseas.

"Make sure you bring your prescription drugs and your over-the-counter medicines because a lot of times you won't be able to get Western standard medical supplies in other countries," Monday says.

Wash your hands, drink only bottled or boiled water or carbonated drinks in cans or bottles, avoid tap water or ice cubes, only eat thoroughly cooked foods, peel fruits and vegetables yourself, and open your own bottles.

"If somebody's going to drug you, they usually will do it in a drink," Monday says.

CDC Travelers' Health	www.cdc.gov/travel
World Health Organization	www.who.int/en
Bureau of Consular Affairs	www.travel.state.gov

Prevent petty crime. Pickpockets and thieves thrive on tourists. They use distractions and the element of surprise to prey on you. Be especially careful around payphones, public restrooms, restaurants, bars, airports, beaches, and pools. Also be extra alert at night.

"Go with your gut. If you feel like you're in danger, you probably are," Monday says.

Travel in groups. There's safety in numbers. Don't carry a briefcase or purse or wear a fanny pack. They're easy to snatch. So are shopping bags. If someone does grab your bag and run, don't chase after them. But you do need to notify the local authorities.

Don't leave jewelry or important documents in your hotel room. If your hotel has a safe, keep your valuables in there.

"Basically, just don't leave anything around that you wouldn't mind losing," Monday says. "You should keep your valuables in separate places underneath your clothing — interior pockets, money belts, that kind of thing."

Dress for success. Don't let your wardrobe announce you're a tourist. "It's not just dressing flashy, it's dressing too casual, too," Monday says. "Try not to stick out. Keep a low profile."

Wear basic clothes, and make sure not to offend the locals. For example, in a Muslim country, a woman shouldn't wear shorts.

Even when traveling domestically or on a cruise ship, safeguard your jewelry. "There are people that are going to steal from you no matter what country you're in," Monday says. "Just don't wear jewelry. There's no point in it, really. If you do wear it, wear something that's small and not easily seen because that's an obvious mark."

Dodge terrorists. It's harder than ever to profile a potential terrorist. Men and women from any ethnic background could be capable of this kind of violence. But you can still limit your risk.

"Stay away from obvious terrorist targets if you're in an area that's dealing with some serious problems," Monday says. These targets include popular congregation spots for Americans and other Westerners.

If you see someone mumbling to himself, you might want to get away. Often, suicide bombers say a prayer just before detonating themselves.

"Follow your instincts, use your powers of observation, keep a low profile, and just stay alert at all times, and you're going to be fine," Monday says.

Dial in on great deals

How are you going to keep in touch with family and friends during your travels?

If you're thinking of using the calling card your telephone company gave you, think again. Unless sky-high rates and hidden connection charges don't bother you.

Instead, try BigZoo, a prepaid long-distance phone service. Calls are only 2.9 cents per minute if you use a local access code and 3.9 cents a minute otherwise. There's also a monthly fee of 75 cents. Check it out at www.bigzoo.com.

Another place to save is Sam's Club, which sells prepaid calling cards with rates of 3.47 cents a minute.

Choose a cruise — you can't lose

Chances are you haven't been on a cruise — but chances are you'd enjoy it.

While only 10 percent of the population has been on a cruise, a whopping 80 percent of those people cruise again. Why should they have all the fun?

Tim Kangas, accredited cruise counselor and owner of the Cruise Planners franchise in Sharpsburg, Georgia, explains the benefits of cruising and offers tips for planning — and saving money on — your next vacation.

Enjoy a wide-variety of options. Unlike other forms of travel, cruises let you visit several places in a single vacation. You also eat great food, meet new friends, and enjoy a wide range of entertainment and activities. Best of all, most everything, including your accommodations, is included in the price. "I think it's really one of the best values out there when you add it all up," says Kangas.

"When you look at other all-inclusive vacations, they're not anywhere near the standard you would find on a cruise line. You're comparing a four- or five-star ship to, basically, a very moderate or poor resort when you look at the same cost."

On a cruise ship, you can find spas, state-of-the-art exercise facilities, casinos, discos, music and comedy acts, piano bars, miniature golf courses, skating rinks, rock climbing walls, shuffleboard, Ping-Pong, bingo games, art auctions, duty-free shopping centers, movie theaters, libraries, game rooms, Internet cafes, sports bars, and swimming pools.

"It just offers people so many choices," Kangas says. "You can literally do everything or do nothing at all."

Get an agent. You have countless options when choosing a cruise. Let a travel agent help you find the one that's right for you.

"There's really no disadvantage to going through a travel agent," Kangas says. "You're not paying a travel agent anything. We get paid by the cruise line. In most cases, you're going to pay less going through a travel agent than going through a cruise line directly."

Kangas admits you might be able to save some money by booking your cruise online, but you don't get the same personal service — and you have no one to call if something goes wrong.

"I highly recommend using an agent — and make sure the agent knows what he's talking about," says Kangas. Before choosing an agent, check if he is accredited through the Cruise Lines International Association (CLIA).

Exchange information. Help your travel agent help you. Tell your agent exactly when you want to travel, where you want to go, how long you can travel, and if you prefer to fly or drive to the port. Your age, state of residence, number of people in your party, and interests will also be helpful.

"Once I find out about the individual, I pick out the ship and itinerary that's best for them," Kangas says.

You can sail on a luxury, mainstream, or small ship. Accommodations vary from interior staterooms with no view to oceanview or balcony cabins.

"Telling us what your budget is is a big help," says Kangas, adding that many people don't like to disclose that information. "It's just a range we're looking for. Having an idea what you want to spend helps expedite the process."

Discover discounts. Why pay full fare when there are so many ways to save on cruises? Seniors and children often qualify for discount rates. So do large groups and military personnel.

You can save money, and get the pick of the cabins, by booking your cruise well in advance. But you can also find good last-minute deals.

"If you're willing to sail during the off-season, you can save a considerable amount of money," Kangas says. Keep in mind the off-season varies with each destination.

You might even qualify for a discount just by living where you do. Cruise lines offer resident discounts to people who live in certain states. Make sure you let your travel agent know where you — and your cruising companions — live.

"Always ask. You can't always assume your travel agent's going to be on top of everything," Kangas says. "It never hurts to ask if there's any other discount available. It might help remind the person of a promotion out there."

Kangas, who runs his business with his wife Sherry, doesn't need to be reminded of cruising's appeal.

"Definitely one of the advantages of being in this business is the travel perks," he says. "You just have to find time to use them."

4 reasons to hit the road in an RV

Recreational vehicles are more popular than ever. In fact, one in every 12 U.S. households owns an RV. Find out what all the excitement's about — and how to get in on it.

Ken Sommer, spokesman for the Recreational Vehicle Industry Association (RVIA), points out the following benefits of RV travel.

Be spontaneous. Pack up and go whenever you want. You don't have to book flights or make hotel reservations in advance. Or wait in long lines at the airport. Just hop in and drive. "With an RV, every weekend can be a mini-vacation," Sommer says.

Feel at home. Bring the comforts of home on the road. RVs feature complete living, cooking, dining, sleeping, and bathroom facilities. Some models even include slideout rooms, satellite TV, washers and dryers, microwaves, queen-size beds, and a place for your computer.

Bond with your family. RV travel brings families closer together — and to other families. You'll meet new friends in RV campgrounds during your travels.

Save money. Even after factoring in the cost of owning an RV, you still save. Campground fees average about $22 a night, much less than most hotels. And you don't have to spend a dime on airfare, rental cars, or eating out.

"RVs deliver true value," Sommer says. "A family of four traveling by RV can spend up to 70 percent less than traveling by car, plane, or cruise ship."

Now that you know all about RVs, here's how to get started on your own RV travel adventure.

Go online. Check out *www.GoRVing.com*. This Web site features tips on purchasing and renting RVs, including searchable campground listings. You can even order a free video or CD-ROM of RV shopping and travel tips. Order online or call 888-467-8464.

Rent. Rent an RV for your next vacation. You know you've always wanted to try it. It's easy with this advice. Just look in the Yellow Pages under "Recreational Vehicles-Rentals" for a rental outlet near you. Or go to the Recreational Vehicle Rental Association's Web site at *www.rvra.org* for a directory of more than 340 rental companies in the United States and Canada.

Rental costs vary depending on the season and size of the unit. Motorhomes, the most popular rental model, cost between $90 and $200 a day. But you can sample a variety of models to see what suits you best. "Renting an RV is a great way to try before you buy," Sommer says.

Read up on it. Go to the library or bookstore to consult RV buyers guides and campground directories.

Visit a dealer. Most dealerships offer test drives. Check the Yellow Pages under "Recreation Vehicle-Sales" or go to *www.GoRVing.com* for a directory of RV dealers.

See the show. Local RV shows give you a chance to walk through various RVs and compare prices in one convenient location. For a listing of RV shows, go to *www.rvia.org/rvshows*.

Once you decide which RV is right for you, you're ready for a whole new travel experience.

"RVs offer a comfortable, convenient, affordable, and hassle-free way to see America," says Sommer. "You have the freedom and flexibility to go where you want, when you want."

Grab good food on the go

Just because you're traveling doesn't mean your diet is on vacation. You can still eat healthy on the road — even if you eat all your meals in restaurants.

Michael F. Jacobson, Executive Director of Center for Science in the Public Interest and co-author of *Restaurant Confidential,* offers these tips for healthy restaurant dining.

Avoid fried foods. Just stay away from these diet disasters. "They are usually fried in hydrogenated shortening that is terrible for one's arteries," Jacobson says. Not to mention one's waistline.

Watch portion sizes. You don't need to clean your plate. As soon as your food arrives, get a doggie bag from your server. "Ask if half the food could be packed away for you to bring home for lunch tomorrow," Jacobson says.

Veg out. Look for dishes with fruits and vegetables. This might be harder than it sounds. "Chinese restaurants are one of the best places to get vegetables," Jacobson says. They usually cook to order, so you can ask them to use very little oil. And they don't use hydrogenated oil.

Sneak a peek. Before you enter the restaurant, check the menu for healthy choices. If you can't find any, go to another place.

Make requests. Don't be afraid to special order your meal. You're paying for it, after all. "When you're figuring out what to order, you should assume that you can ask for anything and let the waiter say you can't do it," says Jacobson.

"So ask for the salad dressing on the side. Ask if you can substitute a side order of vegetables for a side order of French fries. Ask if they can bake it instead of frying it. The servers will generally try to do what you want."

Save at supermarkets. Of course, if your travel accommodations include a kitchen, you can save lots of money and aggravation by cooking your own meals.

But whether you cook or not, the local supermarket can be a great resource for quick, cheap meals. Grab some yogurt or a muffin and orange juice for breakfast, order a sandwich from the deli counter for lunch, or even get a ready-made hot meal for dinner. Stocking up at the supermarket can also help you make healthy choices during the day.

"If you are going to be out on the road for a day, take some snacks with you so you're not dependent on whatever fast food restaurant is on the corner or at the shopping mall," Jacobson says. "We should try to avoid situations where the only choice is restaurant food that isn't terribly healthful for us."

Cash in on cafeterias. If you're looking to save money and time while visiting a new city, try eating at cafeterias in museums or other public attractions. You'll find cheap, sometimes surprisingly good food. And you won't have to take much time away from sightseeing, shopping, or just exploring.

Get the scoop. Regardless of your price range or diet goals, you want to go to a good restaurant. Ask some locals for a recommendation, or pick up a copy of a local newspaper or dining guide. Another great resource is the Internet. You can read reviews of restaurants in your vacation destination on Web sites like *www.citysearch.com.*

Index